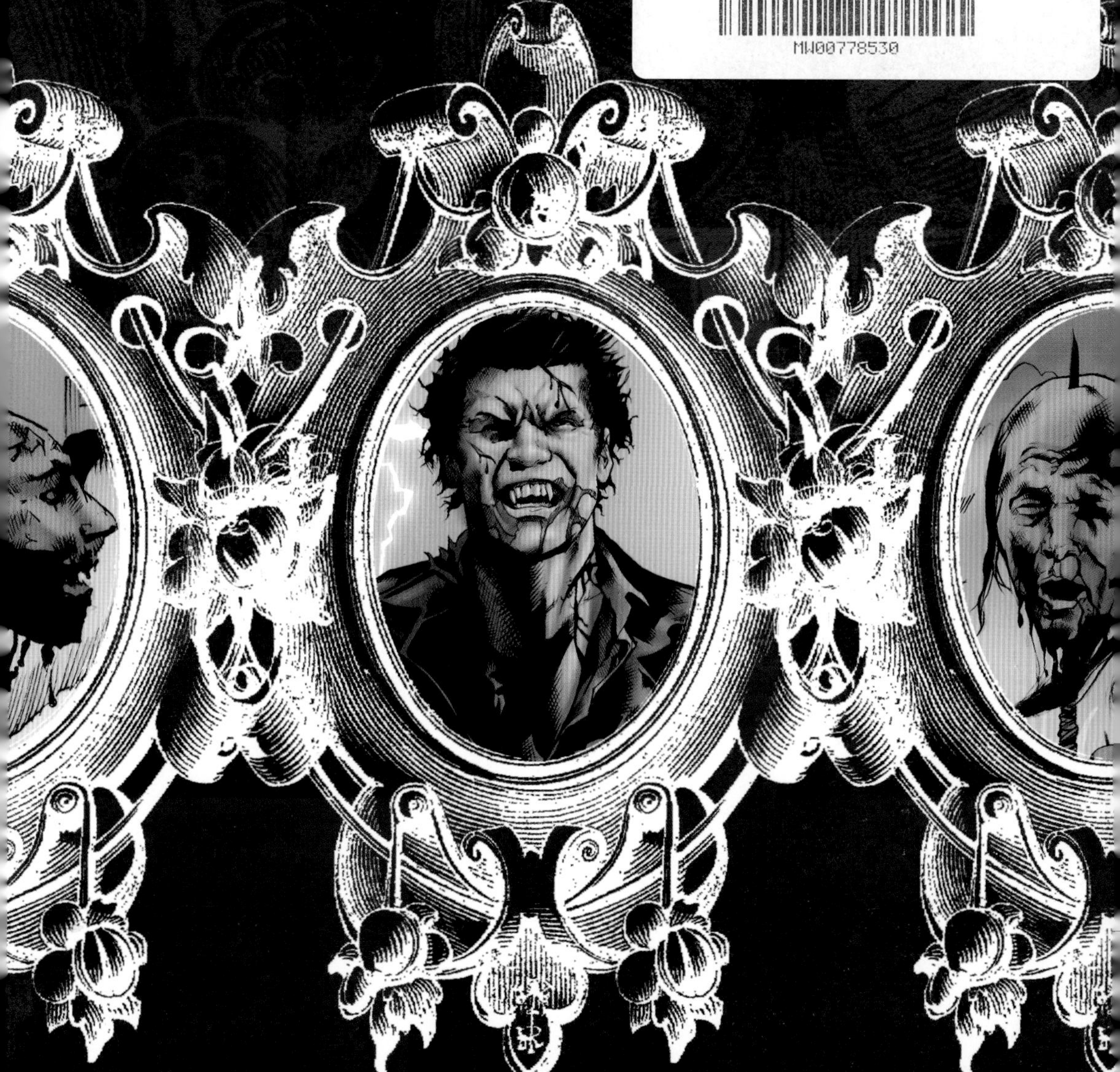

ANGEL™
—AFTER THE FALL—
VOLUME 3

Plotted by

Joss Whedon and Brian Lynch

Scripted by Brian Lynch

Collection Edits by Justin Eisinger

Collection Design by Neil Uyetake

Angel created by Joss Whedon and David Greenwalt.
Special thanks to our Watcher, Joss Whedon, and Fox Worldwide Publishing's Debbie Olshan for their invaluable assistance.

ISBN: 978-1-61377-059-7

14 13 12 11 1 2 3 4

IDW

Ted Adams, CEO & Publisher
Greg Goldstein, Chief Operating Officer
Robbie Robbins, EVP/Sr. Graphic Artist
Chris Ryall, Chief Creative Officer/Editor-in-Chief
Matthew Ruzicka, CPA, Chief Financial Officer
Alan Payne, VP of Sales

Become our fan on Facebook **facebook.com/idwpublishing**
Follow us on Twitter **@idwpublishing**
Check us out on YouTube **youtube.com/idwpublishing**
www.IDWPUBLISHING.com

Originally published as ANGEL: AFTER THE FALL Issues #9–12.

PREVIOUSLY IN

ANGEL™

— AFTER THE FALL —

LOS ANGELES HAS GONE TO HELL.

The entire city was sent to hell as punishment for ANGEL taking a stand against Wolfram & Hart. The town has been divided by Demon Lords, the human civilians enslaved.

But Wolfram & Hart wasn't done there. They made Angel human for that added dose of helplessness and forced a recently deceased WESLEY to stand by Angel's side as an incorporeal ghost. Rounding out the trio is a giant DRAGON sent to kill Angel that instead became his pet, chief mode of transportation, and confidant. Wesley and the Dragon are the only other living beings aware that Angel is no longer a vampire, his secret kept by potions and glamours.

The remaining members of Angel's former crew have gone their separate ways, each one not knowing what has become of the other. For instance, everyone thinks CHARLES GUNN has died. This is not the case. Gunn, who was mortally wounded in the moments before the city's descent into hell, has been turned into a vampire. Still thinking himself a hero, Gunn has since done the following:

1) Honed his abilities by training with what appears to be kidnapped slayer prisoners.

2) Killed the Lord of Westwood, the Lord's followers, and stole a magical item that boosted the Lord's powers.

3) Kidnapped the telekinetic fish BETTA GEORGE.

4) Framed SPIKE and ILLYRIA for deaths of humans Gunn himself killed.

Which leads Angel to head to Beverly Hills, where Spike and Illyria have taken over as Lords. From outward appearances, it seems as though Spike and Illyria have returned to their old ways—Spike spending his days hanging out with a supernatural harem, and Illyria spending her days hitting things.

Angel confronts them, but discovers that not only is Spike NOT murdering anyone, he's secretly saving humans with CONNOR. Connor is running a safe haven for the citizens of Los Angeles, working alongside NINA (the werelady ex-girlfriend of Angel) and GWEN (electric powers out of control in hell, making her unable, once again, to touch a human being without killing them).

Angel, perhaps somewhat jealous of Spike and Connor's new relationship, challenges the Lords to combat. If Angel wins, they surrender control of the city. If Angel loses, Angel dies.

Angel and Wesley are summoned by LORNE. Lorne has found his calling in Silverlake, where he rose up and became Lord, creating the only pleasant area of hell. He has enlisted the GROOSALUGG to act as the city's protector. Lorne and Groo arm Angel to the (formerly fanged) teeth…

…which he'll need, as the Lords have assembled a motley crew of champions to fight in their name. And if that's not enough, they each have a mystical device that when triggered will turn Angel's insides out. Spike and Illyria, as Lords, are given one of the devices. Spike's harem wants Spike to use it on Angel and rise up to take over the city.

The day of the battle, after a heartfelt speech where Angel apologizes to all of Los Angeles for sending them to hell, the battle begins...

...and Angel is quickly overpowered. Thankfully, Lorne has assembled the troops, and reunited the band. Angel, Spike, Illyria, Connor, Gwen, Nina, and The Dragon fight side by side. Gunn watches from the rooftops, declaring that he orchestrated the entire thing.

Spike tells Angel he must help with Illyria, who has been causing time-slips whenever emotions get high. But that's just the start of her problems, as demonstrated when Wesley appears before her...

...and Illyria promptly turns right back into Fred.

Surrounded by the Lord's Champions, Fred is scared, confused, and all too human.

chapter

one

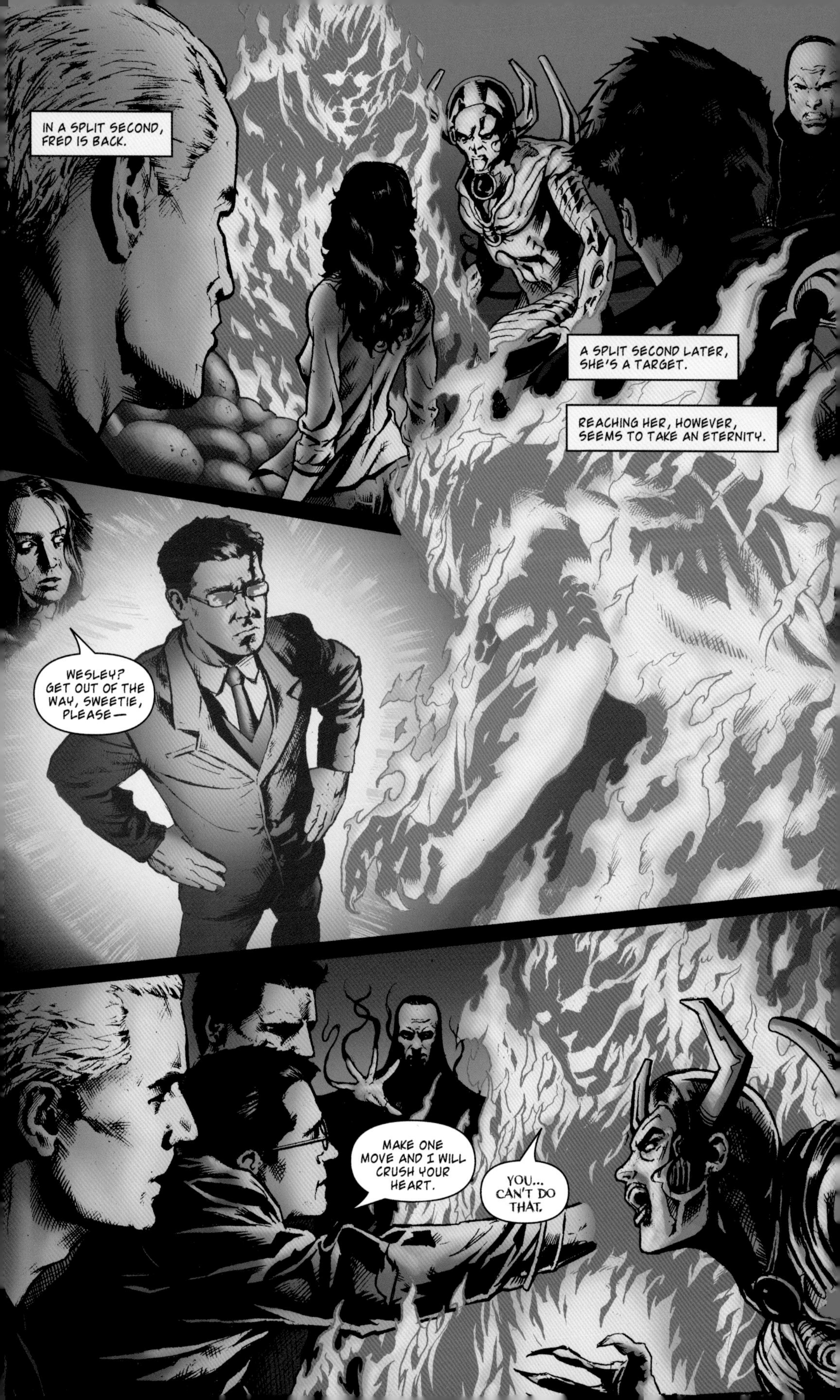
IN A SPLIT SECOND, FRED IS BACK.
A SPLIT SECOND LATER, SHE'S A TARGET.
REACHING HER, HOWEVER, SEEMS TO TAKE AN ETERNITY.
WESLEY? GET OUT OF THE WAY, SWEETIE, PLEASE—
MAKE ONE MOVE AND I WILL CRUSH YOUR HEART.
YOU... CAN'T DO THAT.

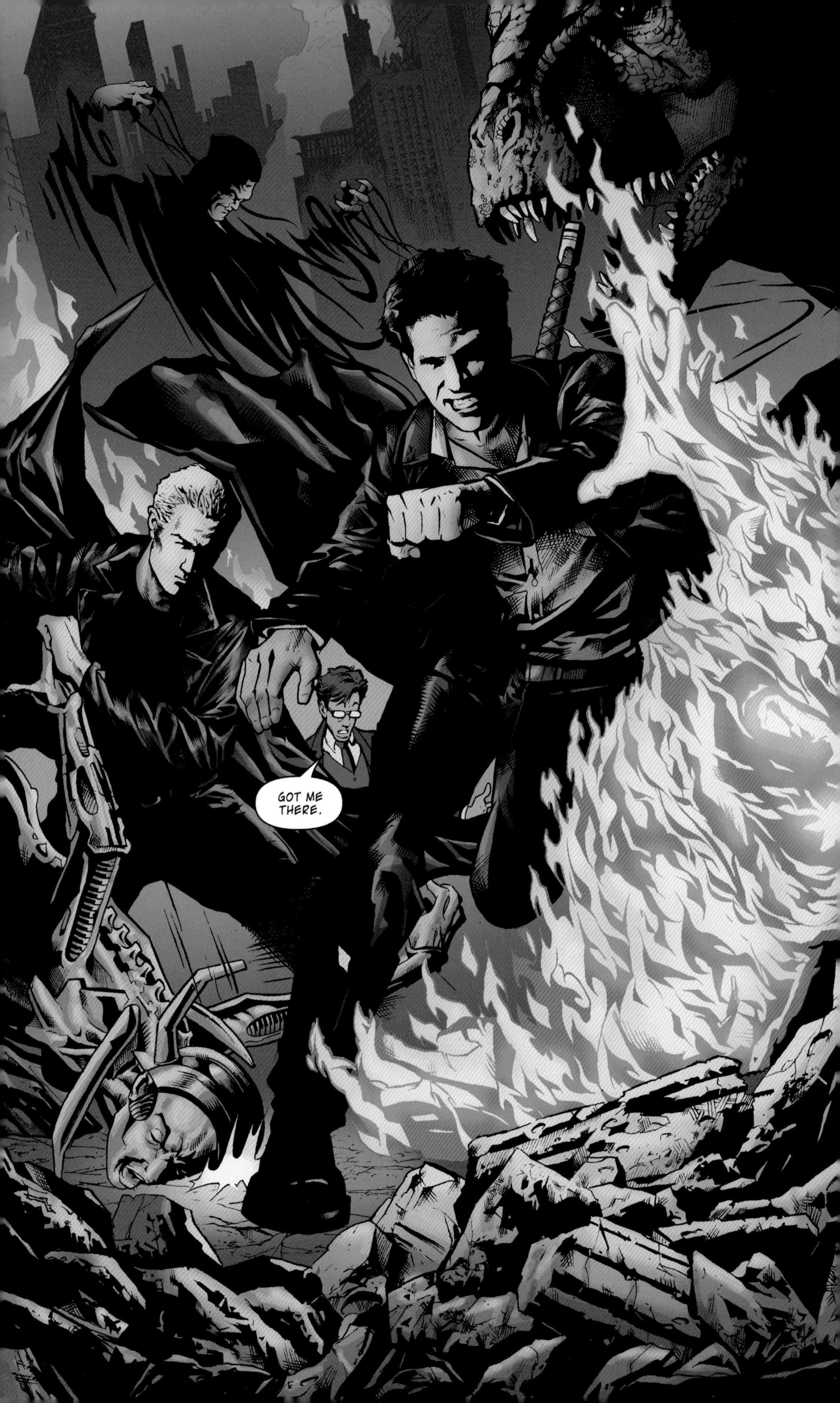
GOT ME THERE.

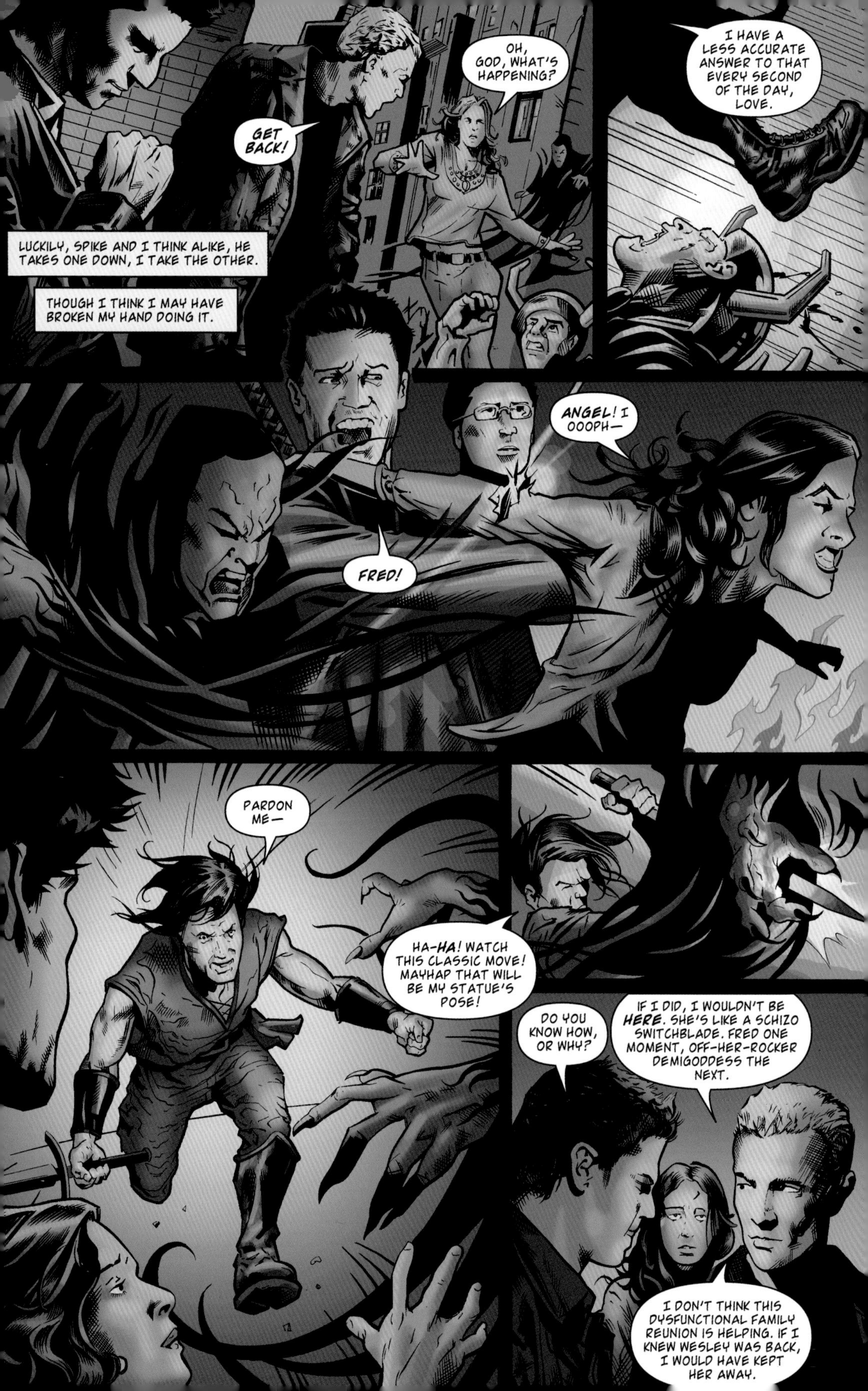
GET BACK!
OH, GOD, WHAT'S HAPPENING?
I HAVE A LESS ACCURATE ANSWER TO THAT EVERY SECOND OF THE DAY, LOVE.
LUCKILY, SPIKE AND I THINK ALIKE, HE TAKES ONE DOWN, I TAKE THE OTHER.
THOUGH I THINK I MAY HAVE BROKEN MY HAND DOING IT.
ANGEL! I OOOPH—
FRED!
PARDON ME—
HA-HA! WATCH THIS CLASSIC MOVE! MAYHAP THAT WILL BE MY STATUE'S POSE!
DO YOU KNOW HOW, OR WHY?
IF I DID, I WOULDN'T BE HERE. SHE'S LIKE A SCHIZO SWITCHBLADE. FRED ONE MOMENT, OFF-HER-ROCKER DEMIGODDESS THE NEXT.
I DON'T THINK THIS DYSFUNCTIONAL FAMILY REUNION IS HELPING. IF I KNEW WESLEY WAS BACK, I WOULD HAVE KEPT HER AWAY.

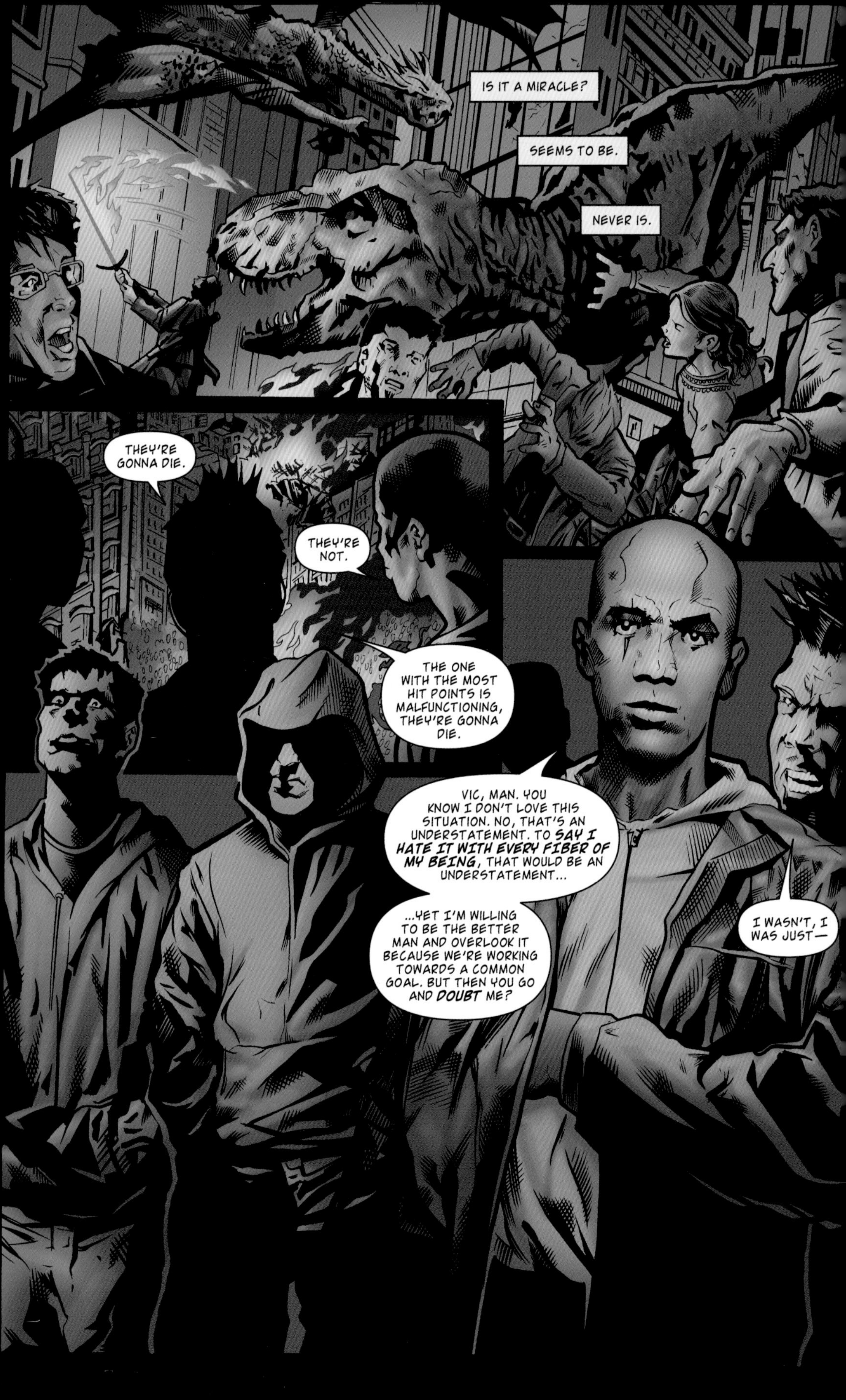
IS IT A MIRACLE?
SEEMS TO BE.
NEVER IS.
THEY'RE GONNA DIE.
THEY'RE NOT.
THE ONE WITH THE MOST HIT POINTS IS MALFUNCTIONING, THEY'RE GONNA DIE.
VIC, MAN. YOU KNOW I DON'T LOVE THIS SITUATION. NO, THAT'S AN UNDERSTATEMENT. TO **SAY I HATE IT WITH EVERY FIBER OF MY BEING**, THAT WOULD BE AN UNDERSTATEMENT...
...YET I'M WILLING TO BE THE BETTER MAN AND OVERLOOK IT BECAUSE WE'RE WORKING TOWARDS A COMMON GOAL. BUT THEN YOU GO AND **DOUBT** ME?
I WASN'T, I WAS JUST—

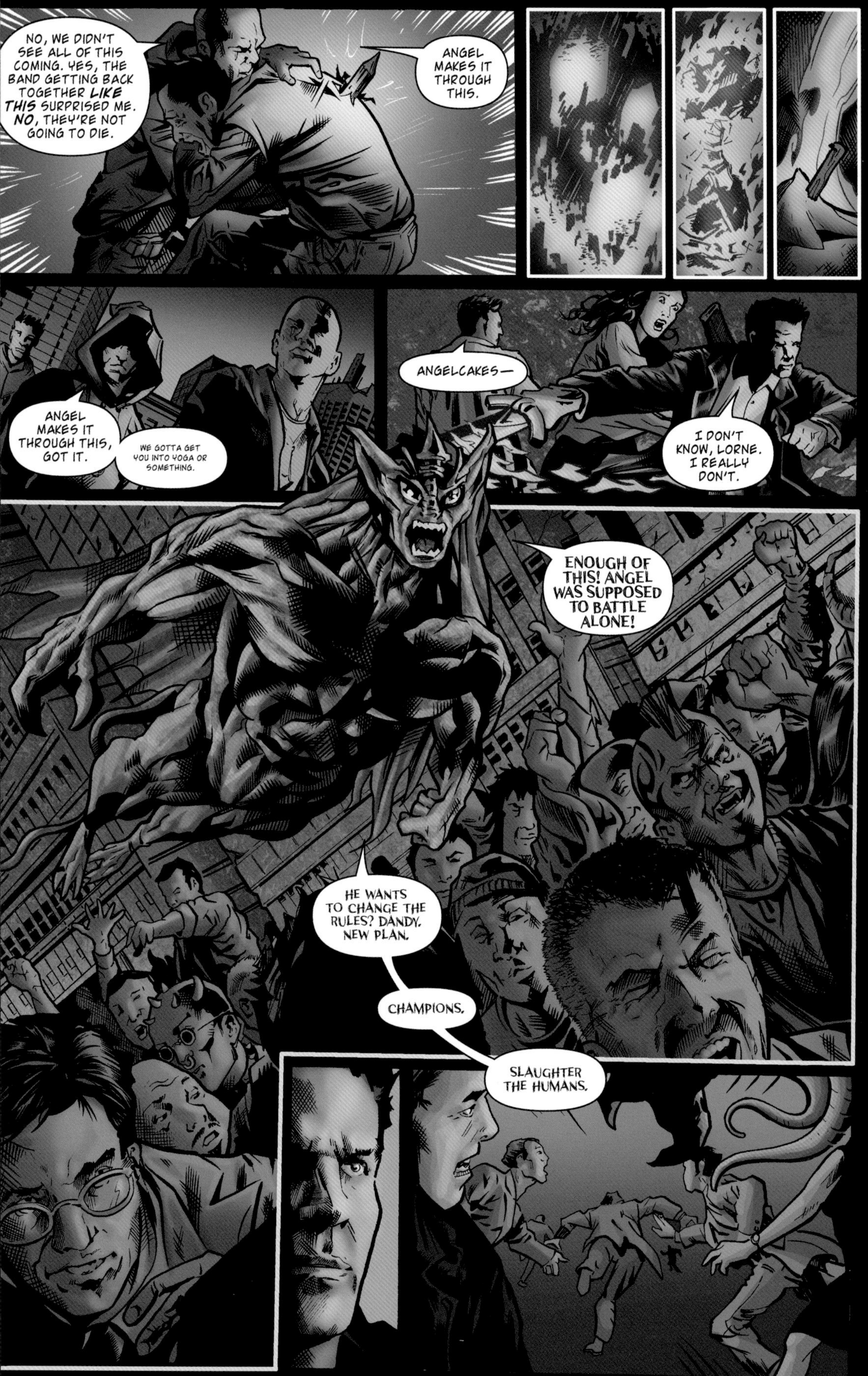
NO, WE DIDN'T SEE ALL OF THIS COMING. YES, THE BAND GETTING BACK TOGETHER LIKE THIS SURPRISED ME. NO, THEY'RE NOT GOING TO DIE.
ANGEL MAKES IT THROUGH THIS.
ANGEL MAKES IT THROUGH THIS, GOT IT.
WE GOTTA GET YOU INTO YOGA OR SOMETHING.
ANGELCAKES—
I DON'T KNOW, LORNE. I REALLY DON'T.
ENOUGH OF THIS! ANGEL WAS SUPPOSED TO BATTLE ALONE!
HE WANTS TO CHANGE THE RULES? DANDY. NEW PLAN.
CHAMPIONS.
SLAUGHTER THE HUMANS.

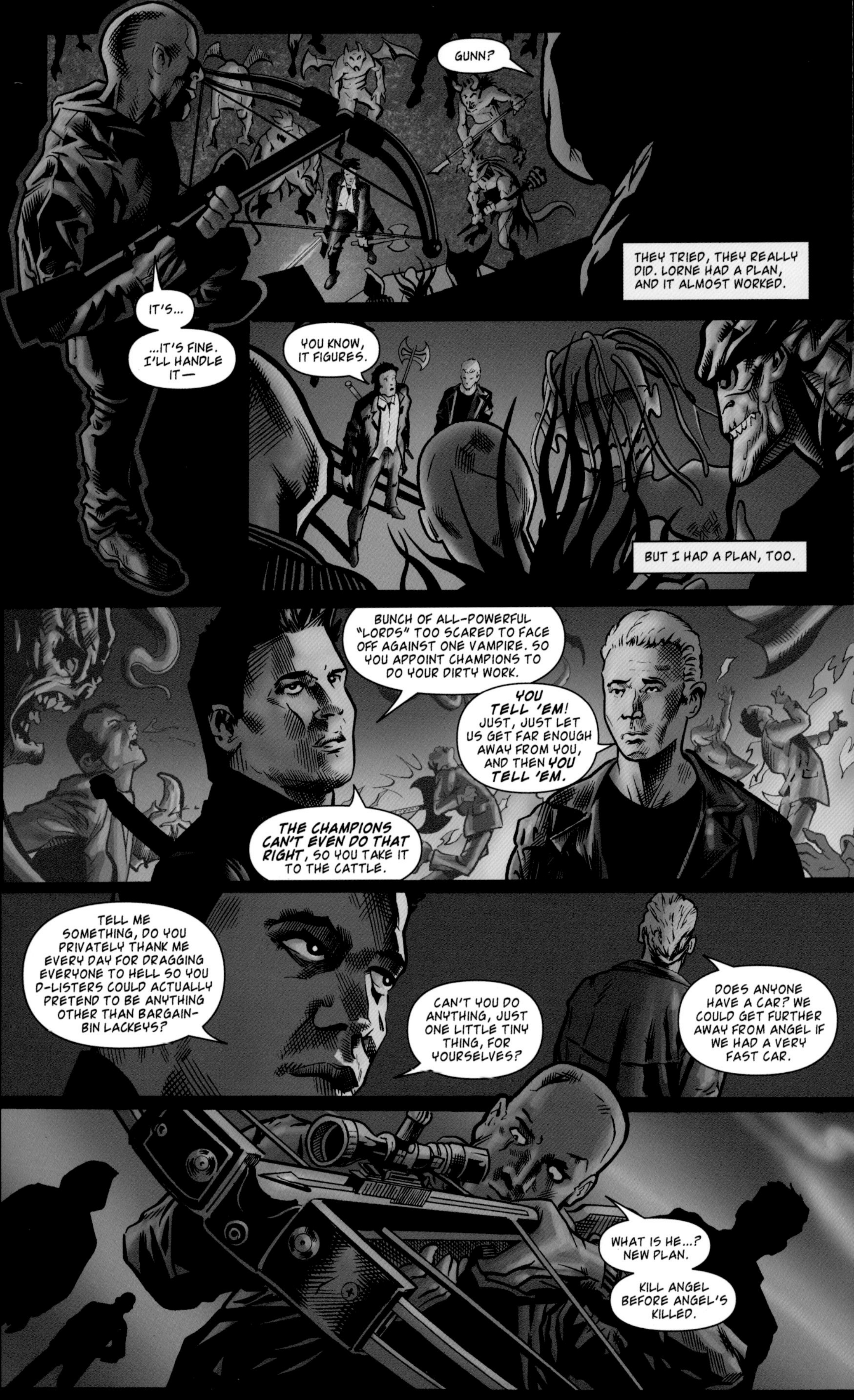
GUNN?
THEY TRIED, THEY REALLY DID. LORNE HAD A PLAN, AND IT ALMOST WORKED.
IT'S...
...IT'S FINE. I'LL HANDLE IT—
YOU KNOW, IT FIGURES.
BUT I HAD A PLAN, TOO.
BUNCH OF ALL-POWERFUL "LORDS" TOO SCARED TO FACE OFF AGAINST ONE VAMPIRE. SO YOU APPOINT CHAMPIONS TO DO YOUR DIRTY WORK.
YOU TELL 'EM! JUST, JUST LET US GET FAR ENOUGH AWAY FROM YOU, AND THEN YOU TELL 'EM.
THE CHAMPIONS CAN'T EVEN DO THAT RIGHT, SO YOU TAKE IT TO THE CATTLE.
TELL ME SOMETHING, DO YOU PRIVATELY THANK ME EVERY DAY FOR DRAGGING EVERYONE TO HELL SO YOU D-LISTERS COULD ACTUALLY PRETEND TO BE ANYTHING OTHER THAN BARGAIN-BIN LACKEYS?
CAN'T YOU DO ANYTHING, JUST ONE LITTLE TINY THING, FOR YOURSELVES?
DOES ANYONE HAVE A CAR? WE COULD GET FURTHER AWAY FROM ANGEL IF WE HAD A VERY FAST CAR.
WHAT IS HE...? NEW PLAN.
KILL ANGEL BEFORE ANGEL'S KILLED.

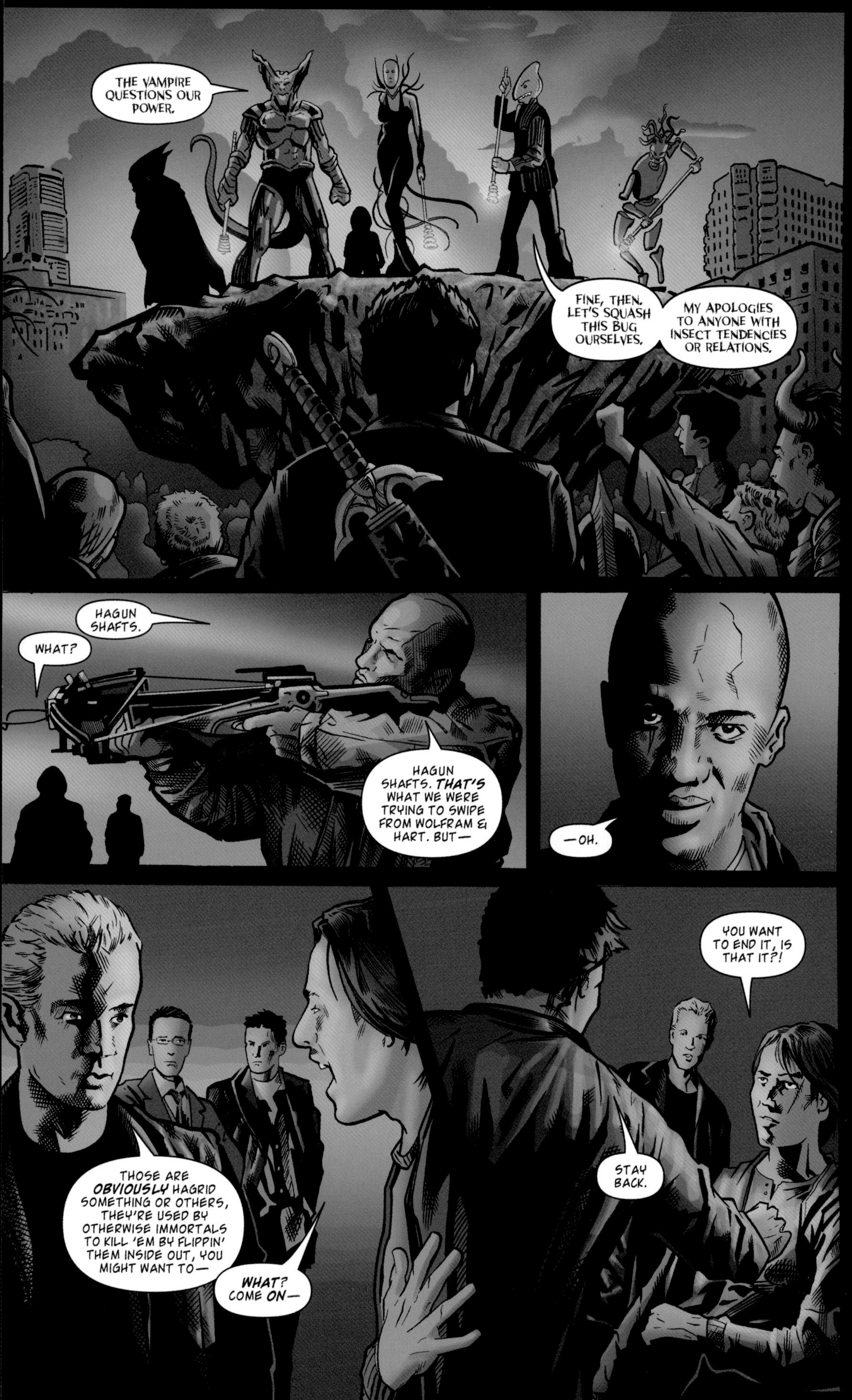
THE VAMPIRE QUESTIONS OUR POWER.
FINE, THEN. LET'S SQUASH THIS BUG OURSELVES.
MY APOLOGIES TO ANYONE WITH INSECT TENDENCIES OR RELATIONS.
HAGUN SHAFTS.
WHAT?
HAGUN SHAFTS. THAT'S WHAT WE WERE TRYING TO SWIPE FROM WOLFRAM & HART. BUT—
—OH.
THOSE ARE OBVIOUSLY HAGRID SOMETHING OR OTHERS, THEY'RE USED BY OTHERWISE IMMORTALS TO KILL 'EM BY FLIPPIN' THEM INSIDE OUT, YOU MIGHT WANT TO—
WHAT? COME ON—
STAY BACK.
YOU WANT TO END IT, IS THAT IT?!

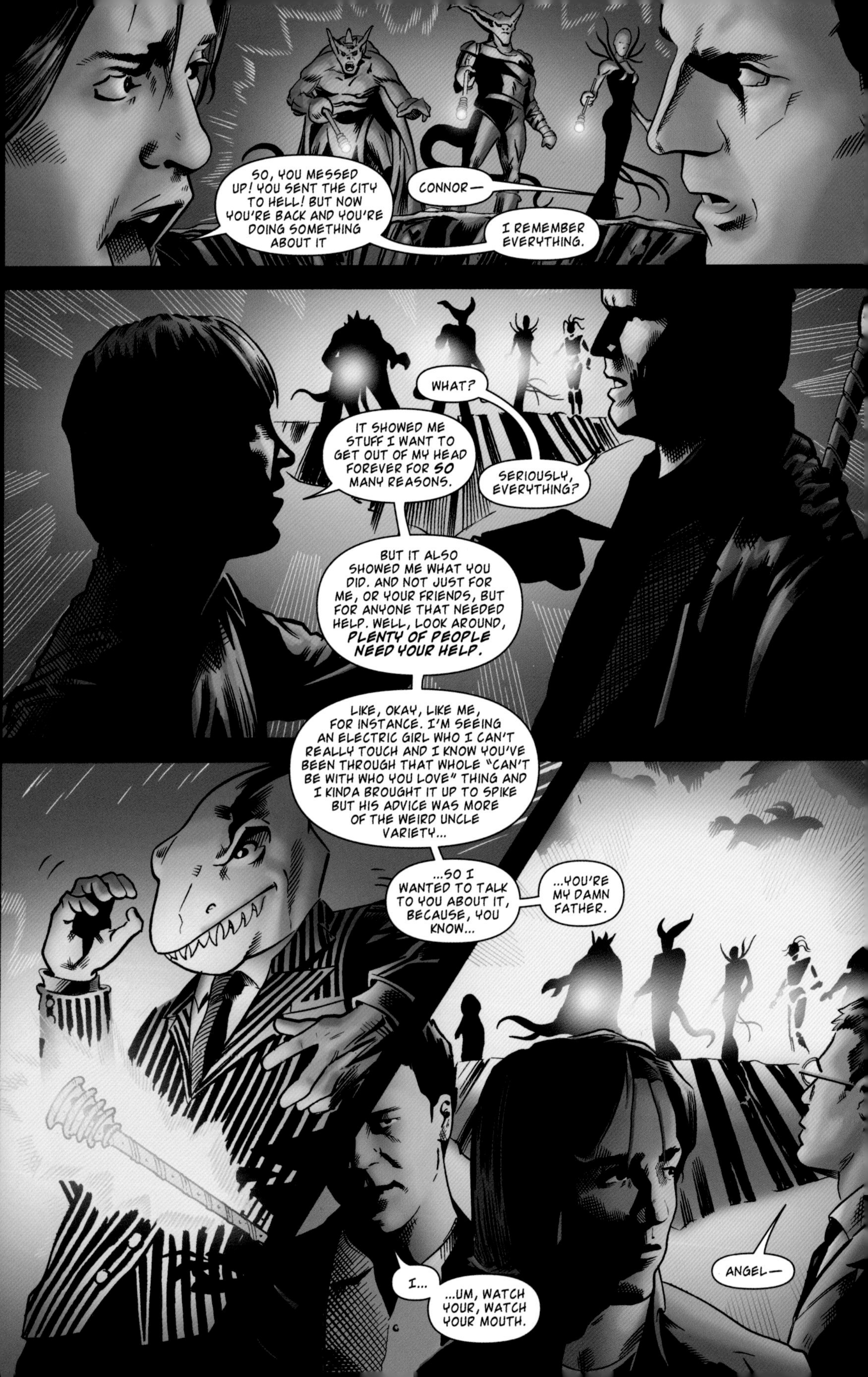
SO, YOU MESSED UP! YOU SENT THE CITY TO HELL! BUT NOW YOU'RE BACK AND YOU'RE DOING SOMETHING ABOUT IT
CONNOR—
I REMEMBER EVERYTHING.
WHAT?
IT SHOWED ME STUFF I WANT TO GET OUT OF MY HEAD FOREVER FOR SO MANY REASONS.
SERIOUSLY, EVERYTHING?
BUT IT ALSO SHOWED ME WHAT YOU DID. AND NOT JUST FOR ME, OR YOUR FRIENDS, BUT FOR ANYONE THAT NEEDED HELP. WELL, LOOK AROUND, PLENTY OF PEOPLE NEED YOUR HELP.
LIKE, OKAY, LIKE ME, FOR INSTANCE. I'M SEEING AN ELECTRIC GIRL WHO I CAN'T REALLY TOUCH AND I KNOW YOU'VE BEEN THROUGH THAT WHOLE "CAN'T BE WITH WHO YOU LOVE" THING AND I KINDA BROUGHT IT UP TO SPIKE BUT HIS ADVICE WAS MORE OF THE WEIRD UNCLE VARIETY...
...SO I WANTED TO TALK TO YOU ABOUT IT, BECAUSE, YOU KNOW...
...YOU'RE MY DAMN FATHER.
I...
...UM, WATCH YOUR, WATCH YOUR MOUTH.
ANGEL—

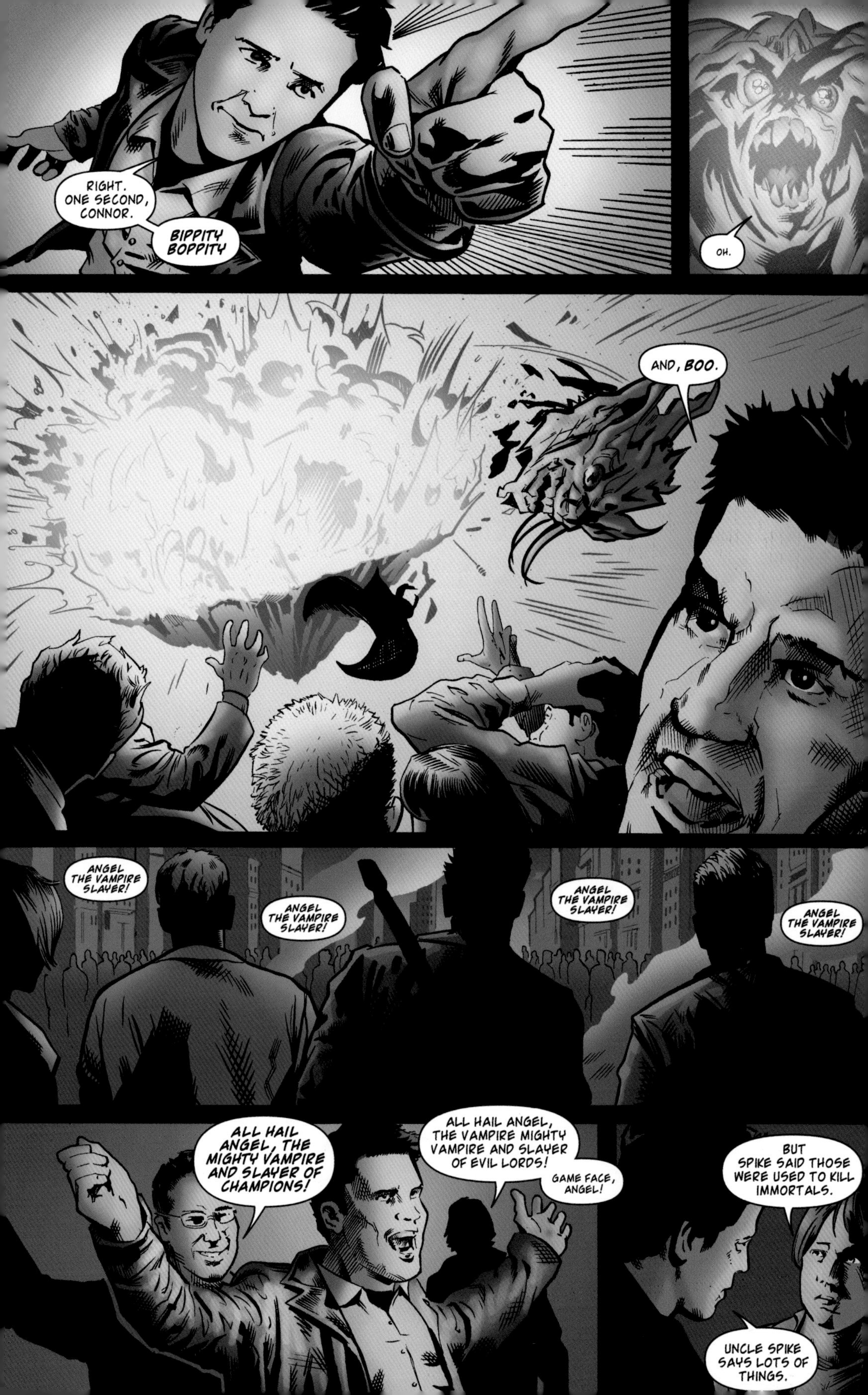
RIGHT. ONE SECOND, CONNOR.
BIPPITY BOPPITY
OH.
AND, BOO.
ANGEL THE VAMPIRE SLAYER!
ANGEL THE VAMPIRE SLAYER!
ANGEL THE VAMPIRE SLAYER!
ANGEL THE VAMPIRE SLAYER!
ALL HAIL ANGEL, THE MIGHTY VAMPIRE AND SLAYER OF CHAMPIONS!
ALL HAIL ANGEL, THE VAMPIRE MIGHTY VAMPIRE AND SLAYER OF EVIL LORDS!
GAME FACE, ANGEL!
BUT SPIKE SAID THOSE WERE USED TO KILL IMMORTALS.
UNCLE SPIKE SAYS LOTS OF THINGS.

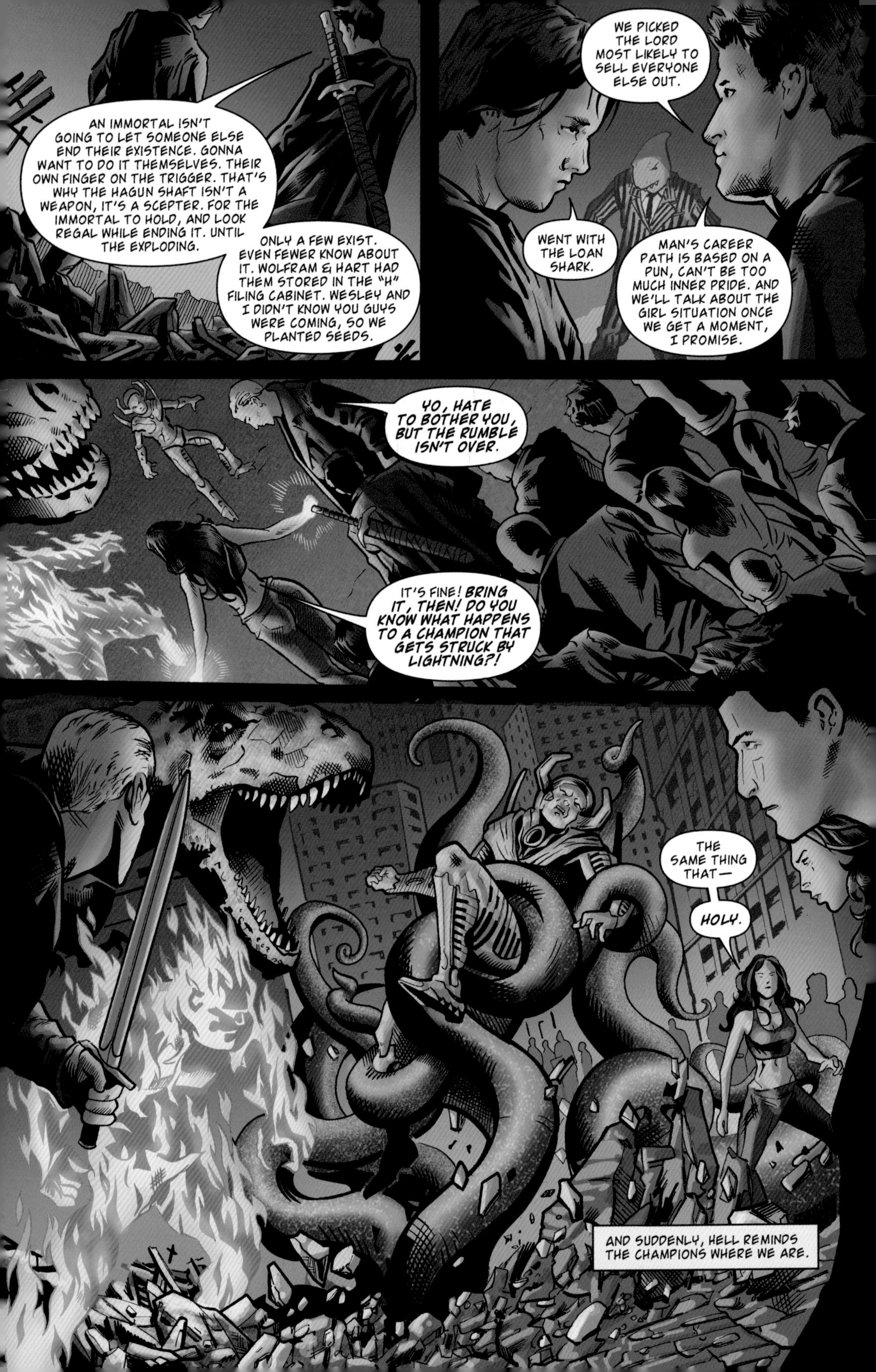
AN IMMORTAL ISN'T GOING TO LET SOMEONE ELSE END THEIR EXISTENCE. GONNA WANT TO DO IT THEMSELVES. THEIR OWN FINGER ON THE TRIGGER. THAT'S WHY THE HAGUN SHAFT ISN'T A WEAPON, IT'S A SCEPTER. FOR THE IMMORTAL TO HOLD, AND LOOK REGAL WHILE ENDING IT. UNTIL THE EXPLODING.
ONLY A FEW EXIST. EVEN FEWER KNOW ABOUT IT. WOLFRAM & HART HAD THEM STORED IN THE "H" FILING CABINET. WESLEY AND I DIDN'T KNOW YOU GUYS WERE COMING, SO WE PLANTED SEEDS.
WE PICKED THE LORD MOST LIKELY TO SELL EVERYONE ELSE OUT.
WENT WITH THE LOAN SHARK.
MAN'S CAREER PATH IS BASED ON A PUN, CAN'T BE TOO MUCH INNER PRIDE. AND WE'LL TALK ABOUT THE GIRL SITUATION ONCE WE GET A MOMENT, I PROMISE.
YO, HATE TO BOTHER YOU, BUT THE RUMBLE ISN'T OVER.
IT'S FINE! BRING IT, THEN! DO YOU KNOW WHAT HAPPENS TO A CHAMPION THAT GETS STRUCK BY LIGHTNING?!
THE SAME THING THAT—
HOLY.
AND SUDDENLY, HELL REMINDS THE CHAMPIONS WHERE WE ARE.

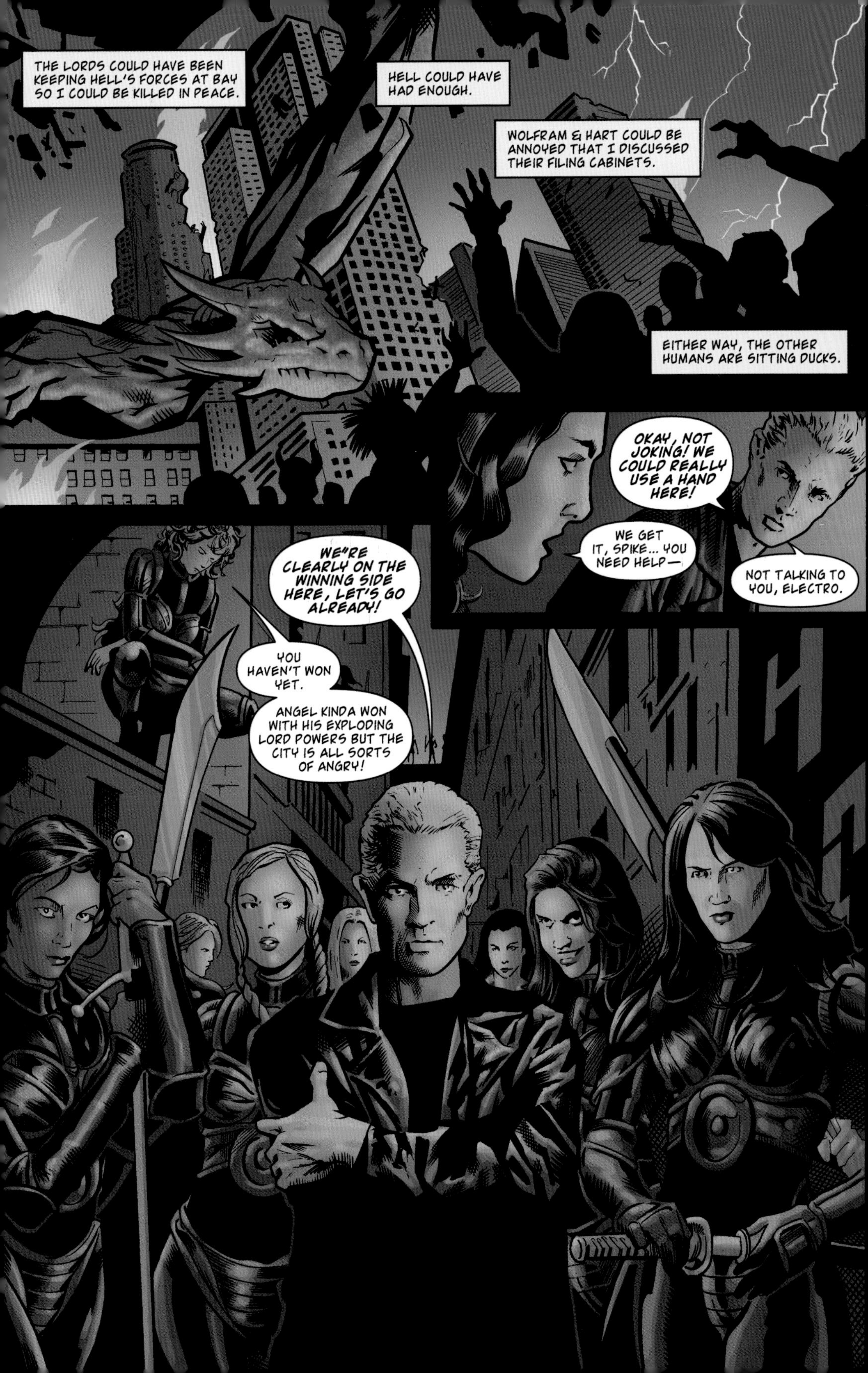
THE LORDS COULD HAVE BEEN KEEPING HELL'S FORCES AT BAY SO I COULD BE KILLED IN PEACE.
HELL COULD HAVE HAD ENOUGH.
WOLFRAM & HART COULD BE ANNOYED THAT I DISCUSSED THEIR FILING CABINETS.
EITHER WAY, THE OTHER HUMANS ARE SITTING DUCKS.
OKAY, NOT JOKING! WE COULD REALLY USE A HAND HERE!
WE GET IT, SPIKE... YOU NEED HELP—
NOT TALKING TO YOU, ELECTRO.
WE"RE CLEARLY ON THE WINNING SIDE HERE, LET'S GO ALREADY!
YOU HAVEN'T WON YET.
ANGEL KINDA WON WITH HIS EXPLODING LORD POWERS BUT THE CITY IS ALL SORTS OF ANGRY!

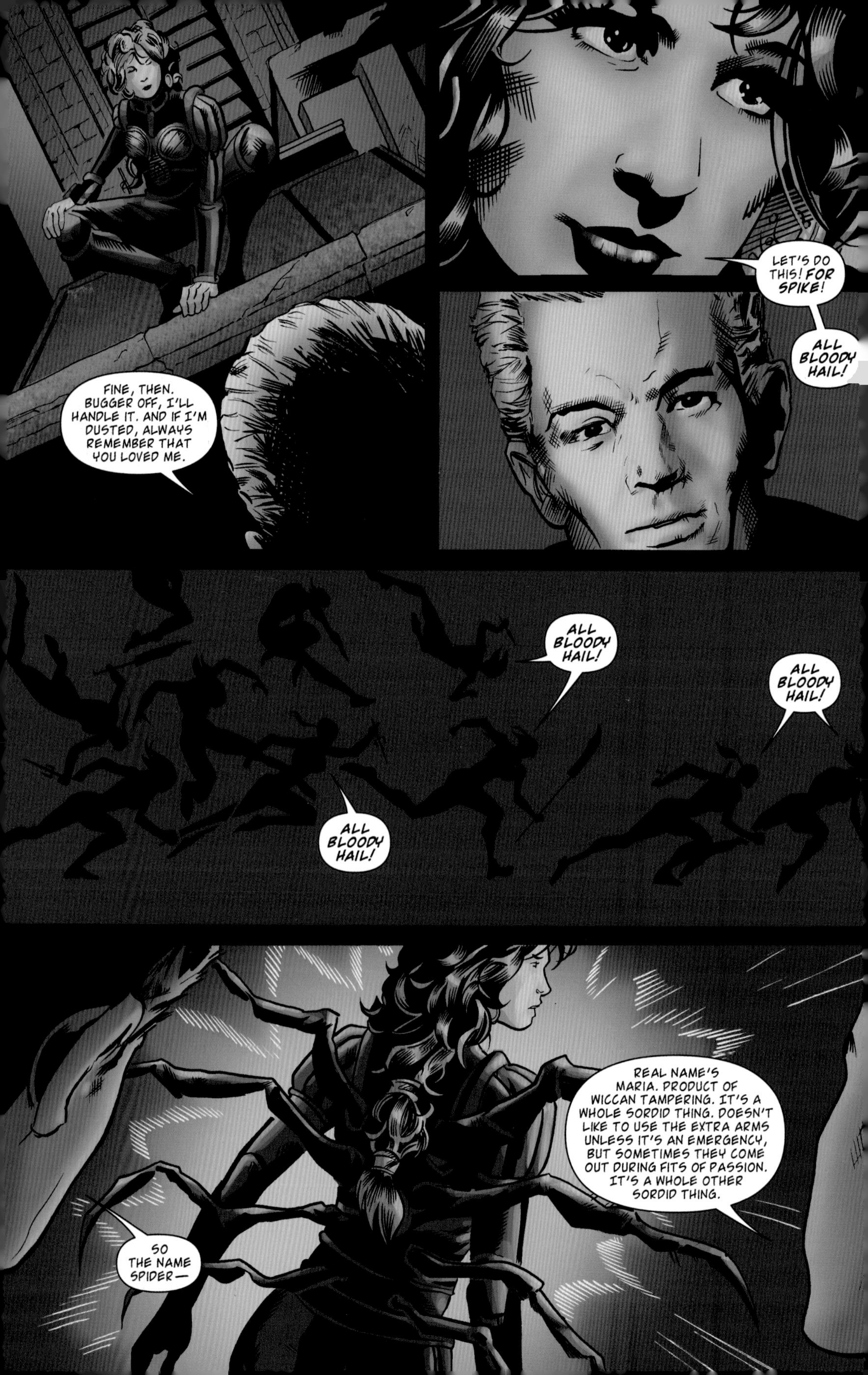
FINE, THEN. BUGGER OFF, I'LL HANDLE IT. AND IF I'M DUSTED, ALWAYS REMEMBER THAT YOU LOVED ME.
LET'S DO THIS! FOR SPIKE!
ALL BLOODY HAIL!
ALL BLOODY HAIL!
ALL BLOODY HAIL!
ALL BLOODY HAIL!
SO THE NAME SPIDER—
REAL NAME'S MARIA. PRODUCT OF WICCAN TAMPERING. IT'S A WHOLE SORDID THING. DOESN'T LIKE TO USE THE EXTRA ARMS UNLESS IT'S AN EMERGENCY, BUT SOMETIMES THEY COME OUT DURING FITS OF PASSION. IT'S A WHOLE OTHER SORDID THING.

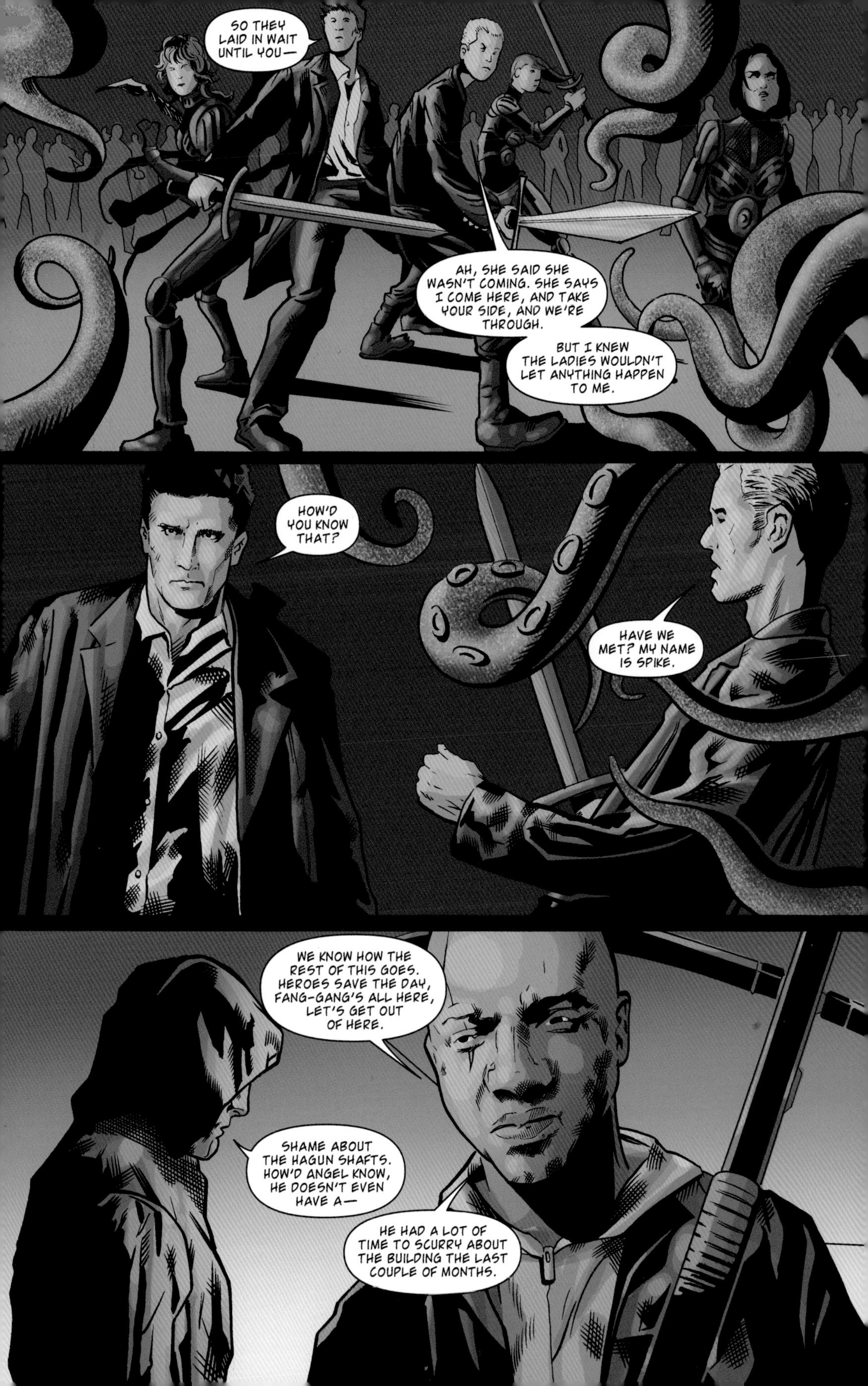
SO THEY LAID IN WAIT UNTIL YOU—
AH, SHE SAID SHE WASN'T COMING. SHE SAYS I COME HERE, AND TAKE YOUR SIDE, AND WE'RE THROUGH.
BUT I KNEW THE LADIES WOULDN'T LET ANYTHING HAPPEN TO ME.
HOW'D YOU KNOW THAT?
HAVE WE MET? MY NAME IS SPIKE.
WE KNOW HOW THE REST OF THIS GOES. HEROES SAVE THE DAY, FANG-GANG'S ALL HERE, LET'S GET OUT OF HERE.
SHAME ABOUT THE HAGUN SHAFTS. HOW'D ANGEL KNOW, HE DOESN'T EVEN HAVE A—
HE HAD A LOT OF TIME TO SCURRY ABOUT THE BUILDING THE LAST COUPLE OF MONTHS.

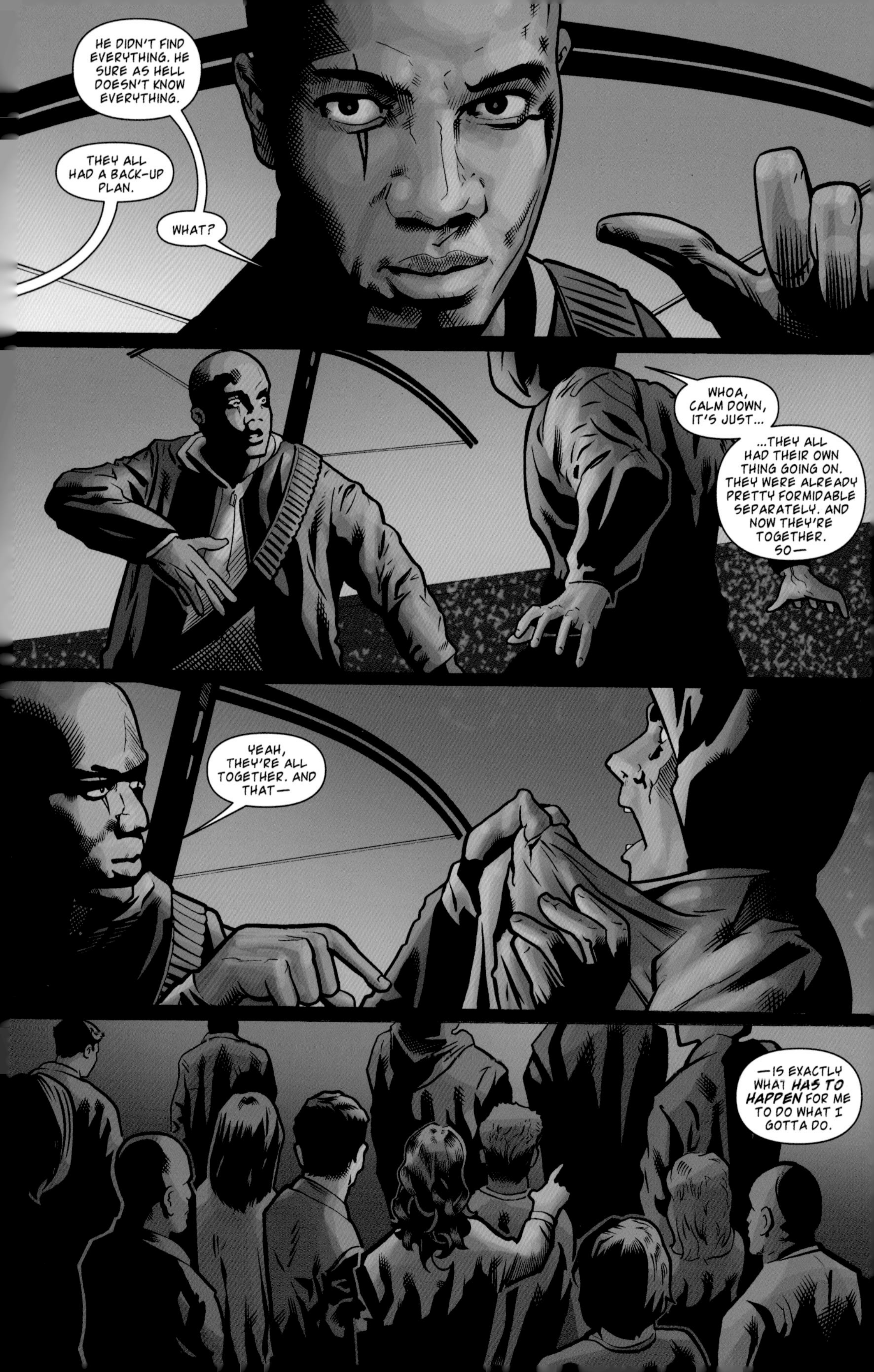
HE DIDN'T FIND EVERYTHING. HE SURE AS HELL DOESN'T KNOW EVERYTHING.
THEY ALL HAD A BACK-UP PLAN.
WHAT?
WHOA, CALM DOWN, IT'S JUST...
...THEY ALL HAD THEIR OWN THING GOING ON. THEY WERE ALREADY PRETTY FORMIDABLE SEPARATELY. AND NOW THEY'RE TOGETHER. SO—
YEAH, THEY'RE ALL TOGETHER. AND THAT—
—IS EXACTLY WHAT HAS TO HAPPEN FOR ME TO DO WHAT I GOTTA DO.

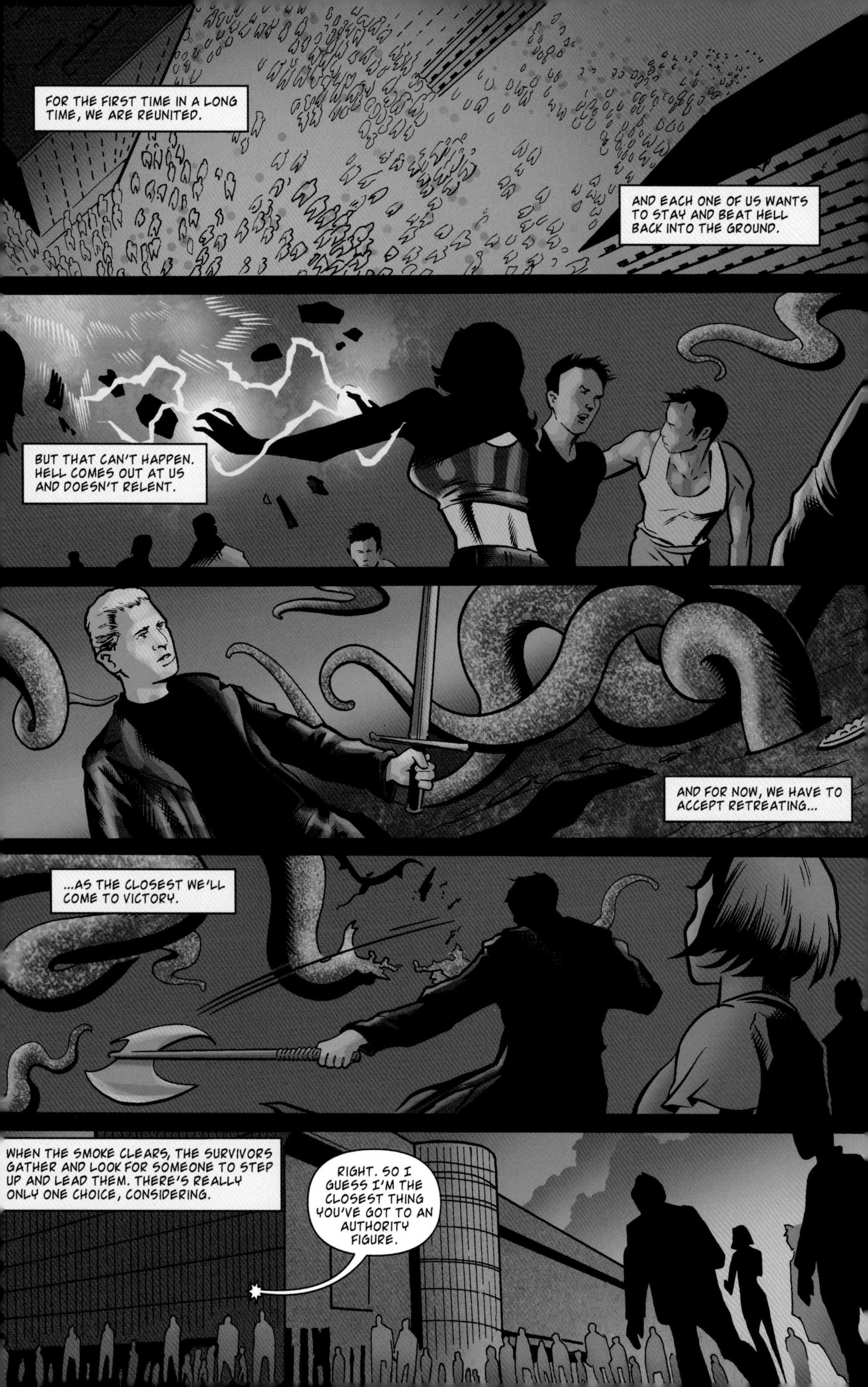
FOR THE FIRST TIME IN A LONG TIME, WE ARE REUNITED.
AND EACH ONE OF US WANTS TO STAY AND BEAT HELL BACK INTO THE GROUND.
BUT THAT CAN'T HAPPEN. HELL COMES OUT AT US AND DOESN'T RELENT.
AND FOR NOW, WE HAVE TO ACCEPT RETREATING...
...AS THE CLOSEST WE'LL COME TO VICTORY.
WHEN THE SMOKE CLEARS, THE SURVIVORS GATHER AND LOOK FOR SOMEONE TO STEP UP AND LEAD THEM. THERE'S REALLY ONLY ONE CHOICE, CONSIDERING.
RIGHT. SO I GUESS I'M THE CLOSEST THING YOU'VE GOT TO AN AUTHORITY FIGURE.

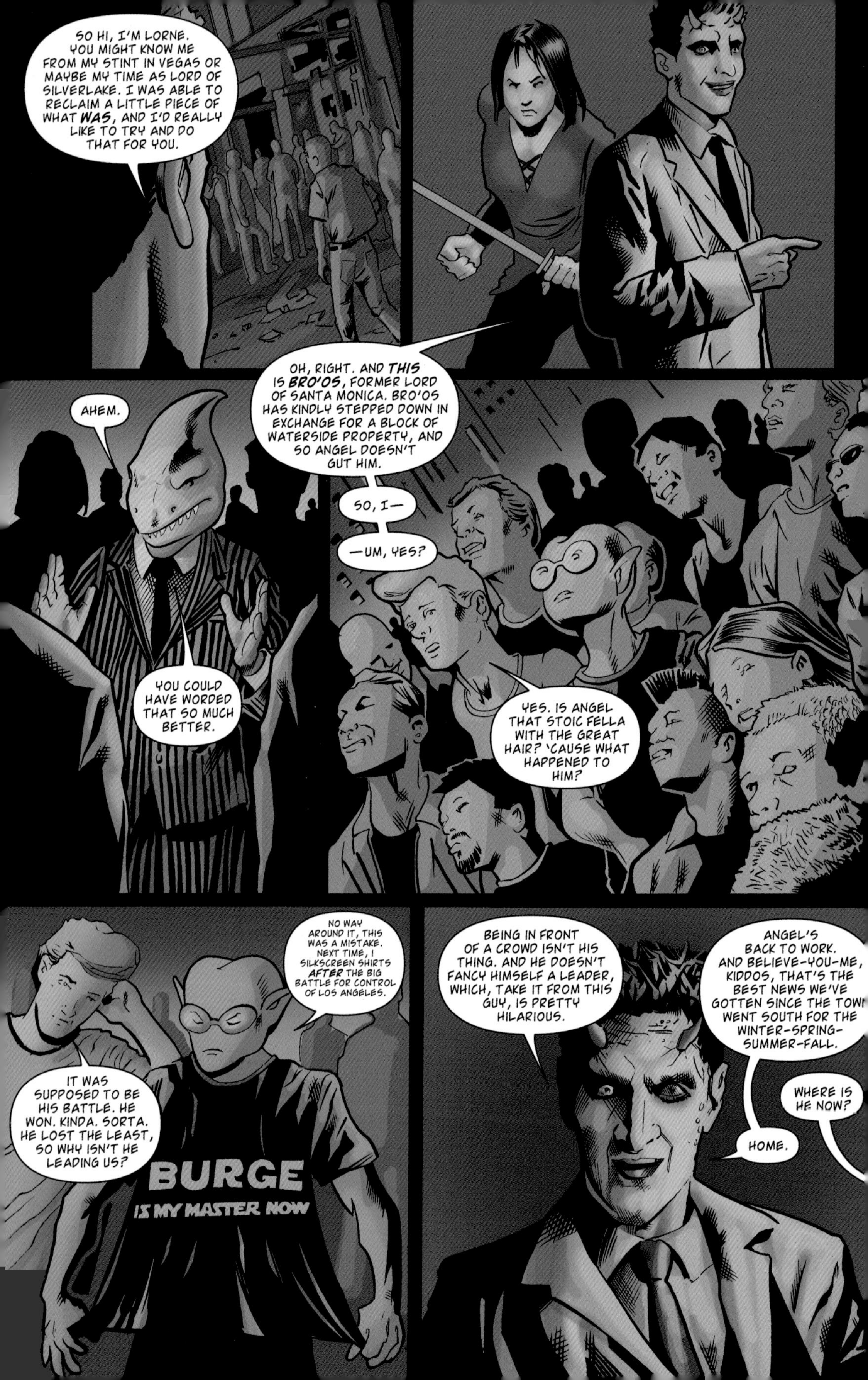
SO HI, I'M LORNE. YOU MIGHT KNOW ME FROM MY STINT IN VEGAS OR MAYBE MY TIME AS LORD OF SILVERLAKE. I WAS ABLE TO RECLAIM A LITTLE PIECE OF WHAT WAS, AND I'D REALLY LIKE TO TRY AND DO THAT FOR YOU.
OH, RIGHT. AND THIS IS BRO'OS, FORMER LORD OF SANTA MONICA. BRO'OS HAS KINDLY STEPPED DOWN IN EXCHANGE FOR A BLOCK OF WATERSIDE PROPERTY, AND SO ANGEL DOESN'T GUT HIM.
AHEM.
SO, I—
—UM, YES?
YOU COULD HAVE WORDED THAT SO MUCH BETTER.
YES. IS ANGEL THAT STOIC FELLA WITH THE GREAT HAIR? 'CAUSE WHAT HAPPENED TO HIM?
NO WAY AROUND IT, THIS WAS A MISTAKE. NEXT TIME, I SILKSCREEN SHIRTS AFTER THE BIG BATTLE FOR CONTROL OF LOS ANGELES.
IT WAS SUPPOSED TO BE HIS BATTLE. HE WON. KINDA. SORTA. HE LOST THE LEAST, SO WHY ISN'T HE LEADING US?
BURGE
IS MY MASTER NOW
BEING IN FRONT OF A CROWD ISN'T HIS THING. AND HE DOESN'T FANCY HIMSELF A LEADER, WHICH, TAKE IT FROM THIS GUY, IS PRETTY HILARIOUS.
ANGEL'S BACK TO WORK. AND BELIEVE-YOU-ME, KIDDOS, THAT'S THE BEST NEWS WE'VE GOTTEN SINCE THE TOWN WENT SOUTH FOR THE WINTER-SPRING-SUMMER-FALL.
WHERE IS HE NOW?
HOME.

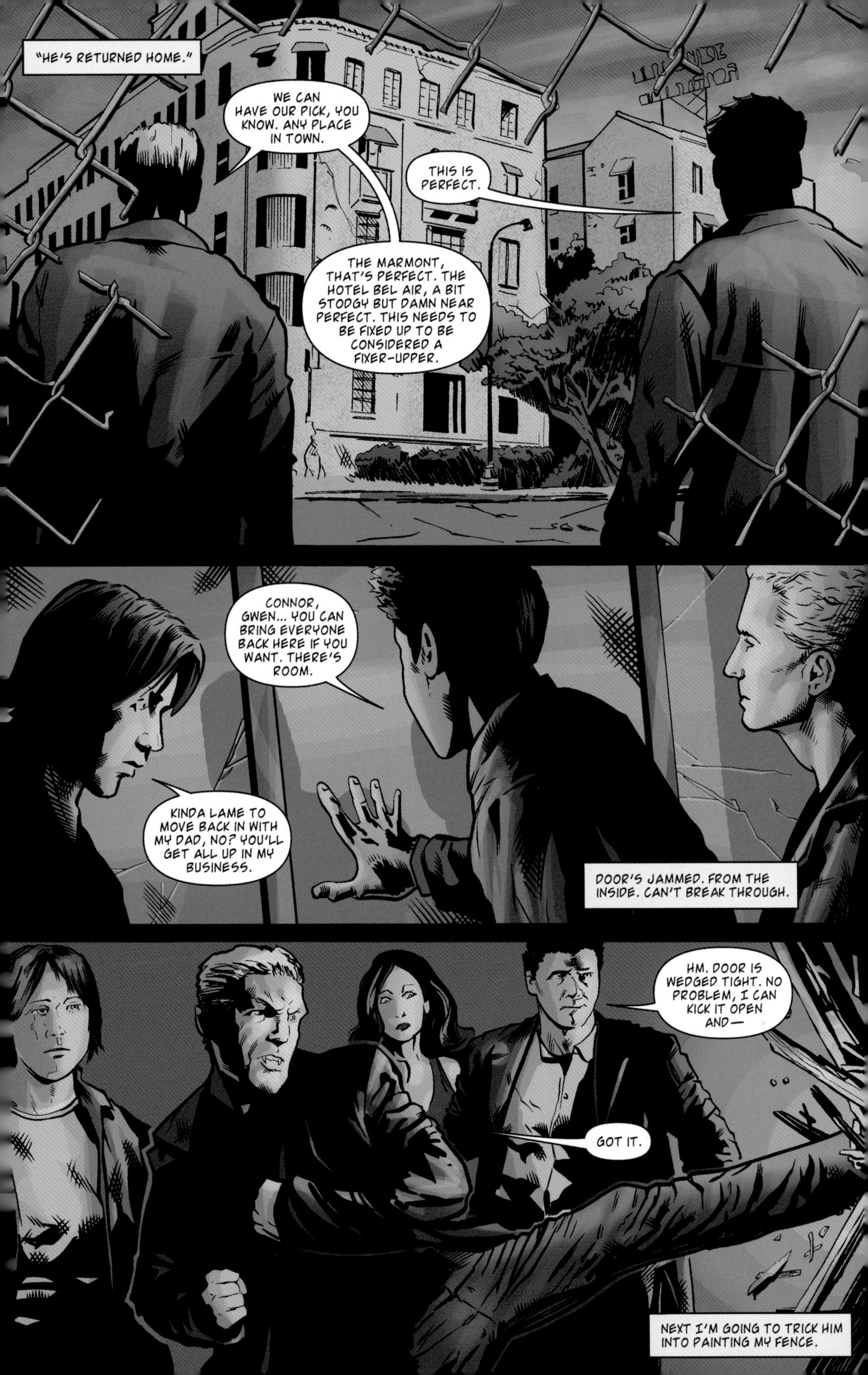
"HE'S RETURNED HOME."
WE CAN HAVE OUR PICK, YOU KNOW. ANY PLACE IN TOWN.
THIS IS PERFECT.
THE MARMONT, THAT'S PERFECT. THE HOTEL BEL AIR, A BIT STODGY BUT DAMN NEAR PERFECT. THIS NEEDS TO BE FIXED UP TO BE CONSIDERED A FIXER-UPPER.
CONNOR, GWEN... YOU CAN BRING EVERYONE BACK HERE IF YOU WANT. THERE'S ROOM.
KINDA LAME TO MOVE BACK IN WITH MY DAD, NO? YOU'LL GET ALL UP IN MY BUSINESS.
DOOR'S JAMMED. FROM THE INSIDE. CAN'T BREAK THROUGH.
HM. DOOR IS WEDGED TIGHT. NO PROBLEM, I CAN KICK IT OPEN AND—
GOT IT.
NEXT I'M GOING TO TRICK HIM INTO PAINTING MY FENCE.

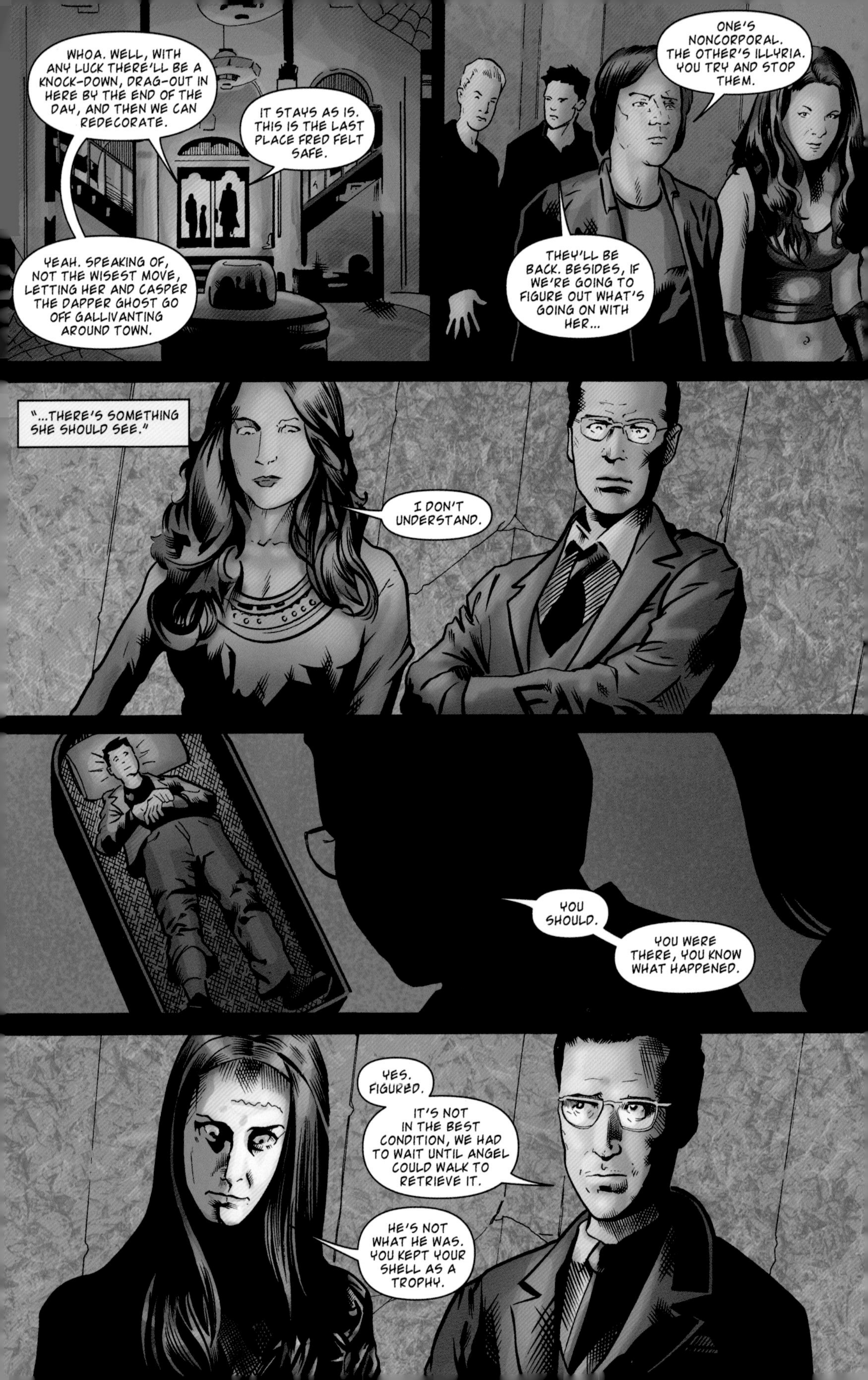
WHOA. WELL, WITH ANY LUCK THERE'LL BE A KNOCK-DOWN, DRAG-OUT IN HERE BY THE END OF THE DAY, AND THEN WE CAN REDECORATE.
IT STAYS AS IS. THIS IS THE LAST PLACE FRED FELT SAFE.
YEAH. SPEAKING OF, NOT THE WISEST MOVE, LETTING HER AND CASPER THE DAPPER GHOST GO OFF GALLIVANTING AROUND TOWN.
ONE'S NONCORPORAL. THE OTHER'S ILLYRIA. YOU TRY AND STOP THEM.
THEY'LL BE BACK. BESIDES, IF WE'RE GOING TO FIGURE OUT WHAT'S GOING ON WITH HER...
"...THERE'S SOMETHING SHE SHOULD SEE."
I DON'T UNDERSTAND.
YOU SHOULD.
YOU WERE THERE, YOU KNOW WHAT HAPPENED.
YES. FIGURED.
IT'S NOT IN THE BEST CONDITION, WE HAD TO WAIT UNTIL ANGEL COULD WALK TO RETRIEVE IT.
HE'S NOT WHAT HE WAS. YOU KEPT YOUR SHELL AS A TROPHY.

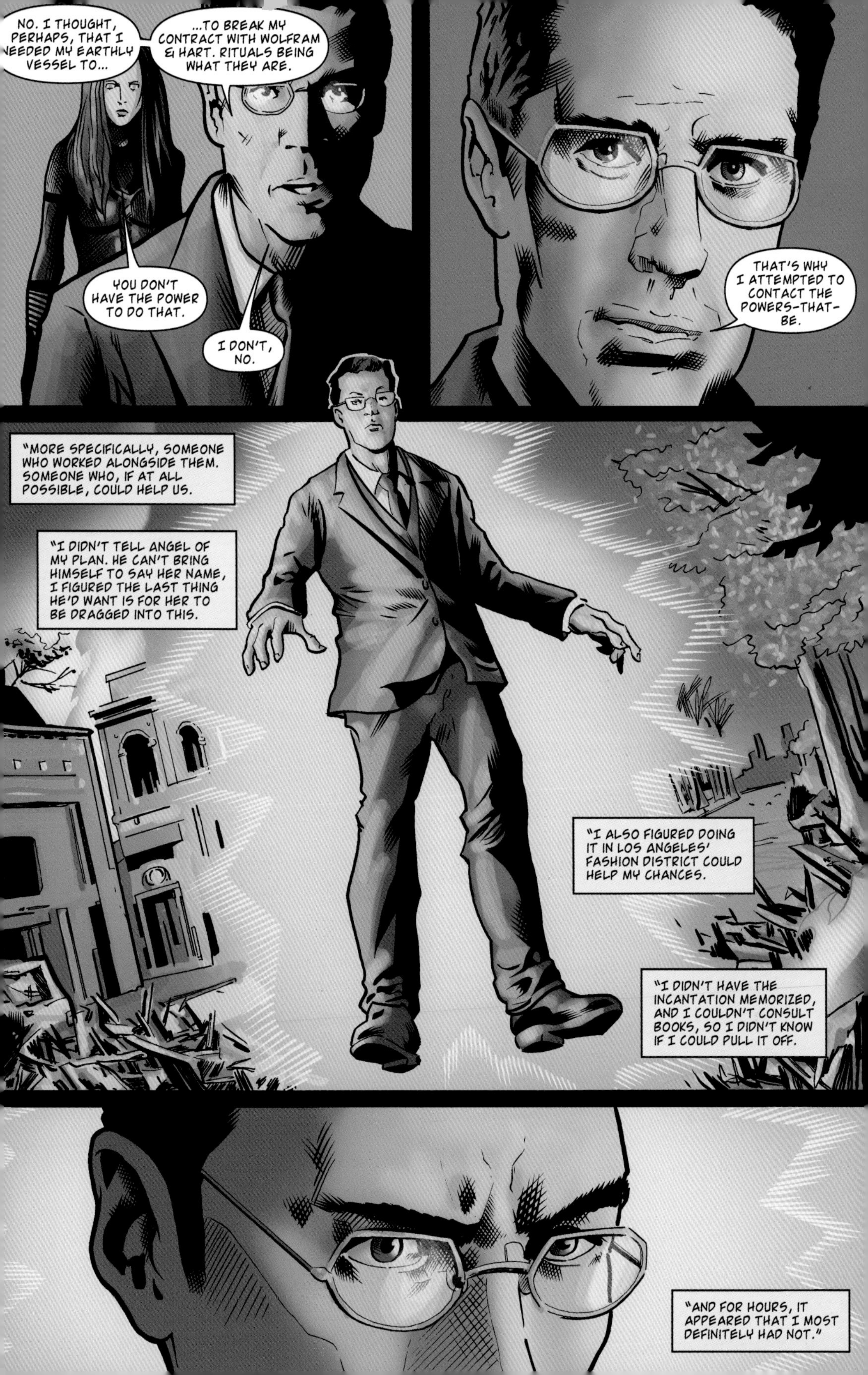
NO. I THOUGHT, PERHAPS, THAT I NEEDED MY EARTHLY VESSEL TO...
...TO BREAK MY CONTRACT WITH WOLFRAM & HART. RITUALS BEING WHAT THEY ARE.
YOU DON'T HAVE THE POWER TO DO THAT.
I DON'T, NO.
THAT'S WHY I ATTEMPTED TO CONTACT THE POWERS-THAT-BE.
"MORE SPECIFICALLY, SOMEONE WHO WORKED ALONGSIDE THEM. SOMEONE WHO, IF AT ALL POSSIBLE, COULD HELP US.
"I DIDN'T TELL ANGEL OF MY PLAN. HE CAN'T BRING HIMSELF TO SAY HER NAME, I FIGURED THE LAST THING HE'D WANT IS FOR HER TO BE DRAGGED INTO THIS.
"I ALSO FIGURED DOING IT IN LOS ANGELES' FASHION DISTRICT COULD HELP MY CHANCES.
"I DIDN'T HAVE THE INCANTATION MEMORIZED, AND I COULDN'T CONSULT BOOKS, SO I DIDN'T KNOW IF I COULD PULL IT OFF.
"AND FOR HOURS, IT APPEARED THAT I MOST DEFINITELY HAD NOT."

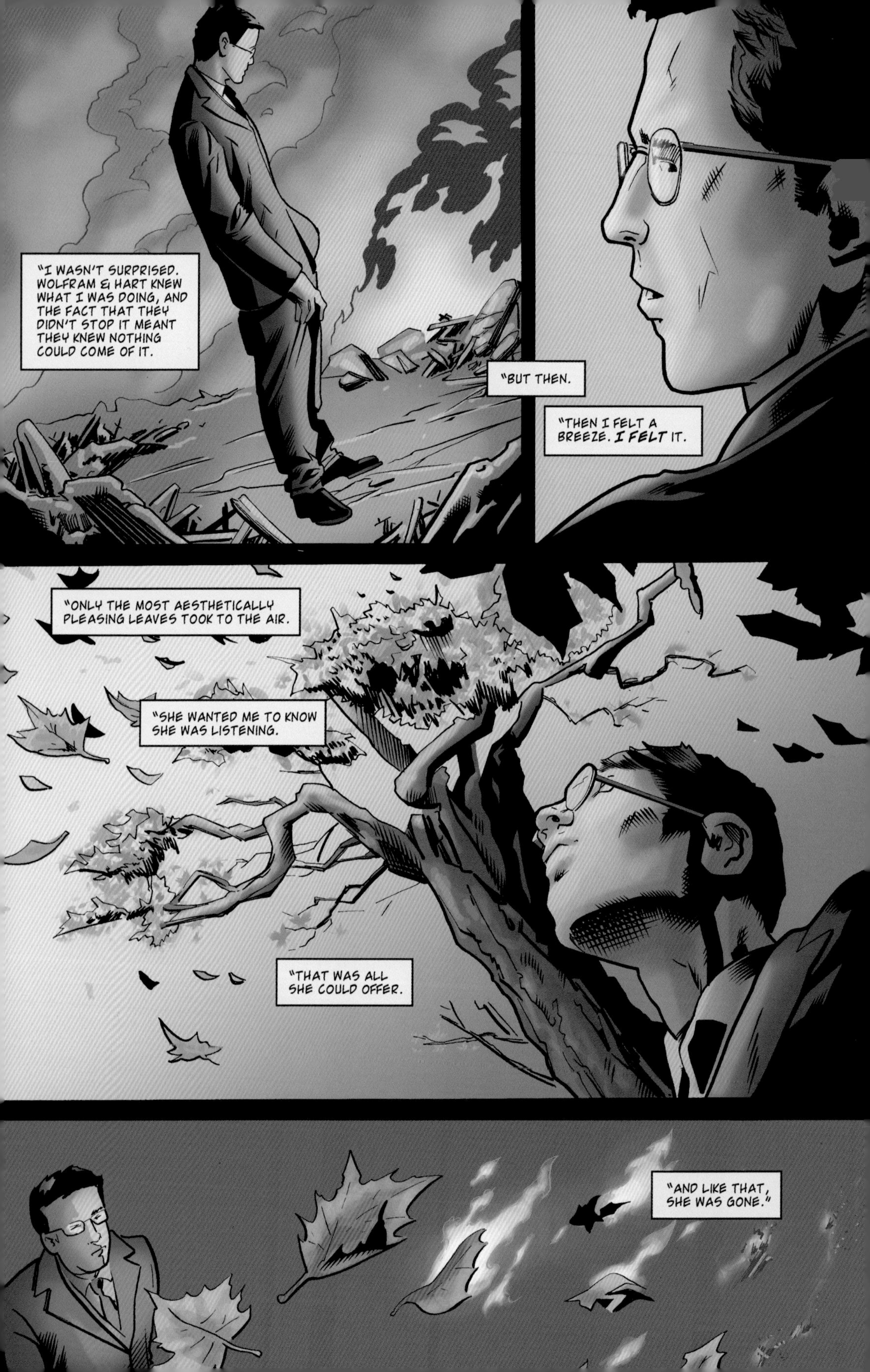
"I WASN'T SURPRISED. WOLFRAM & HART KNEW WHAT I WAS DOING, AND THE FACT THAT THEY DIDN'T STOP IT MEANT THEY KNEW NOTHING COULD COME OF IT.
"BUT THEN.
"THEN I FELT A BREEZE. I FELT IT.
"ONLY THE MOST AESTHETICALLY PLEASING LEAVES TOOK TO THE AIR.
"SHE WANTED ME TO KNOW SHE WAS LISTENING.
"THAT WAS ALL SHE COULD OFFER.
"AND LIKE THAT, SHE WAS GONE."

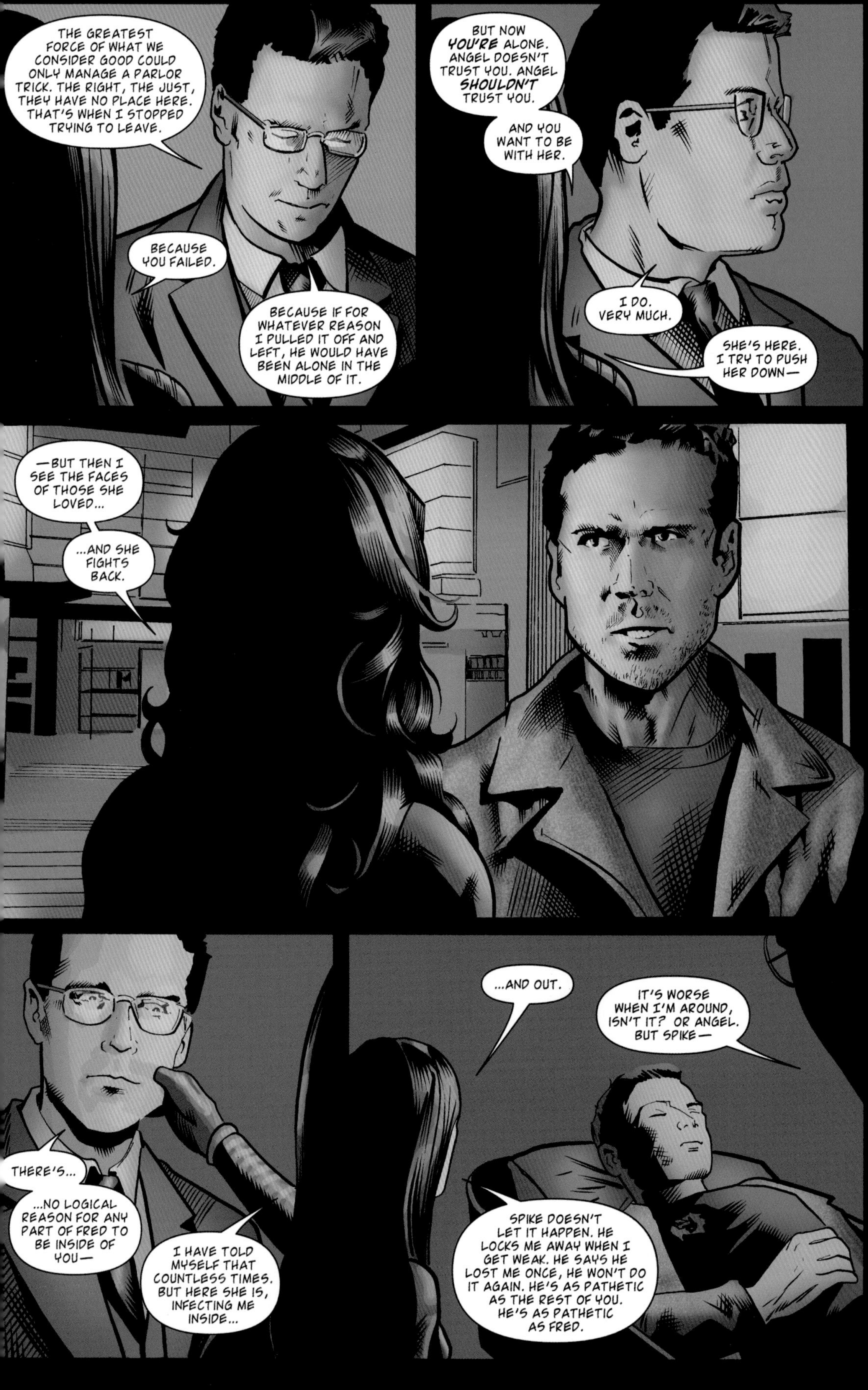
THE GREATEST FORCE OF WHAT WE CONSIDER GOOD COULD ONLY MANAGE A PARLOR TRICK. THE RIGHT, THE JUST, THEY HAVE NO PLACE HERE. THAT'S WHEN I STOPPED TRYING TO LEAVE.
BECAUSE YOU FAILED.
BECAUSE IF FOR WHATEVER REASON I PULLED IT OFF AND LEFT, HE WOULD HAVE BEEN ALONE IN THE MIDDLE OF IT.
BUT NOW YOU'RE ALONE. ANGEL DOESN'T TRUST YOU. ANGEL SHOULDN'T TRUST YOU.
AND YOU WANT TO BE WITH HER.
I DO. VERY MUCH.
SHE'S HERE. I TRY TO PUSH HER DOWN—
—BUT THEN I SEE THE FACES OF THOSE SHE LOVED...
...AND SHE FIGHTS BACK.
THERE'S...
...NO LOGICAL REASON FOR ANY PART OF FRED TO BE INSIDE OF YOU—
I HAVE TOLD MYSELF THAT COUNTLESS TIMES. BUT HERE SHE IS, INFECTING ME INSIDE...
...AND OUT.
IT'S WORSE WHEN I'M AROUND, ISN'T IT? OR ANGEL. BUT SPIKE—
SPIKE DOESN'T LET IT HAPPEN. HE LOCKS ME AWAY WHEN I GET WEAK. HE SAYS HE LOST ME ONCE, HE WON'T DO IT AGAIN. HE'S AS PATHETIC AS THE REST OF YOU. HE'S AS PATHETIC AS FRED.

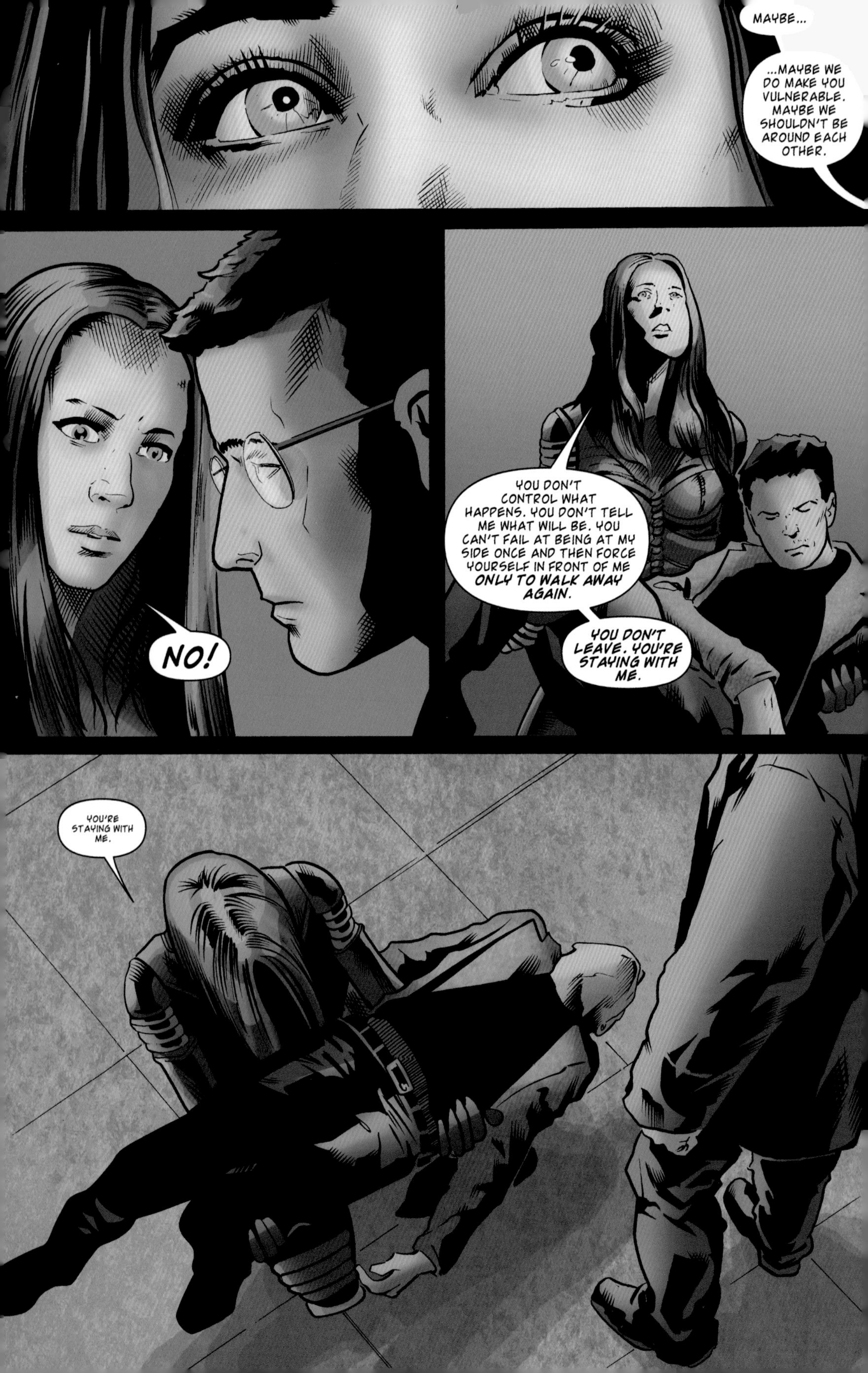
MAYBE...
...MAYBE WE DO MAKE YOU VULNERABLE. MAYBE WE SHOULDN'T BE AROUND EACH OTHER.
NO!
YOU DON'T CONTROL WHAT HAPPENS. YOU DON'T TELL ME WHAT WILL BE. YOU CAN'T FAIL AT BEING AT MY SIDE ONCE AND THEN FORCE YOURSELF IN FRONT OF ME ONLY TO WALK AWAY AGAIN.
YOU DON'T LEAVE. YOU'RE STAYING WITH ME.
YOU'RE STAYING WITH ME.

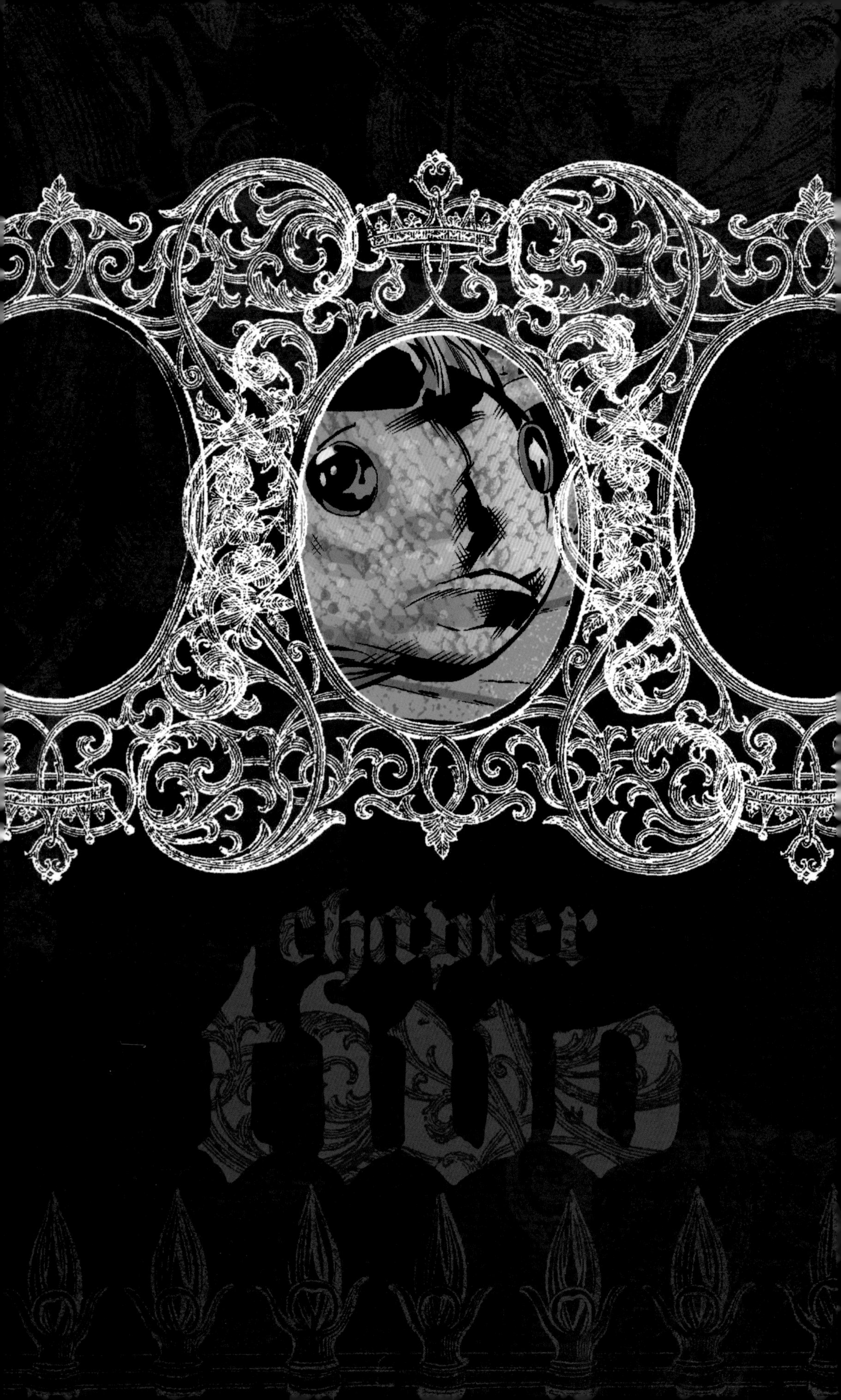
chapter
two

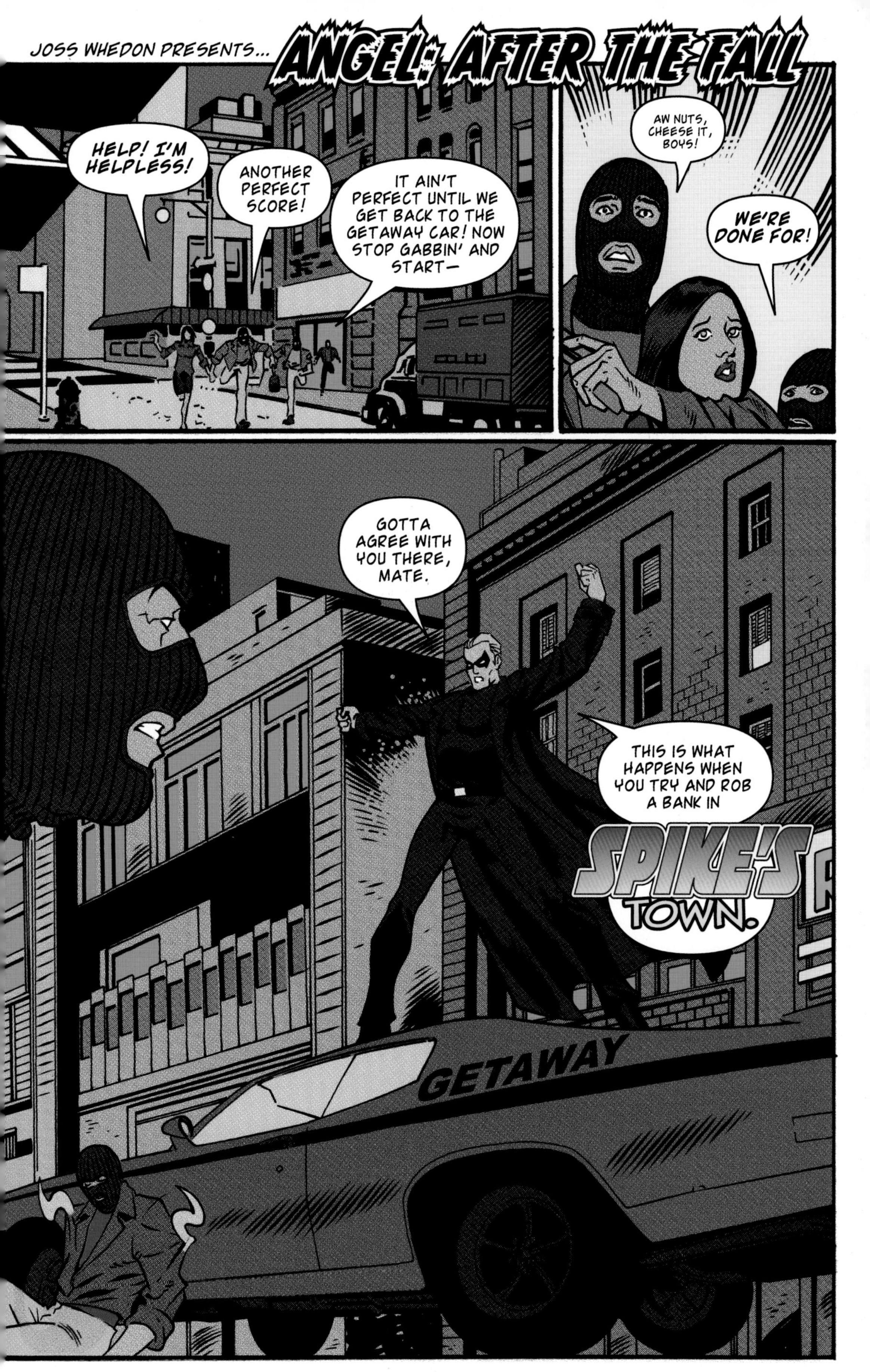
JOSS WHEDON PRESENTS...
ANGEL: AFTER THE FALL
HELP! I'M HELPLESS!
ANOTHER PERFECT SCORE!
IT AIN'T PERFECT UNTIL WE GET BACK TO THE GETAWAY CAR! NOW STOP GABBIN' AND START—
AW NUTS, CHEESE IT, BOYS!
WE'RE DONE FOR!
GOTTA AGREE WITH YOU THERE, MATE.
THIS IS WHAT HAPPENS WHEN YOU TRY AND ROB A BANK IN
SPIKE'S TOWN.
GETAWAY

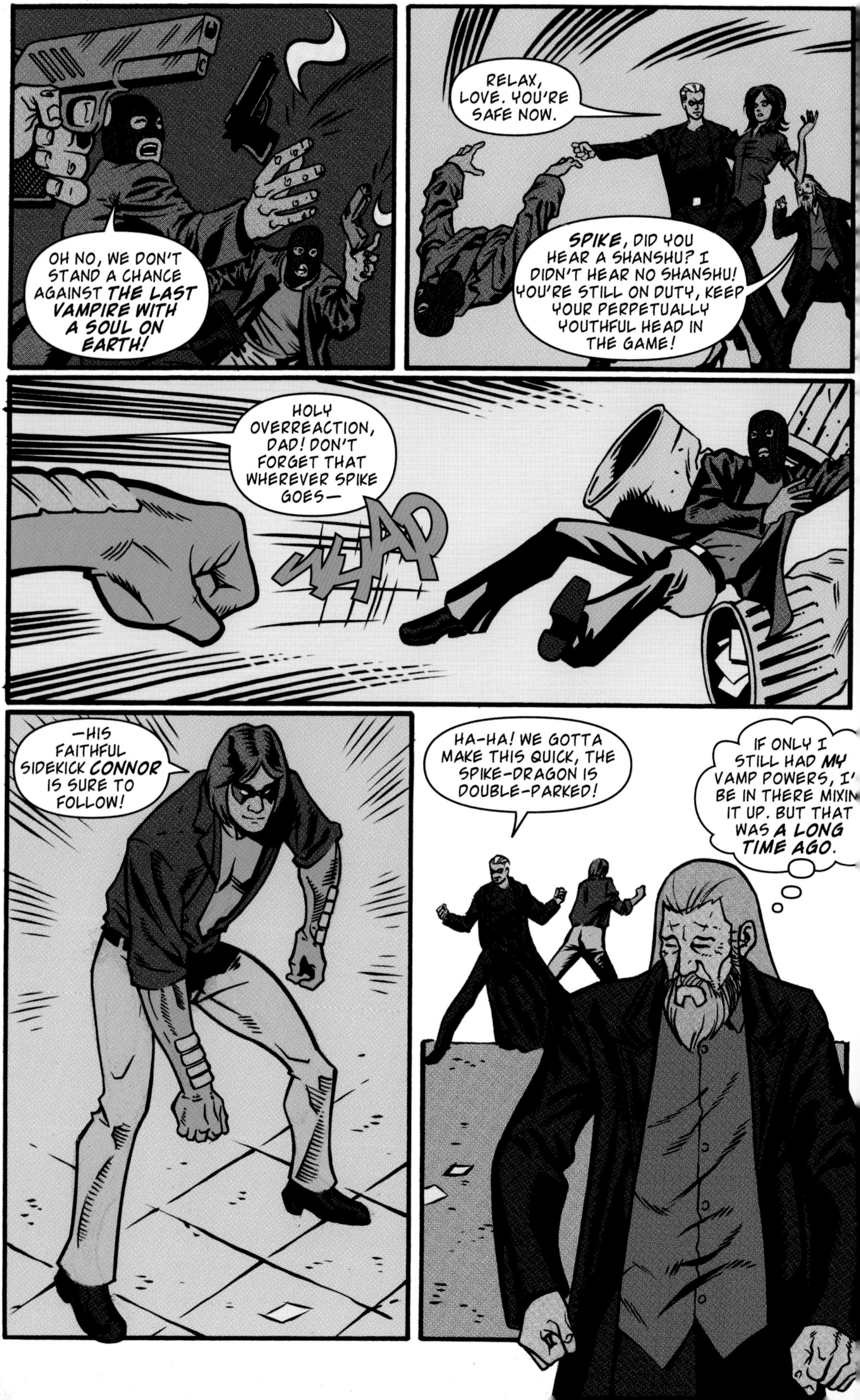
OH NO, WE DON'T STAND A CHANCE AGAINST THE LAST VAMPIRE WITH A SOUL ON EARTH!
RELAX, LOVE. YOU'RE SAFE NOW.
SPIKE, DID YOU HEAR A SHANSHU? I DIDN'T HEAR NO SHANSHU! YOU'RE STILL ON DUTY, KEEP YOUR PERPETUALLY YOUTHFUL HEAD IN THE GAME!
HOLY OVERREACTION, DAD! DON'T FORGET THAT WHEREVER SPIKE GOES—
WHAP
—HIS FAITHFUL SIDEKICK CONNOR IS SURE TO FOLLOW!
HA-HA! WE GOTTA MAKE THIS QUICK, THE SPIKE-DRAGON IS DOUBLE-PARKED!
IF ONLY I STILL HAD MY VAMP POWERS, I' BE IN THERE MIXIN IT UP. BUT THAT WAS A LONG TIME AGO.

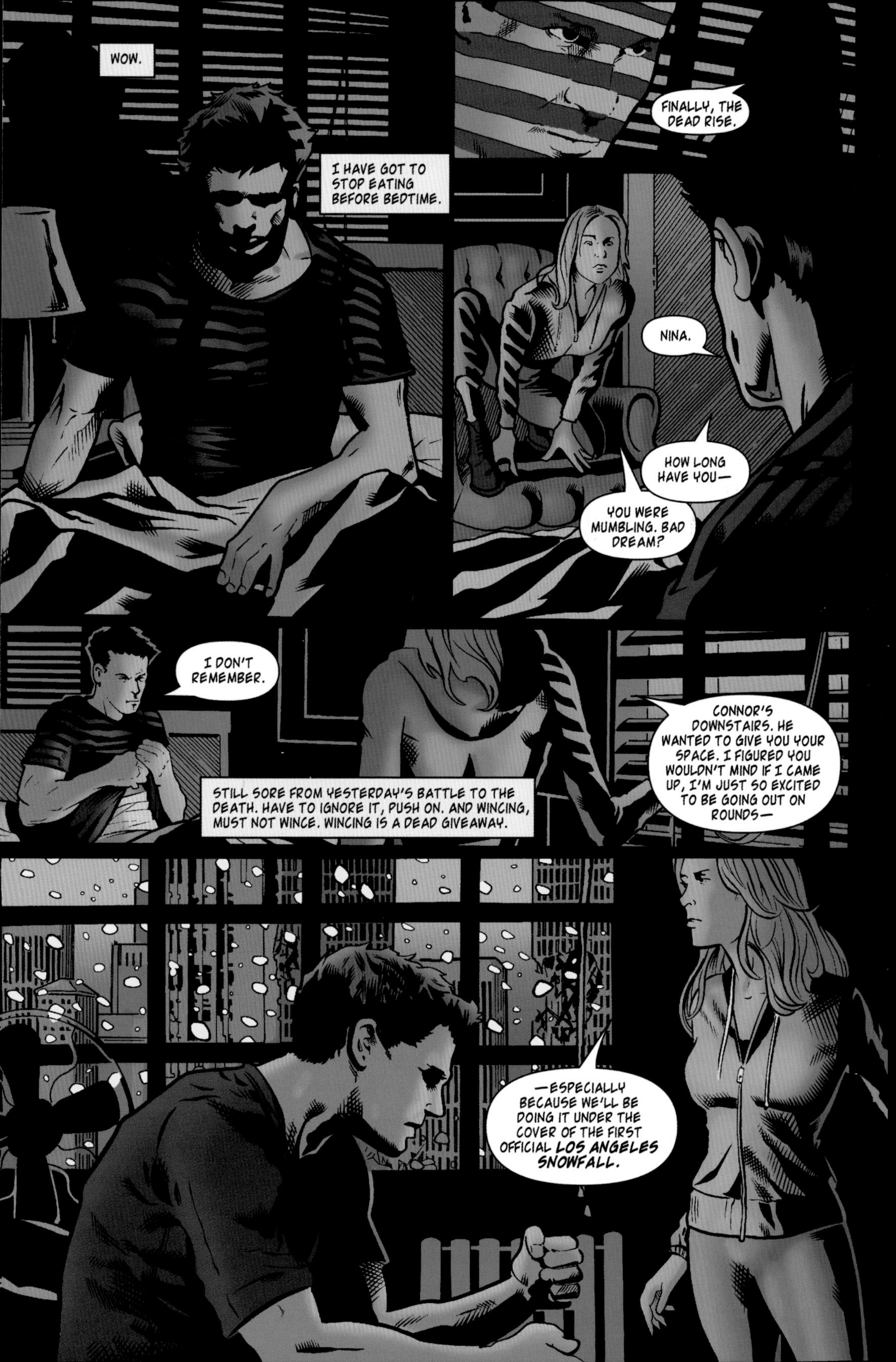
WOW.
I HAVE GOT TO STOP EATING BEFORE BEDTIME.
FINALLY, THE DEAD RISE.
NINA.
HOW LONG HAVE YOU—
YOU WERE MUMBLING. BAD DREAM?
I DON'T REMEMBER.
STILL SORE FROM YESTERDAY'S BATTLE TO THE DEATH. HAVE TO IGNORE IT, PUSH ON. AND WINCING, MUST NOT WINCE. WINCING IS A DEAD GIVEAWAY.
CONNOR'S DOWNSTAIRS. HE WANTED TO GIVE YOU YOUR SPACE. I FIGURED YOU WOULDN'T MIND IF I CAME UP, I'M JUST SO EXCITED TO BE GOING OUT ON ROUNDS—
—ESPECIALLY BECAUSE WE'LL BE DOING IT UNDER THE COVER OF THE FIRST OFFICIAL **LOS ANGELES SNOWFALL.**

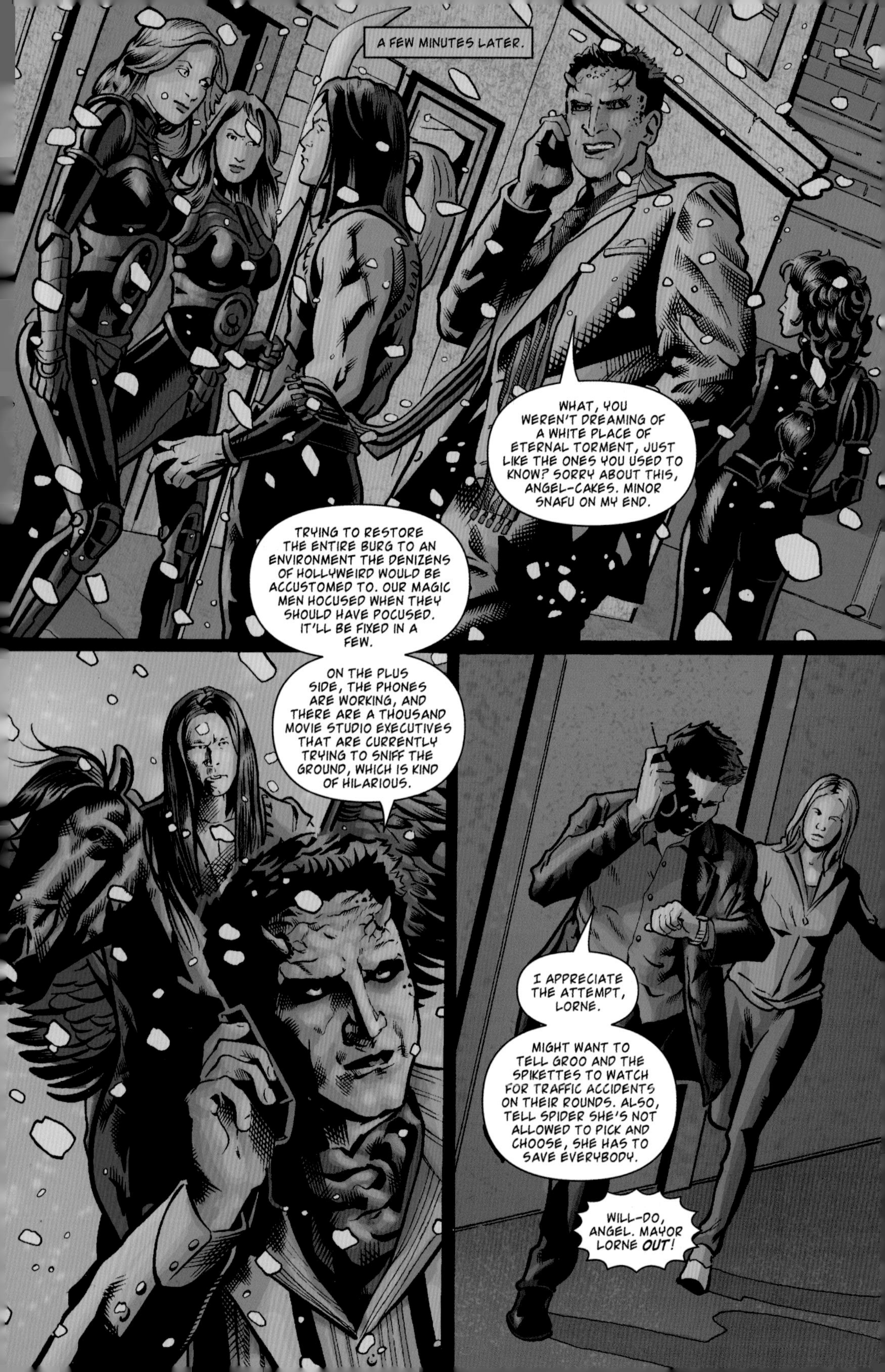
A FEW MINUTES LATER.
WHAT, YOU WEREN'T DREAMING OF A WHITE PLACE OF ETERNAL TORMENT, JUST LIKE THE ONES YOU USED TO KNOW? SORRY ABOUT THIS, ANGEL-CAKES. MINOR SNAFU ON MY END.
TRYING TO RESTORE THE ENTIRE BURG TO AN ENVIRONMENT THE DENIZENS OF HOLLYWEIRD WOULD BE ACCUSTOMED TO. OUR MAGIC MEN HOCUSED WHEN THEY SHOULD HAVE POCUSED. IT'LL BE FIXED IN A FEW.
ON THE PLUS SIDE, THE PHONES ARE WORKING, AND THERE ARE A THOUSAND MOVIE STUDIO EXECUTIVES THAT ARE CURRENTLY TRYING TO SNIFF THE GROUND, WHICH IS KIND OF HILARIOUS.
I APPRECIATE THE ATTEMPT, LORNE.
MIGHT WANT TO TELL GROO AND THE SPIKETTES TO WATCH FOR TRAFFIC ACCIDENTS ON THEIR ROUNDS. ALSO, TELL SPIDER SHE'S NOT ALLOWED TO PICK AND CHOOSE, SHE HAS TO SAVE EVERYBODY.
WILL-DO, ANGEL. MAYOR LORNE OUT!

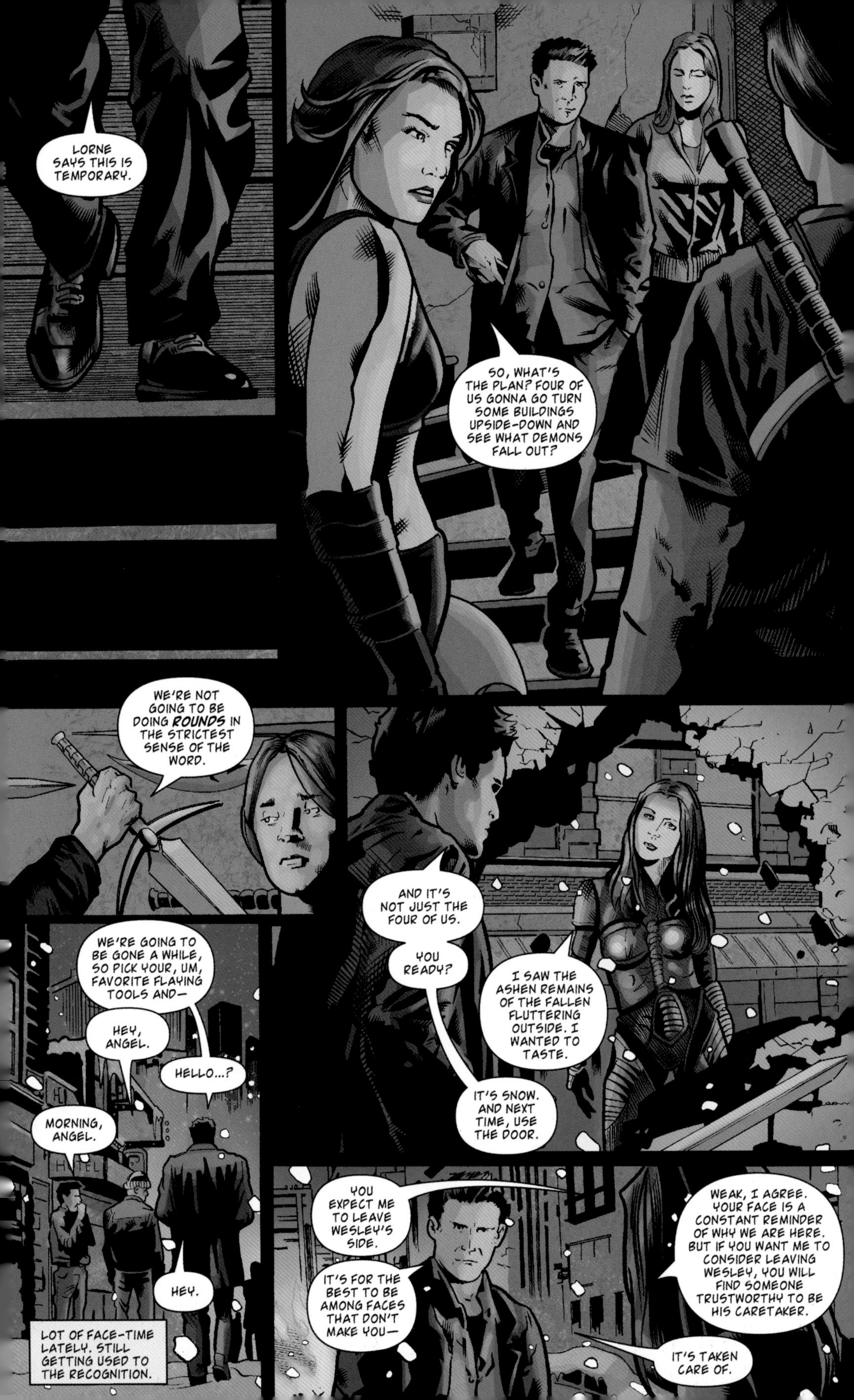
LORNE SAYS THIS IS TEMPORARY.
SO, WHAT'S THE PLAN? FOUR OF US GONNA GO TURN SOME BUILDINGS UPSIDE-DOWN AND SEE WHAT DEMONS FALL OUT?
WE'RE NOT GOING TO BE DOING ROUNDS IN THE STRICTEST SENSE OF THE WORD.
AND IT'S NOT JUST THE FOUR OF US.
YOU READY?
I SAW THE ASHEN REMAINS OF THE FALLEN FLUTTERING OUTSIDE. I WANTED TO TASTE.
IT'S SNOW. AND NEXT TIME, USE THE DOOR.
WE'RE GOING TO BE GONE A WHILE, SO PICK YOUR, UM, FAVORITE FLAYING TOOLS AND—
HEY, ANGEL.
HELLO...?
MORNING, ANGEL.
HEY.
LOT OF FACE-TIME LATELY. STILL GETTING USED TO THE RECOGNITION.
YOU EXPECT ME TO LEAVE WESLEY'S SIDE.
IT'S FOR THE BEST TO BE AMONG FACES THAT DON'T MAKE YOU—
WEAK, I AGREE. YOUR FACE IS A CONSTANT REMINDER OF WHY WE ARE HERE. BUT IF YOU WANT ME TO CONSIDER LEAVING WESLEY, YOU WILL FIND SOMEONE TRUSTWORTHY TO BE HIS CARETAKER.
IT'S TAKEN CARE OF.

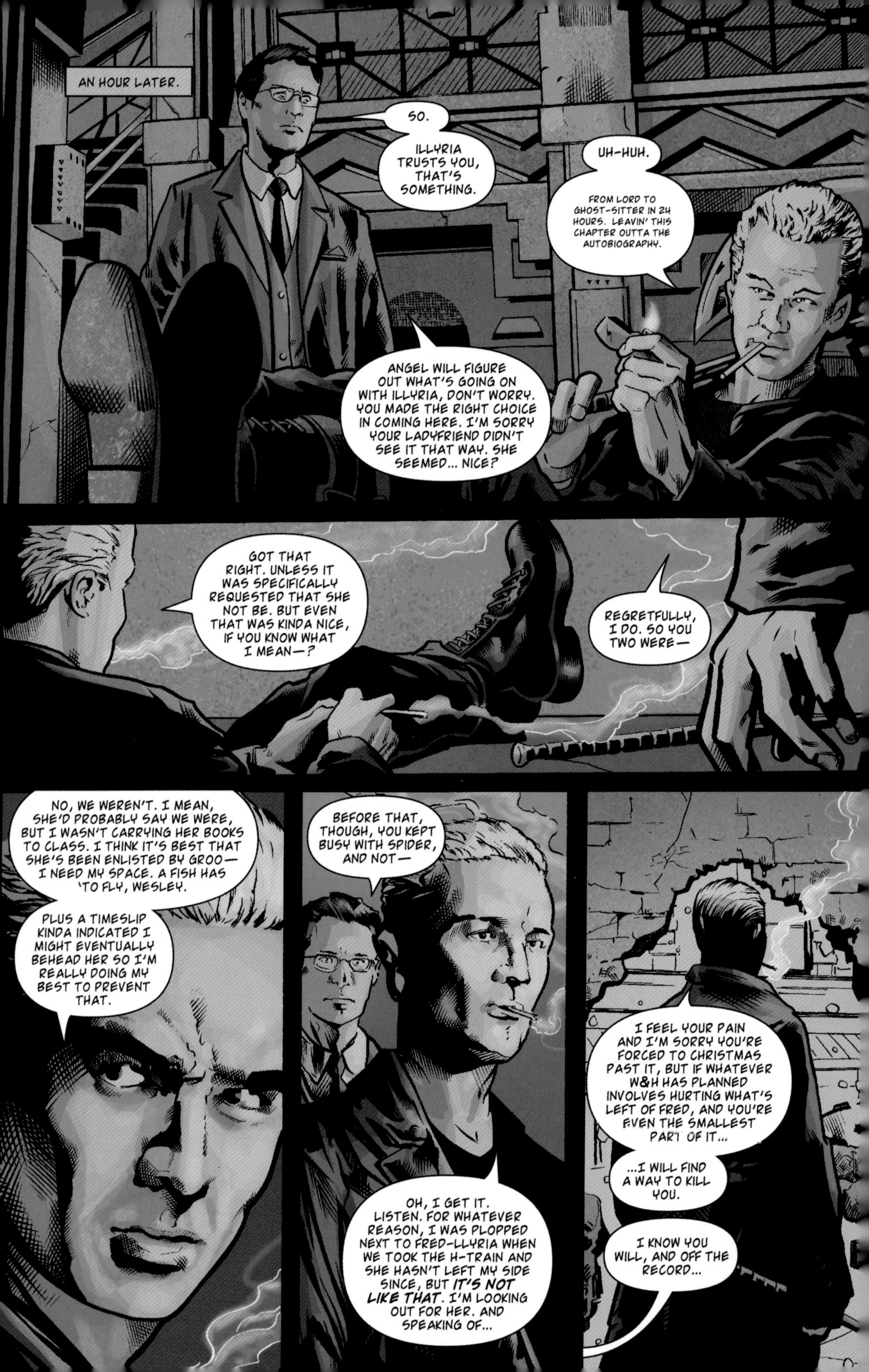
AN HOUR LATER.
SO.
ILLYRIA TRUSTS YOU, THAT'S SOMETHING.
UH-HUH.
FROM LORD TO GHOST-SITTER IN 24 HOURS. LEAVIN' THIS CHAPTER OUTTA THE AUTOBIOGRAPHY.
ANGEL WILL FIGURE OUT WHAT'S GOING ON WITH ILLYRIA, DON'T WORRY. YOU MADE THE RIGHT CHOICE IN COMING HERE. I'M SORRY YOUR LADYFRIEND DIDN'T SEE IT THAT WAY. SHE SEEMED... NICE?
GOT THAT RIGHT. UNLESS IT WAS SPECIFICALLY REQUESTED THAT SHE NOT BE. BUT EVEN THAT WAS KINDA NICE, IF YOU KNOW WHAT I MEAN—?
REGRETFULLY, I DO. SO YOU TWO WERE—
NO, WE WEREN'T. I MEAN, SHE'D PROBABLY SAY WE WERE, BUT I WASN'T CARRYING HER BOOKS TO CLASS. I THINK IT'S BEST THAT SHE'S BEEN ENLISTED BY GROO— I NEED MY SPACE. A FISH HAS 'TO FLY, WESLEY.
PLUS A TIMESLIP KINDA INDICATED I MIGHT EVENTUALLY BEHEAD HER SO I'M REALLY DOING MY BEST TO PREVENT THAT.
BEFORE THAT, THOUGH, YOU KEPT BUSY WITH SPIDER, AND NOT—
OH, I GET IT. LISTEN. FOR WHATEVER REASON, I WAS PLOPPED NEXT TO FRED-LLYRIA WHEN WE TOOK THE H-TRAIN AND SHE HASN'T LEFT MY SIDE SINCE, BUT IT'S NOT LIKE THAT. I'M LOOKING OUT FOR HER. AND SPEAKING OF...
I FEEL YOUR PAIN AND I'M SORRY YOU'RE FORCED TO CHRISTMAS PAST IT, BUT IF WHATEVER W&H HAS PLANNED INVOLVES HURTING WHAT'S LEFT OF FRED, AND YOU'RE EVEN THE SMALLEST PART OF IT...
...I WILL FIND A WAY TO KILL YOU.
I KNOW YOU WILL, AND OFF THE RECORD...

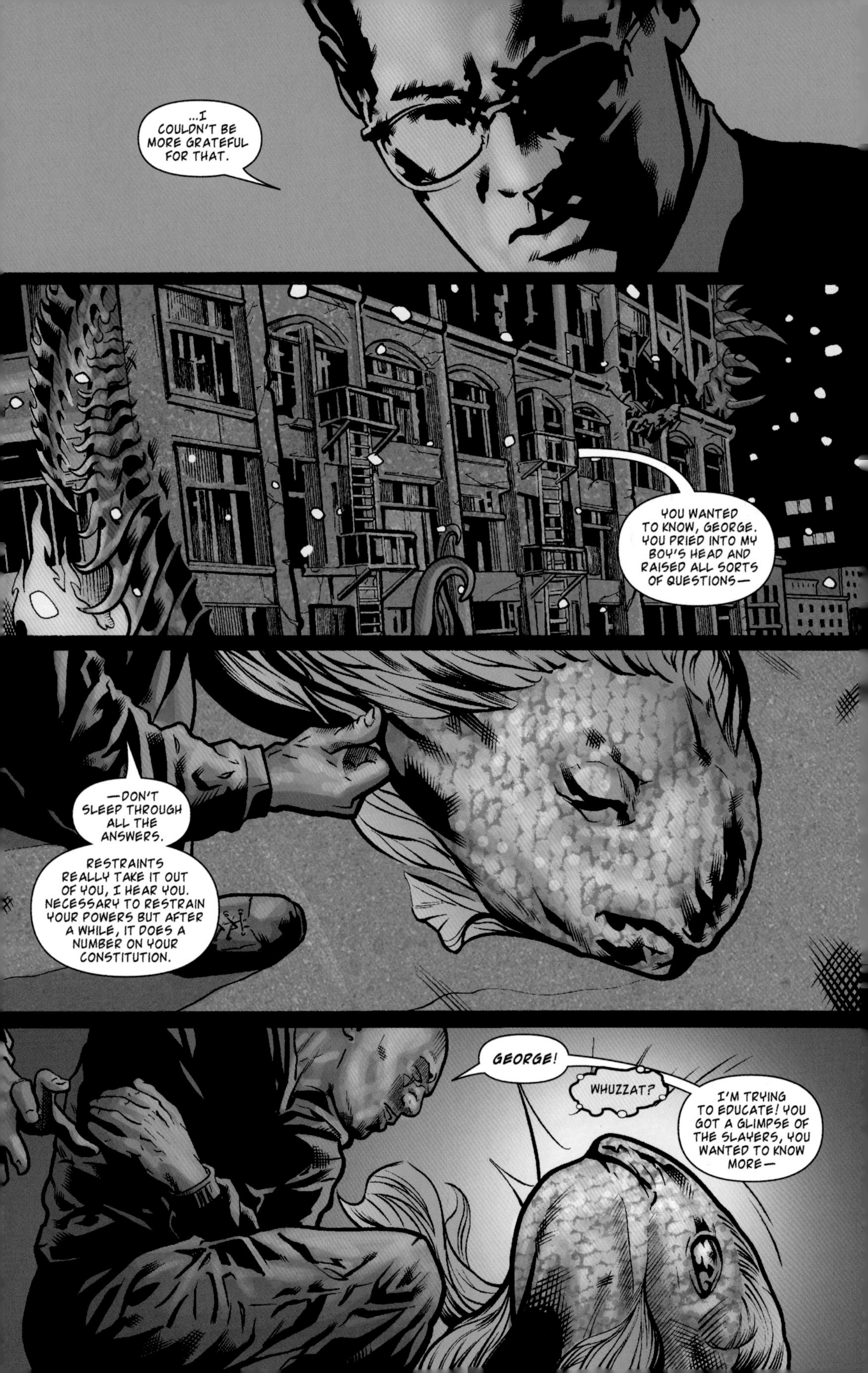
...I COULDN'T BE MORE GRATEFUL FOR THAT.
YOU WANTED TO KNOW, GEORGE. YOU PRIED INTO MY BOY'S HEAD AND RAISED ALL SORTS OF QUESTIONS—
—DON'T SLEEP THROUGH ALL THE ANSWERS.
RESTRAINTS REALLY TAKE IT OUT OF YOU, I HEAR YOU. NECESSARY TO RESTRAIN YOUR POWERS BUT AFTER A WHILE, IT DOES A NUMBER ON YOUR CONSTITUTION.
GEORGE!
WHUZZAT?
I'M TRYING TO EDUCATE! YOU GOT A GLIMPSE OF THE SLAYERS, YOU WANTED TO KNOW MORE—

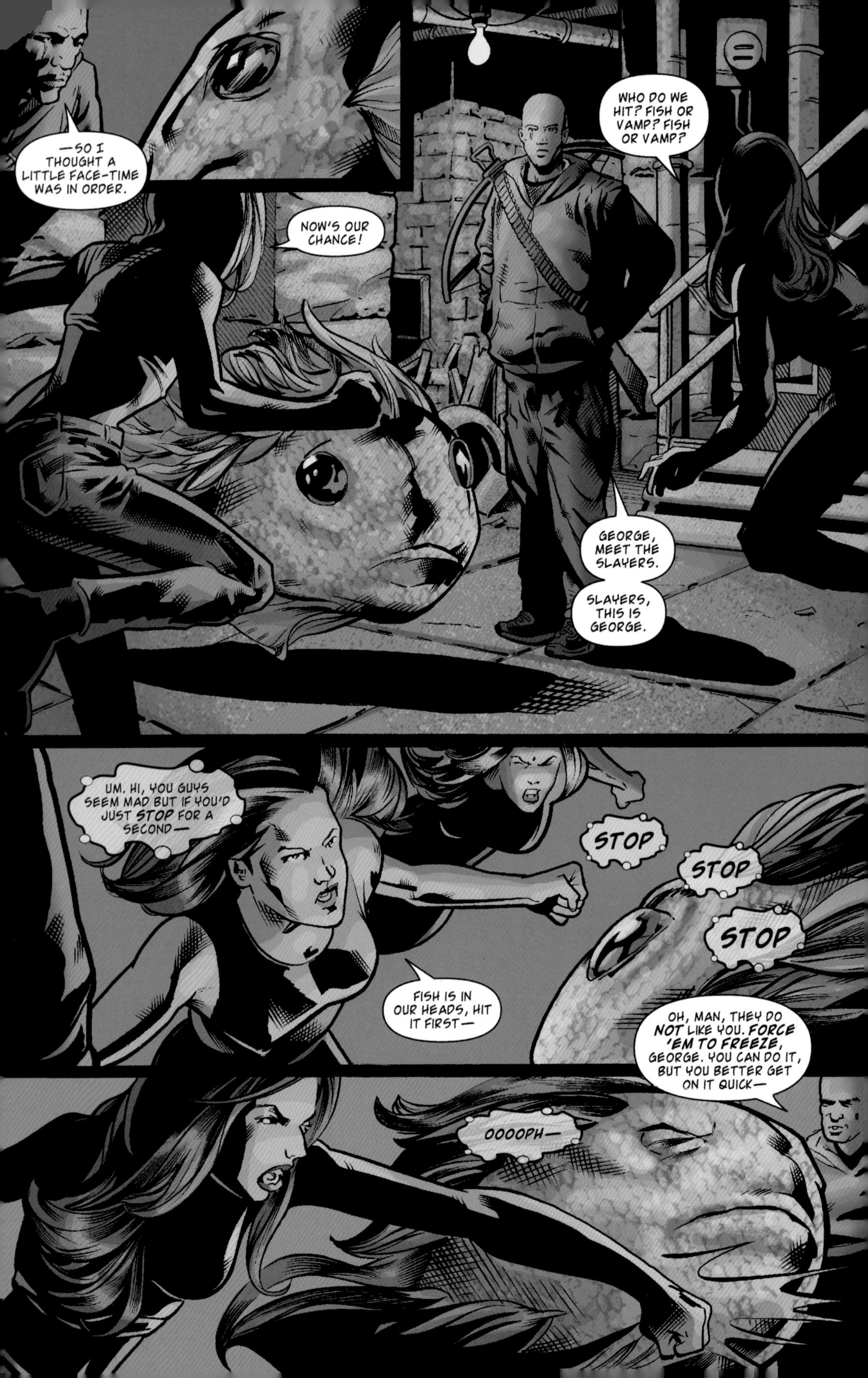
—SO I THOUGHT A LITTLE FACE-TIME WAS IN ORDER.
WHO DO WE HIT? FISH OR VAMP? FISH OR VAMP?
NOW'S OUR CHANCE!
GEORGE, MEET THE SLAYERS.
SLAYERS, THIS IS GEORGE.
UM. HI, YOU GUYS SEEM MAD BUT IF YOU'D JUST ***STOP*** FOR A SECOND—
STOP
STOP
STOP
FISH IS IN OUR HEADS, HIT IT FIRST—
OH, MAN, THEY DO ***NOT*** LIKE YOU. ***FORCE 'EM TO FREEZE***, GEORGE. YOU CAN DO IT, BUT YOU BETTER GET ON IT QUICK—
OOOOPH—

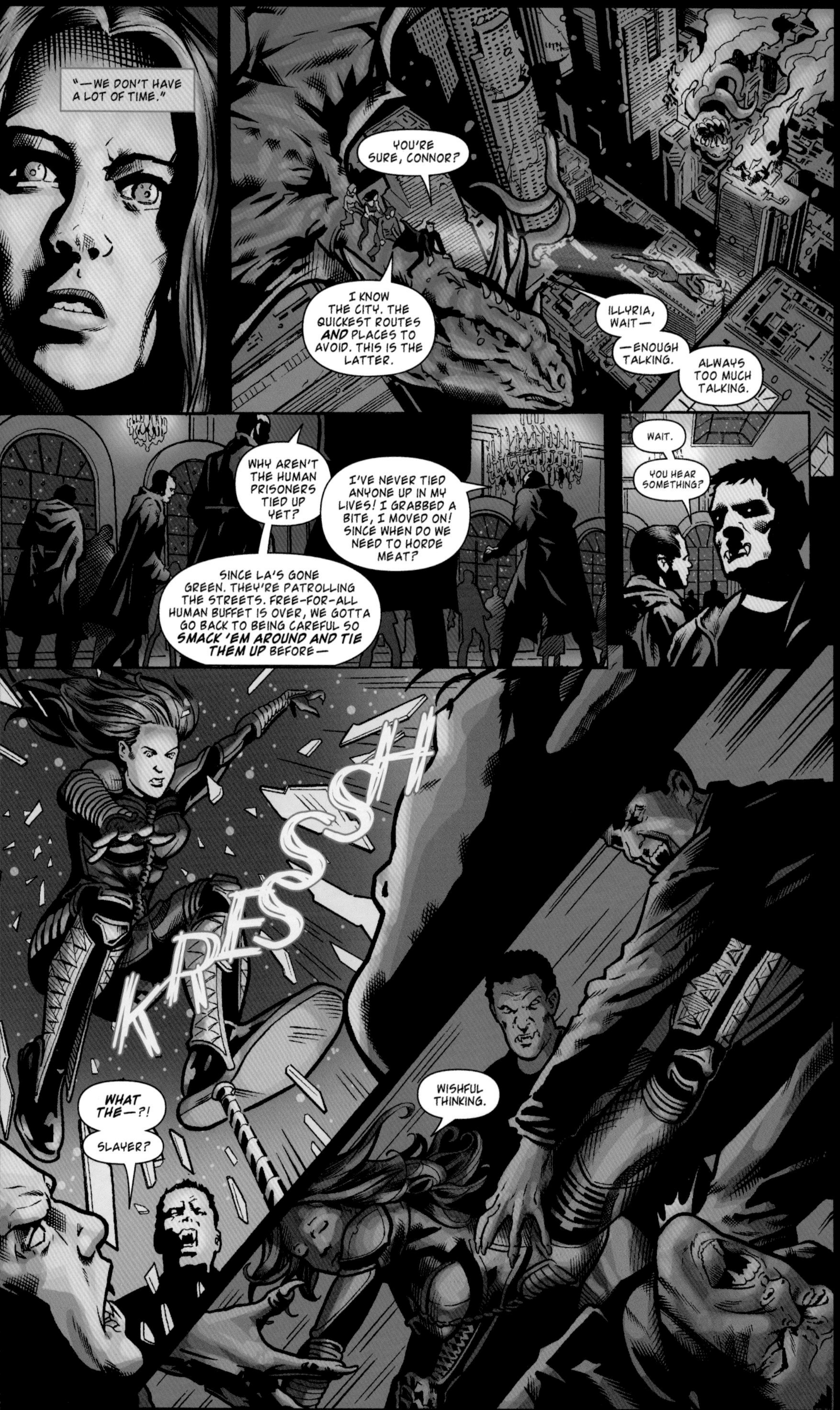
"—WE DON'T HAVE A LOT OF TIME."
YOU'RE SURE, CONNOR?
I KNOW THE CITY. THE QUICKEST ROUTES AND PLACES TO AVOID. THIS IS THE LATTER.
ILLYRIA, WAIT—
—ENOUGH TALKING.
ALWAYS TOO MUCH TALKING.
WHY AREN'T THE HUMAN PRISONERS TIED UP YET?
I'VE NEVER TIED ANYONE UP IN MY LIVES! I GRABBED A BITE, I MOVED ON! SINCE WHEN DO WE NEED TO HORDE MEAT?
SINCE LA'S GONE GREEN. THEY'RE PATROLLING THE STREETS. FREE-FOR-ALL HUMAN BUFFET IS OVER, WE GOTTA GO BACK TO BEING CAREFUL SO SMACK 'EM AROUND AND TIE THEM UP BEFORE—
WAIT.
YOU HEAR SOMETHING?
KRESSSH
WHAT THE—?!
SLAYER?
WISHFUL THINKING.

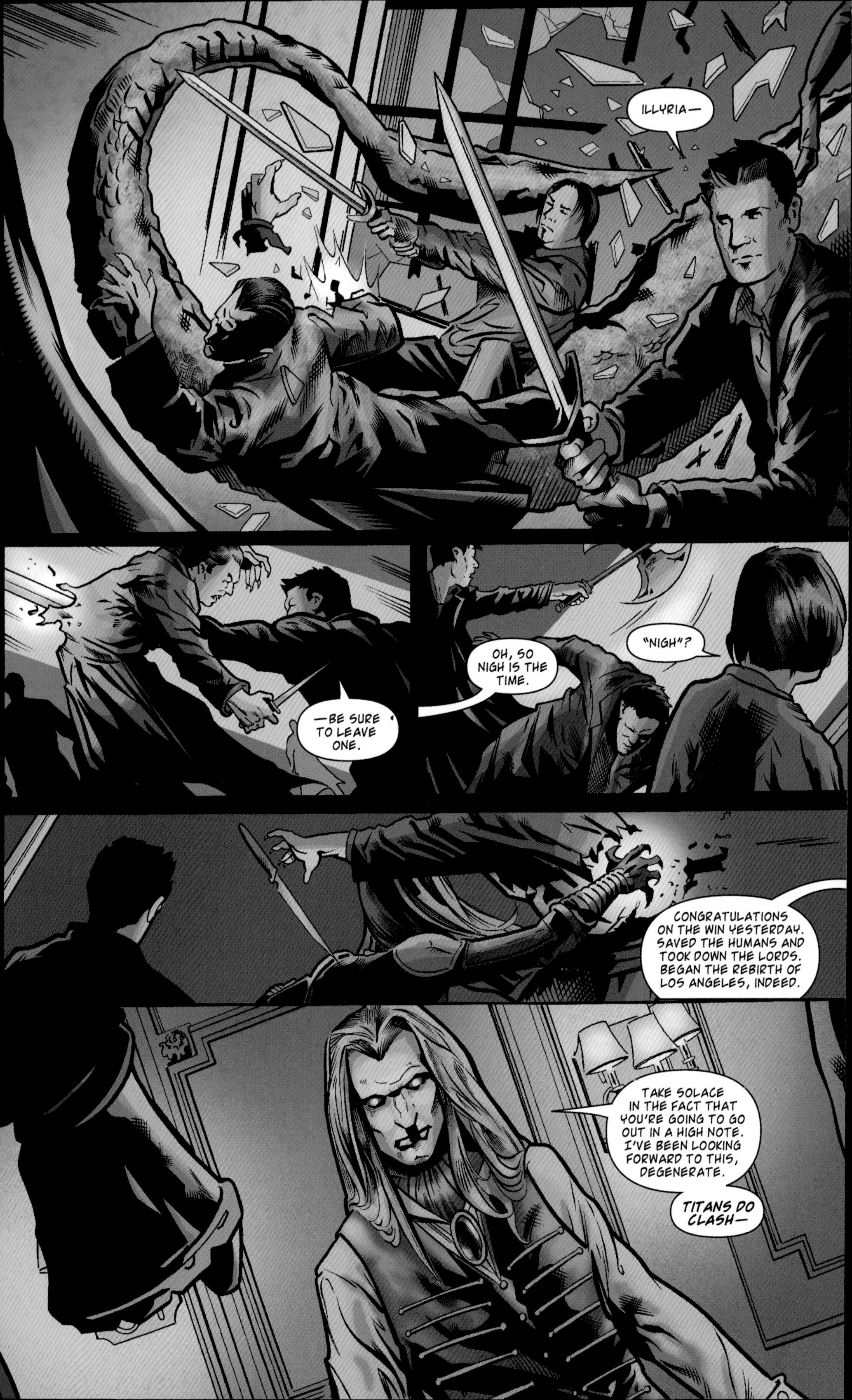
ILLYRIA—
—BE SURE TO LEAVE ONE.
OH, SO NIGH IS THE TIME.
"NIGH"?
CONGRATULATIONS ON THE WIN YESTERDAY. SAVED THE HUMANS AND TOOK DOWN THE LORDS. BEGAN THE REBIRTH OF LOS ANGELES, INDEED.
TAKE SOLACE IN THE FACT THAT YOU'RE GOING TO GO OUT IN A HIGH NOTE. I'VE BEEN LOOKING FORWARD TO THIS, DEGENERATE.
TITANS DO CLASH—

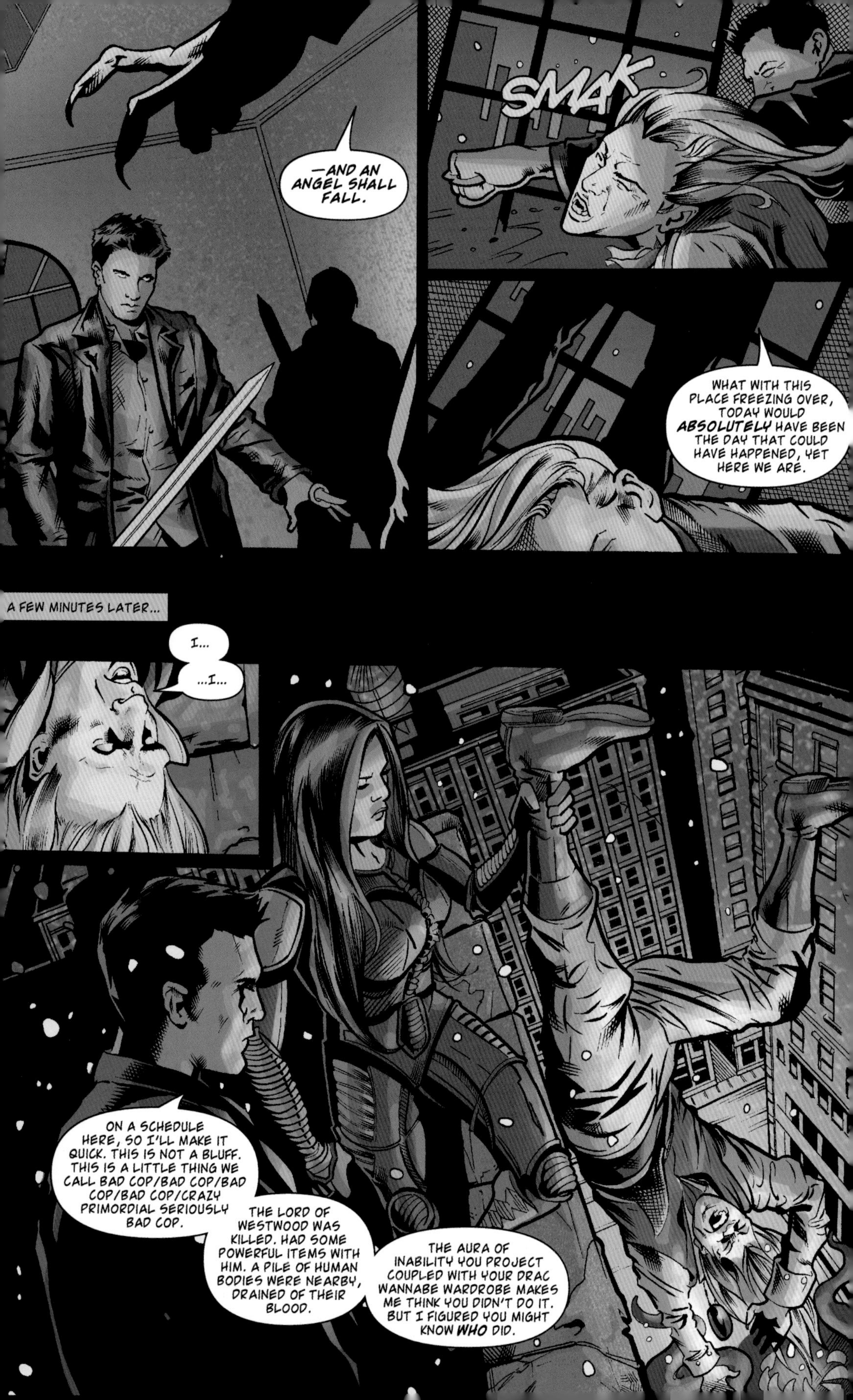
—AND AN ANGEL SHALL FALL.
SMAK
WHAT WITH THIS PLACE FREEZING OVER, TODAY WOULD ABSOLUTELY HAVE BEEN THE DAY THAT COULD HAVE HAPPENED, YET HERE WE ARE.
A FEW MINUTES LATER...
I...
...I...
ON A SCHEDULE HERE, SO I'LL MAKE IT QUICK. THIS IS NOT A BLUFF. THIS IS A LITTLE THING WE CALL BAD COP/BAD COP/BAD COP/BAD COP/CRAZY PRIMORDIAL SERIOUSLY BAD COP.
THE LORD OF WESTWOOD WAS KILLED. HAD SOME POWERFUL ITEMS WITH HIM. A PILE OF HUMAN BODIES WERE NEARBY, DRAINED OF THEIR BLOOD.
THE AURA OF INABILITY YOU PROJECT COUPLED WITH YOUR DRAC WANNABE WARDROBE MAKES ME THINK YOU DIDN'T DO IT. BUT I FIGURED YOU MIGHT KNOW WHO DID.

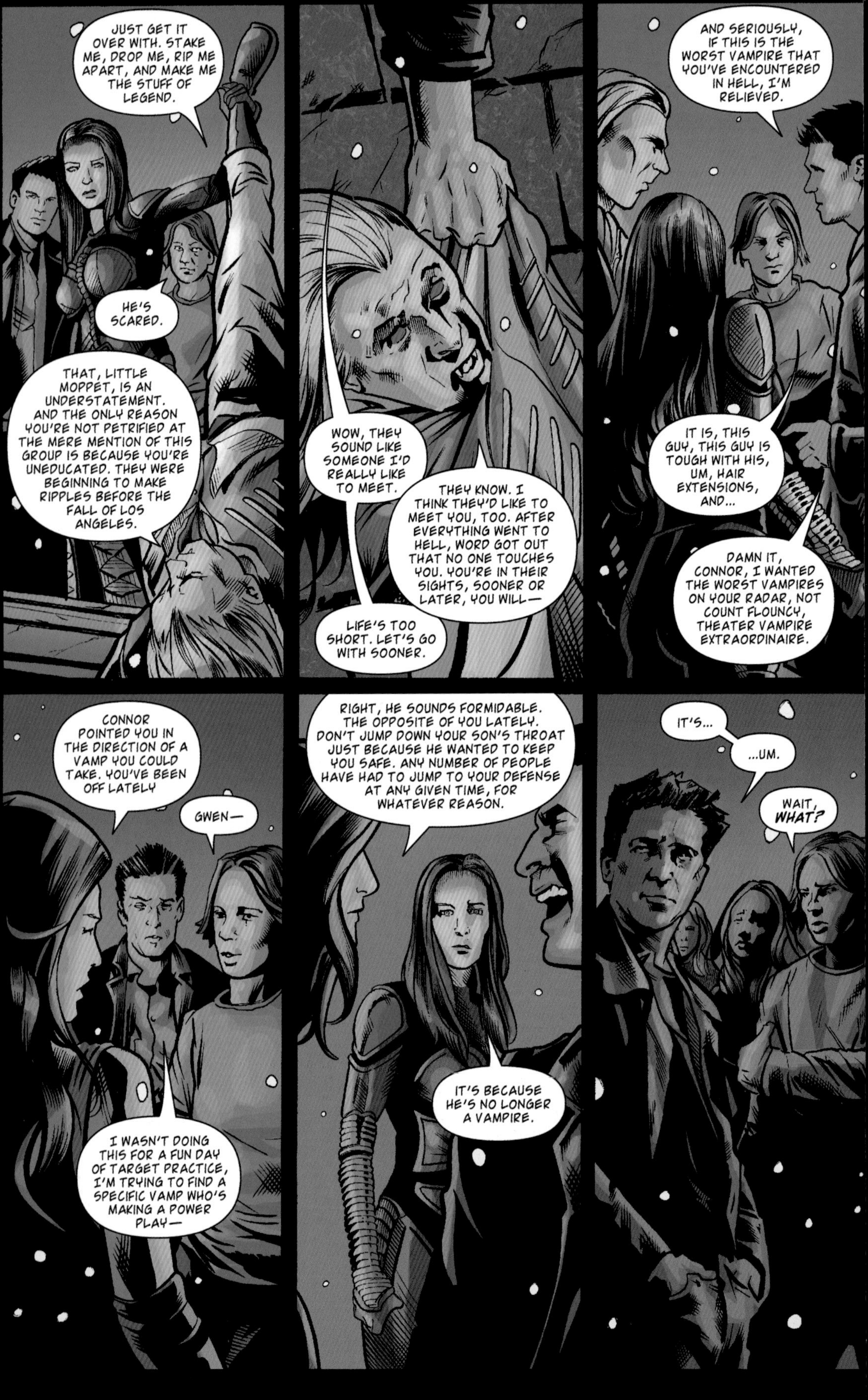
JUST GET IT OVER WITH. STAKE ME, DROP ME, RIP ME APART, AND MAKE ME THE STUFF OF LEGEND.
HE'S SCARED.
THAT, LITTLE MOPPET, IS AN UNDERSTATEMENT. AND THE ONLY REASON YOU'RE NOT PETRIFIED AT THE MERE MENTION OF THIS GROUP IS BECAUSE YOU'RE UNEDUCATED. THEY WERE BEGINNING TO MAKE RIPPLES BEFORE THE FALL OF LOS ANGELES.
WOW, THEY SOUND LIKE SOMEONE I'D REALLY LIKE TO MEET.
THEY KNOW. I THINK THEY'D LIKE TO MEET YOU, TOO. AFTER EVERYTHING WENT TO HELL, WORD GOT OUT THAT NO ONE TOUCHES YOU. YOU'RE IN THEIR SIGHTS, SOONER OR LATER, YOU WILL—
LIFE'S TOO SHORT. LET'S GO WITH SOONER.
AND SERIOUSLY, IF THIS IS THE WORST VAMPIRE THAT YOU'VE ENCOUNTERED IN HELL, I'M RELIEVED.
IT IS, THIS GUY, THIS GUY IS TOUGH WITH HIS, UM, HAIR EXTENSIONS, AND...
DAMN IT, CONNOR, I WANTED THE WORST VAMPIRES ON YOUR RADAR, NOT COUNT FLOUNCY, THEATER VAMPIRE EXTRAORDINAIRE.
CONNOR POINTED YOU IN THE DIRECTION OF A VAMP YOU COULD TAKE. YOU'VE BEEN OFF LATELY
GWEN—
I WASN'T DOING THIS FOR A FUN DAY OF TARGET PRACTICE, I'M TRYING TO FIND A SPECIFIC VAMP WHO'S MAKING A POWER PLAY—
RIGHT, HE SOUNDS FORMIDABLE. THE OPPOSITE OF YOU LATELY. DON'T JUMP DOWN YOUR SON'S THROAT JUST BECAUSE HE WANTED TO KEEP YOU SAFE. ANY NUMBER OF PEOPLE HAVE HAD TO JUMP TO YOUR DEFENSE AT ANY GIVEN TIME, FOR WHATEVER REASON.
IT'S BECAUSE HE'S NO LONGER A VAMPIRE.
IT'S...
...UM.
WAIT, *WHAT?*

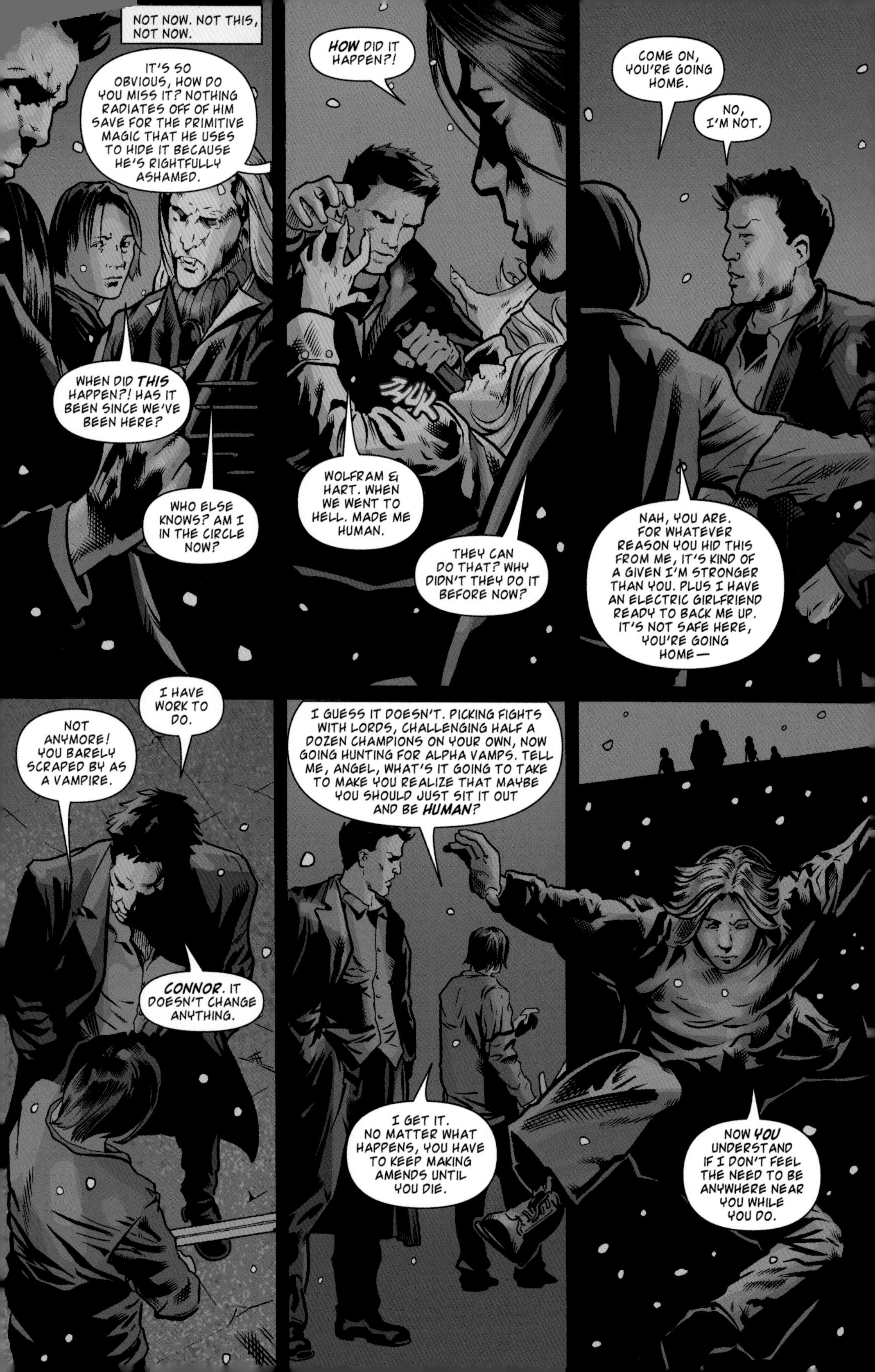
NOT NOW. NOT THIS, NOT NOW.
IT'S SO OBVIOUS, HOW DO YOU MISS IT? NOTHING RADIATES OFF OF HIM SAVE FOR THE PRIMITIVE MAGIC THAT HE USES TO HIDE IT BECAUSE HE'S RIGHTFULLY ASHAMED.
WHEN DID THIS HAPPEN?! HAS IT BEEN SINCE WE'VE BEEN HERE?
WHO ELSE KNOWS? AM I IN THE CIRCLE NOW?
HOW DID IT HAPPEN?!
THUK
WOLFRAM & HART. WHEN WE WENT TO HELL. MADE ME HUMAN.
THEY CAN DO THAT? WHY DIDN'T THEY DO IT BEFORE NOW?
COME ON, YOU'RE GOING HOME.
NO, I'M NOT.
NAH, YOU ARE. FOR WHATEVER REASON YOU HID THIS FROM ME, IT'S KIND OF A GIVEN I'M STRONGER THAN YOU. PLUS I HAVE AN ELECTRIC GIRLFRIEND READY TO BACK ME UP. IT'S NOT SAFE HERE, YOU'RE GOING HOME—
I HAVE WORK TO DO.
NOT ANYMORE! YOU BARELY SCRAPED BY AS A VAMPIRE.
CONNOR. IT DOESN'T CHANGE ANYTHING.
I GUESS IT DOESN'T. PICKING FIGHTS WITH LORDS, CHALLENGING HALF A DOZEN CHAMPIONS ON YOUR OWN, NOW GOING HUNTING FOR ALPHA VAMPS. TELL ME, ANGEL, WHAT'S IT GOING TO TAKE TO MAKE YOU REALIZE THAT MAYBE YOU SHOULD JUST SIT IT OUT AND BE HUMAN?
I GET IT. NO MATTER WHAT HAPPENS, YOU HAVE TO KEEP MAKING AMENDS UNTIL YOU DIE.
NOW YOU UNDERSTAND IF I DON'T FEEL THE NEED TO BE ANYWHERE NEAR YOU WHILE YOU DO.

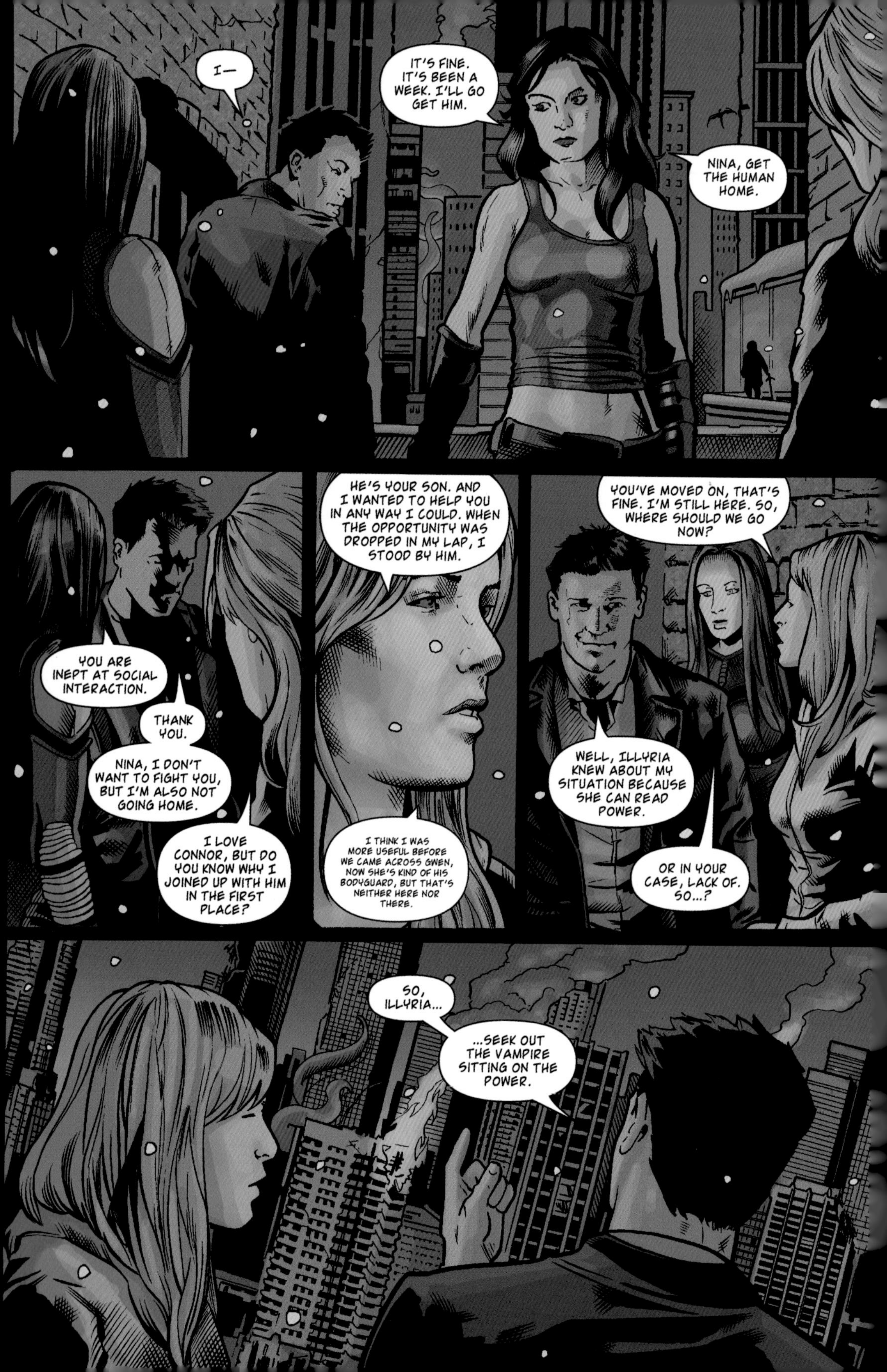
I—
IT'S FINE. IT'S BEEN A WEEK. I'LL GO GET HIM.
NINA, GET THE HUMAN HOME.
YOU ARE INEPT AT SOCIAL INTERACTION.
THANK YOU.
NINA, I DON'T WANT TO FIGHT YOU, BUT I'M ALSO NOT GOING HOME.
I LOVE CONNOR, BUT DO YOU KNOW WHY I JOINED UP WITH HIM IN THE FIRST PLACE?
HE'S YOUR SON. AND I WANTED TO HELP YOU IN ANY WAY I COULD. WHEN THE OPPORTUNITY WAS DROPPED IN MY LAP, I STOOD BY HIM.
I THINK I WAS MORE USEFUL BEFORE WE CAME ACROSS GWEN, NOW SHE'S KIND OF HIS BODYGUARD, BUT THAT'S NEITHER HERE NOR THERE.
YOU'VE MOVED ON, THAT'S FINE. I'M STILL HERE. SO, WHERE SHOULD WE GO NOW?
WELL, ILLYRIA KNEW ABOUT MY SITUATION BECAUSE SHE CAN READ POWER.
OR IN YOUR CASE, LACK OF. SO...?
SO, ILLYRIA...
...SEEK OUT THE VAMPIRE SITTING ON THE POWER.

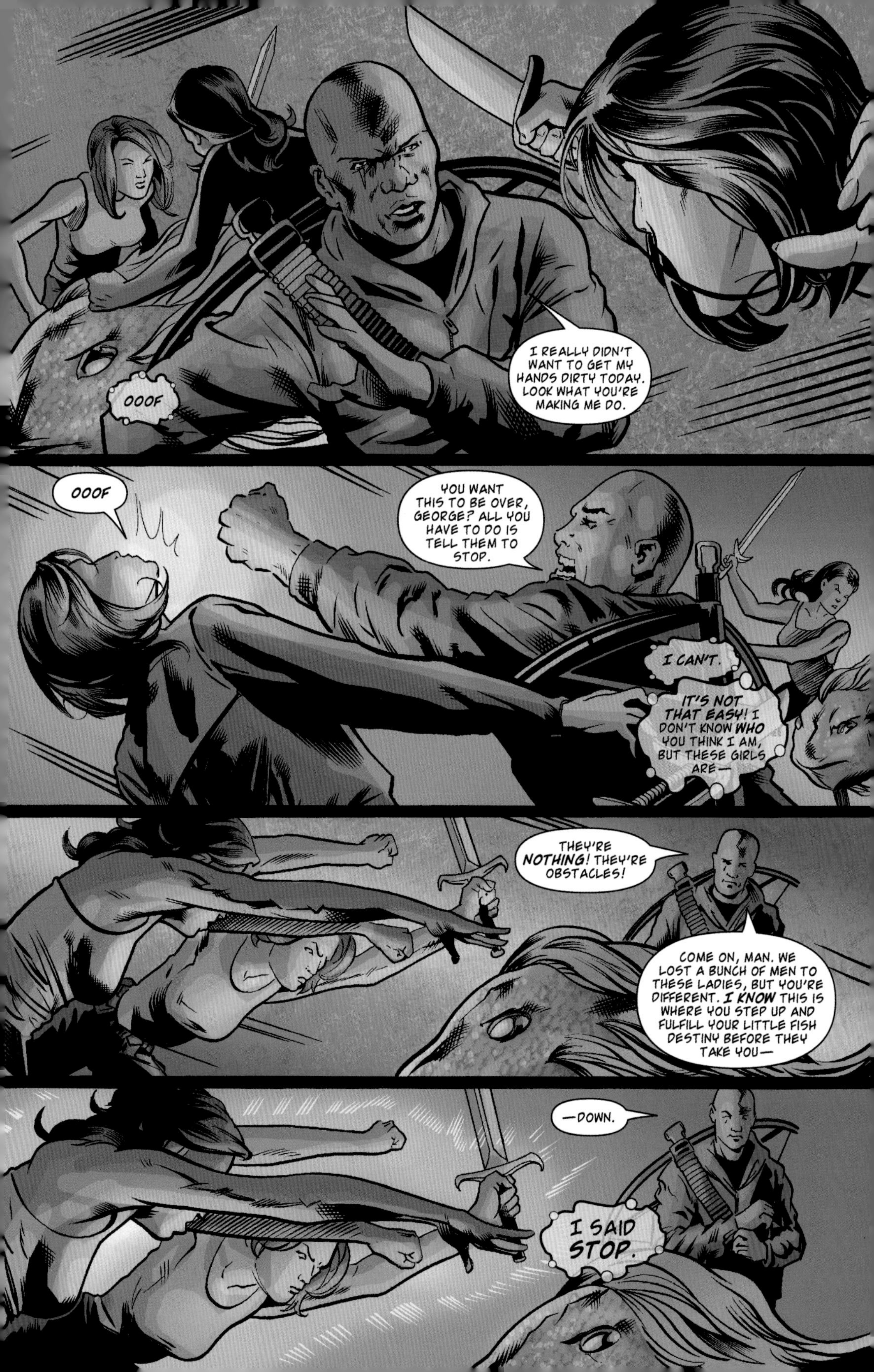

I REALLY DIDN'T WANT TO GET MY HANDS DIRTY TODAY. LOOK WHAT YOU'RE MAKING ME DO.
OOOF
OOOF
YOU WANT THIS TO BE OVER, GEORGE? ALL YOU HAVE TO DO IS TELL THEM TO STOP.
I CAN'T.
IT'S NOT THAT EASY! I DON'T KNOW WHO YOU THINK I AM, BUT THESE GIRLS ARE—
THEY'RE NOTHING! THEY'RE OBSTACLES!
COME ON, MAN. WE LOST A BUNCH OF MEN TO THESE LADIES, BUT YOU'RE DIFFERENT. I KNOW THIS IS WHERE YOU STEP UP AND FULFILL YOUR LITTLE FISH DESTINY BEFORE THEY TAKE YOU—
—DOWN.
I SAID STOP.

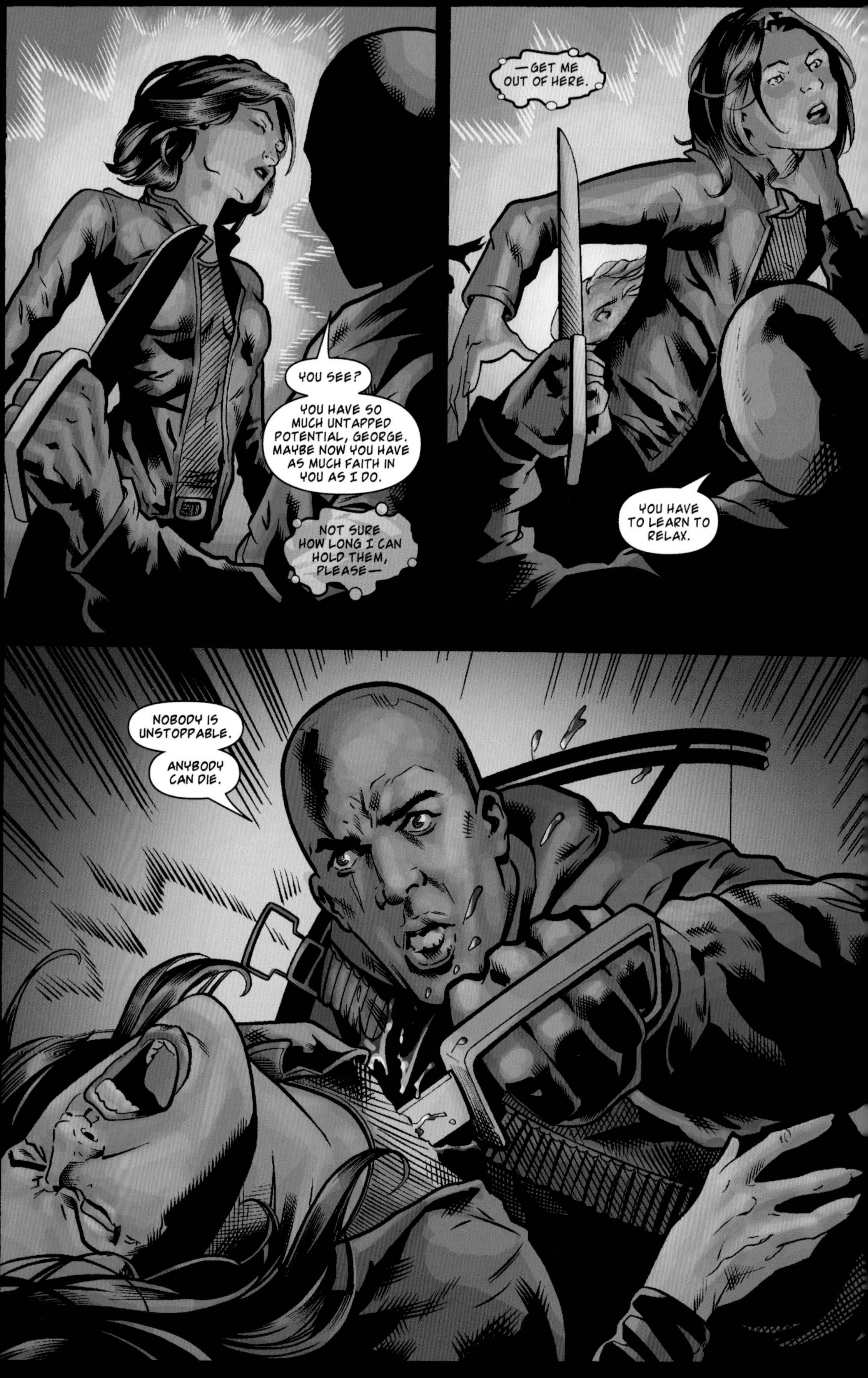
YOU SEE?
YOU HAVE SO MUCH UNTAPPED POTENTIAL, GEORGE. MAYBE NOW YOU HAVE AS MUCH FAITH IN YOU AS I DO.
NOT SURE HOW LONG I CAN HOLD THEM, PLEASE—
—GET ME OUT OF HERE.
YOU HAVE TO LEARN TO RELAX.
NOBODY IS UNSTOPPABLE.
ANYBODY CAN DIE.

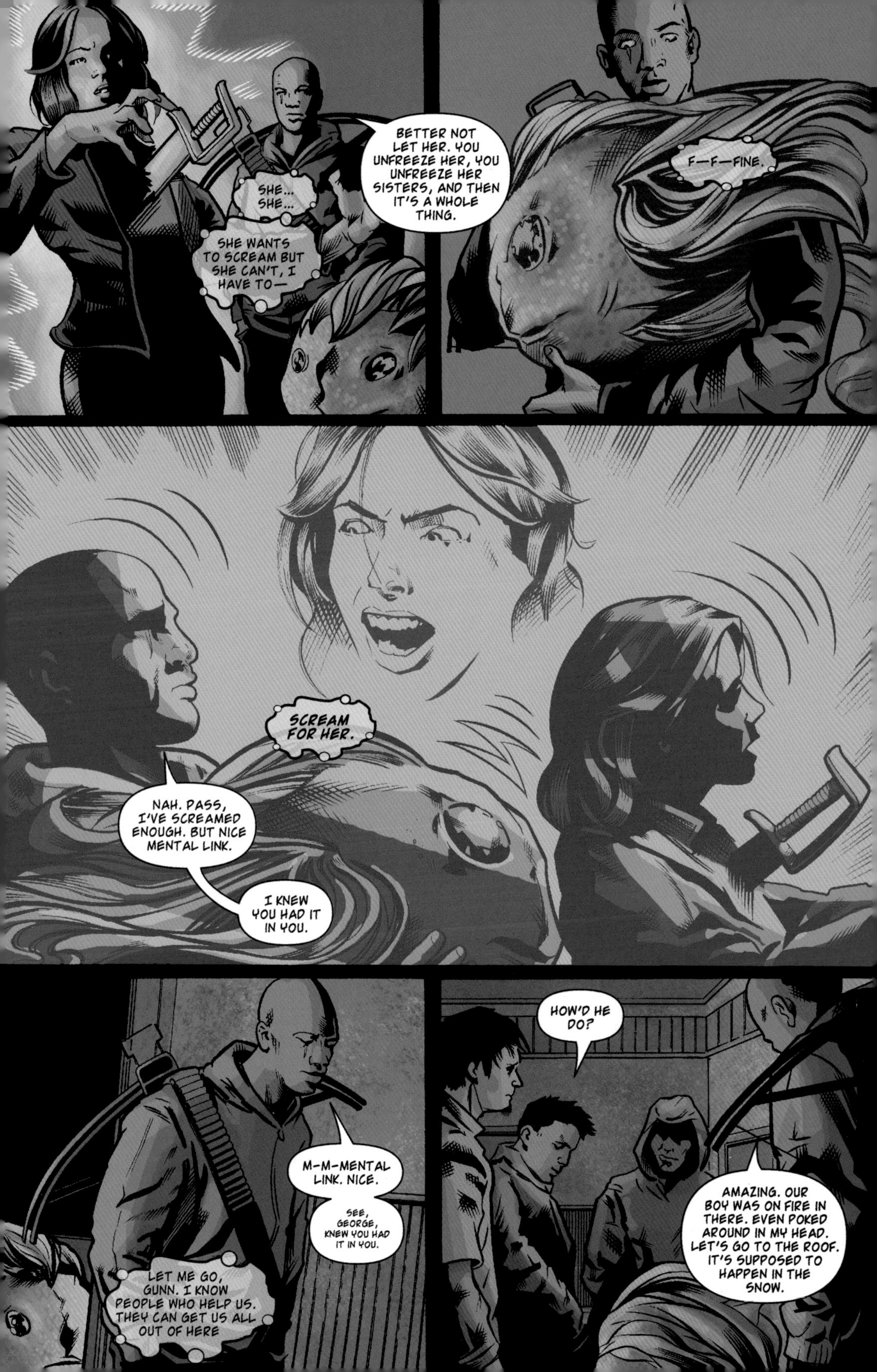
SHE... SHE...
SHE WANTS TO SCREAM BUT SHE CAN'T, I HAVE TO—
BETTER NOT LET HER. YOU UNFREEZE HER, YOU UNFREEZE HER SISTERS, AND THEN IT'S A WHOLE THING.
F—F—FINE.
SCREAM FOR HER.
NAH. PASS, I'VE SCREAMED ENOUGH. BUT NICE MENTAL LINK.
I KNEW YOU HAD IT IN YOU.
M-M-MENTAL LINK. NICE.
SEE, GEORGE, KNEW YOU HAD IT IN YOU.
LET ME GO, GUNN. I KNOW PEOPLE WHO HELP US. THEY CAN GET US ALL OUT OF HERE
HOW'D HE DO?
AMAZING. OUR BOY WAS ON FIRE IN THERE. EVEN POKED AROUND IN MY HEAD. LET'S GO TO THE ROOF. IT'S SUPPOSED TO HAPPEN IN THE SNOW.

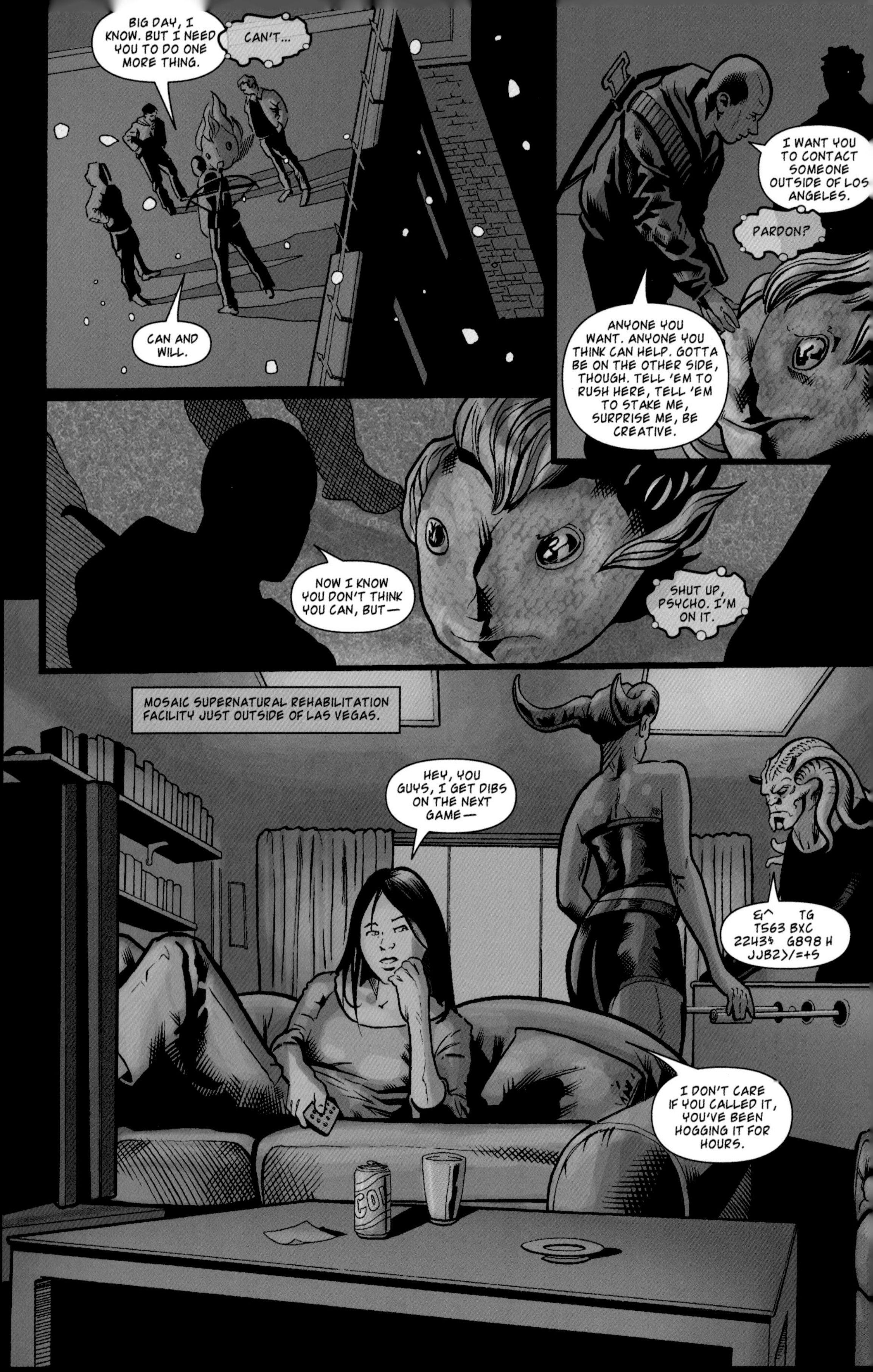
BIG DAY, I KNOW. BUT I NEED YOU TO DO ONE MORE THING.
CAN'T...
CAN AND WILL.
I WANT YOU TO CONTACT SOMEONE OUTSIDE OF LOS ANGELES.
PARDON?
ANYONE YOU WANT. ANYONE YOU THINK CAN HELP. GOTTA BE ON THE OTHER SIDE, THOUGH. TELL 'EM TO RUSH HERE, TELL 'EM TO STAKE ME, SURPRISE ME, BE CREATIVE.
NOW I KNOW YOU DON'T THINK YOU CAN, BUT—
SHUT UP, PSYCHO. I'M ON IT.
MOSAIC SUPERNATURAL REHABILITATION FACILITY JUST OUTSIDE OF LAS VEGAS.
HEY, YOU GUYS, I GET DIBS ON THE NEXT GAME—
&^ TG T563 BXC 2243$ G898 H JJB2>/=+5
I DON'T CARE IF YOU CALLED IT, YOU'VE BEEN HOGGING IT FOR HOURS.

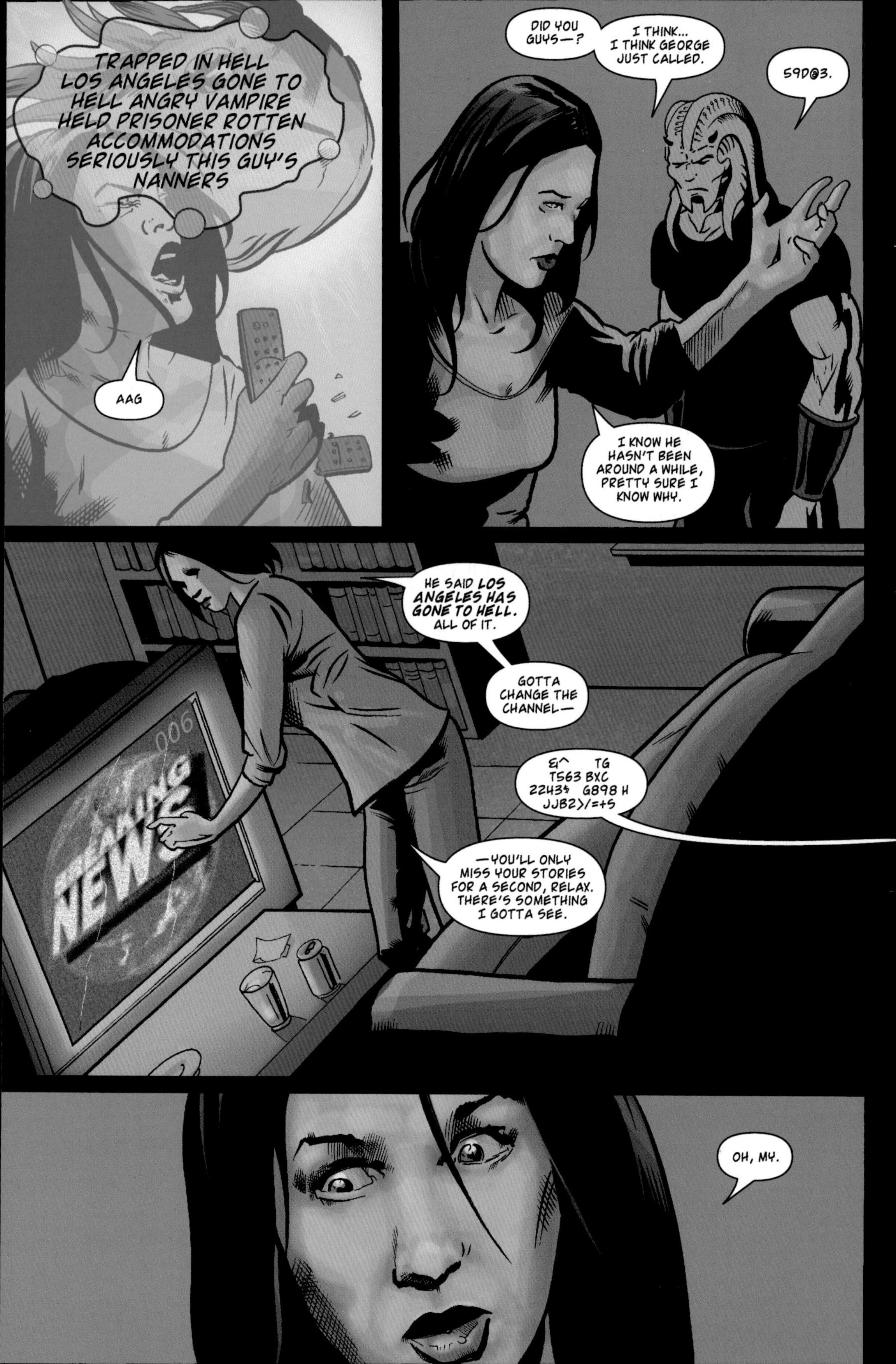
TRAPPED IN HELL LOS ANGELES GONE TO HELL ANGRY VAMPIRE HELD PRISONER ROTTEN ACCOMMODATIONS SERIOUSLY THIS GUY'S NANNERS
AAG
DID YOU GUYS—?
I THINK... I THINK GEORGE JUST CALLED.
59D@3.
I KNOW HE HASN'T BEEN AROUND A WHILE, PRETTY SURE I KNOW WHY.
HE SAID LOS ANGELES HAS GONE TO HELL. ALL OF IT.
GOTTA CHANGE THE CHANNEL—
&^ TG T563 BXC 2243$ G898 H JJB2>/=+S
—YOU'LL ONLY MISS YOUR STORIES FOR A SECOND, RELAX. THERE'S SOMETHING I GOTTA SEE.
NEWS
OH, MY.

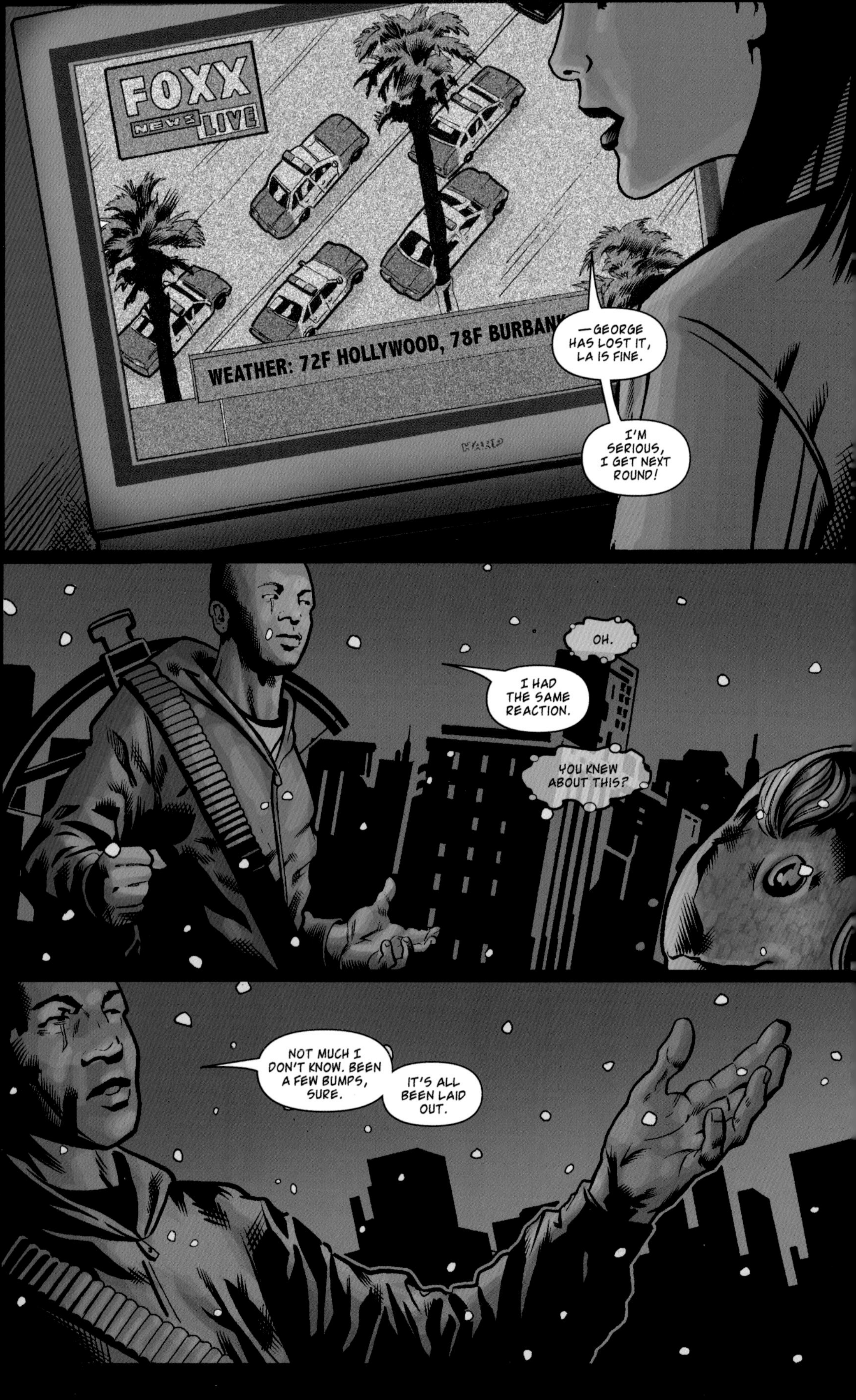
FOXX
NEWS LIVE
WEATHER: 72F HOLLYWOOD, 78F BURBANK
—GEORGE HAS LOST IT, LA IS FINE.
I'M SERIOUS, I GET NEXT ROUND!
OH.
I HAD THE SAME REACTION.
YOU KNEW ABOUT THIS?
NOT MUCH I DON'T KNOW. BEEN A FEW BUMPS, SURE.
IT'S ALL BEEN LAID OUT.

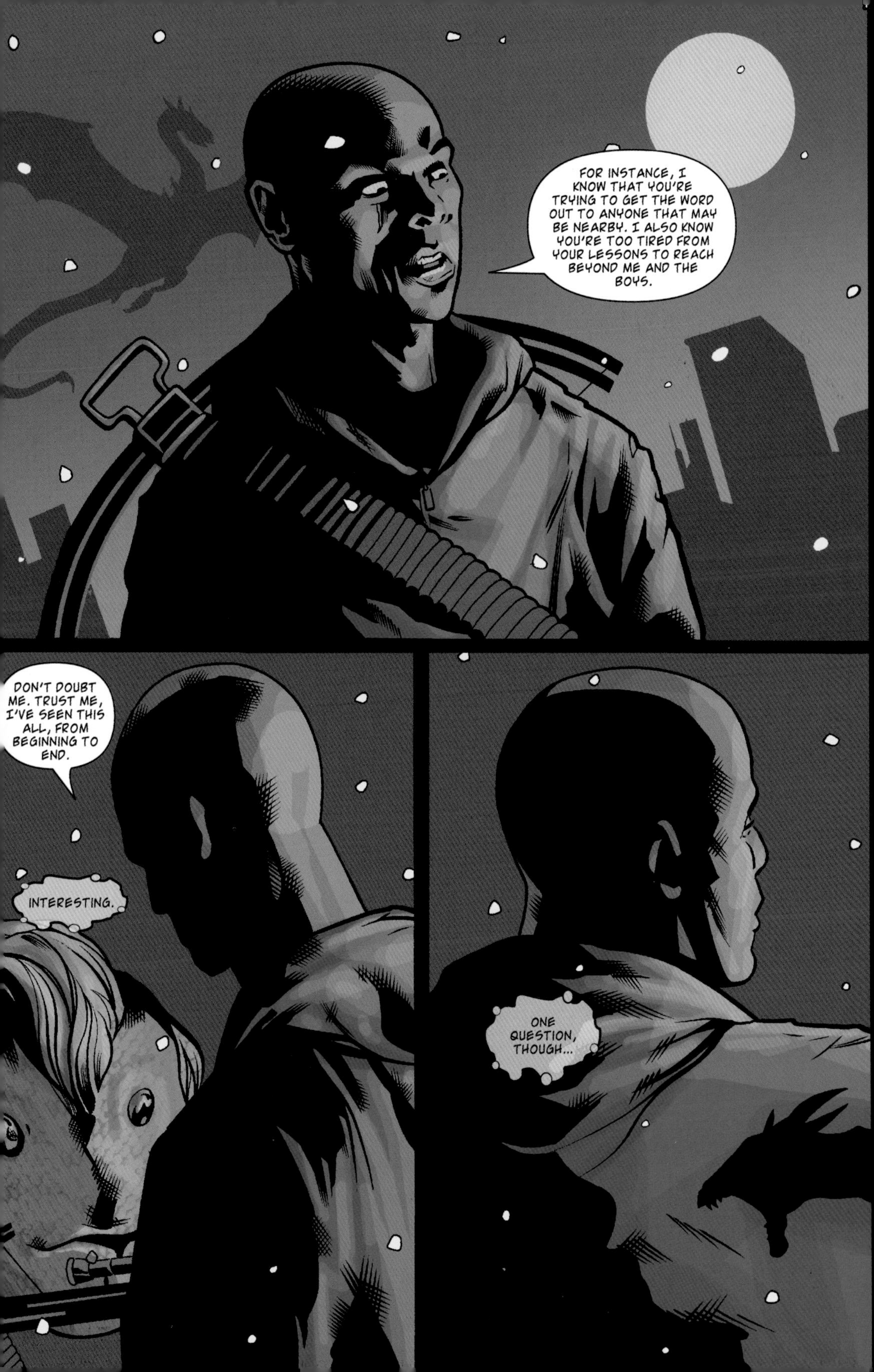
FOR INSTANCE, I KNOW THAT YOU'RE TRYING TO GET THE WORD OUT TO ANYONE THAT MAY BE NEARBY. I ALSO KNOW YOU'RE TOO TIRED FROM YOUR LESSONS TO REACH BEYOND ME AND THE BOYS.
DON'T DOUBT ME. TRUST ME, I'VE SEEN THIS ALL, FROM BEGINNING TO END.
INTERESTING.
ONE QUESTION, THOUGH...

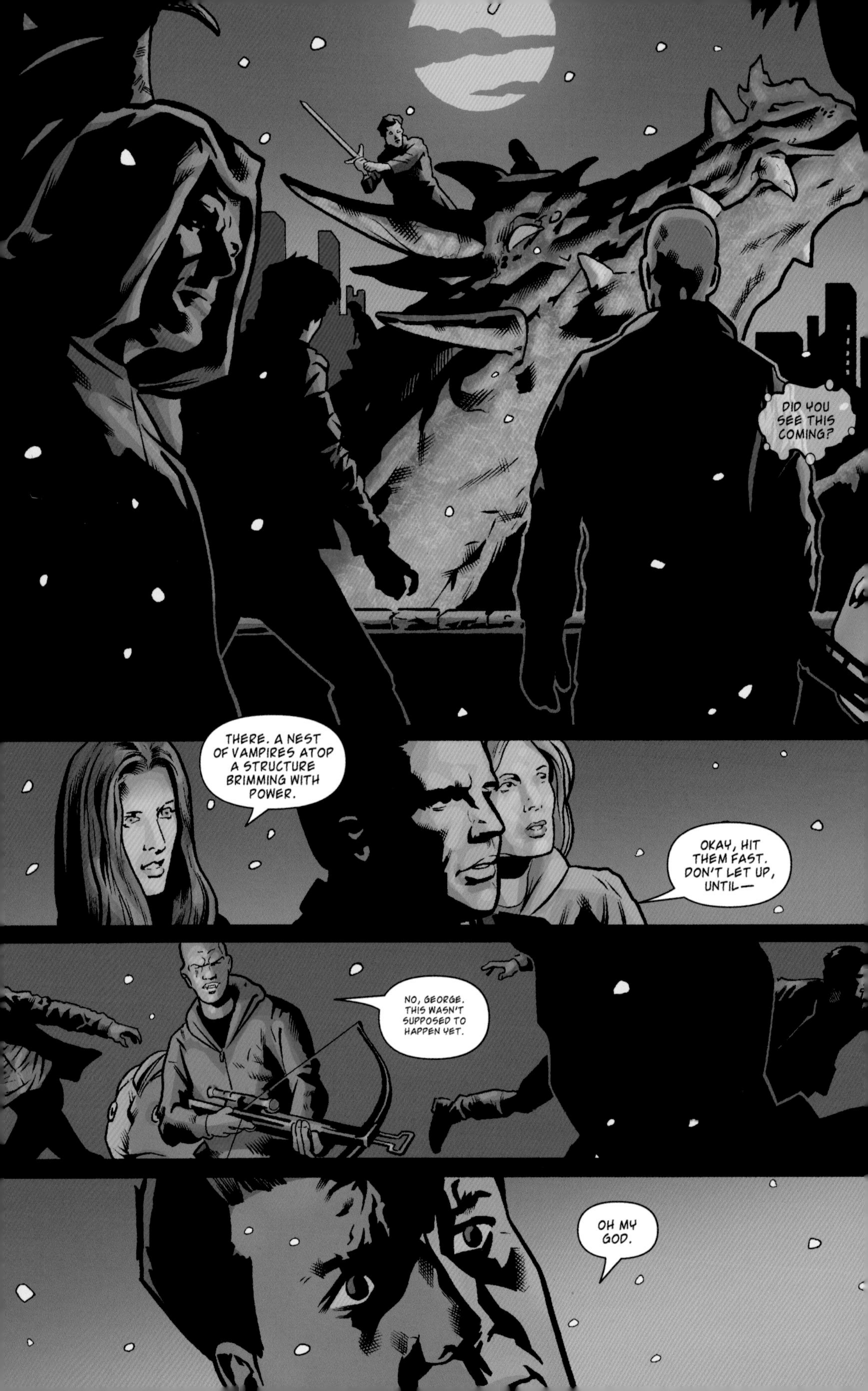
DID YOU SEE THIS COMING?
THERE. A NEST OF VAMPIRES ATOP A STRUCTURE BRIMMING WITH POWER.
OKAY, HIT THEM FAST. DON'T LET UP, UNTIL—
NO, GEORGE. THIS WASN'T SUPPOSED TO HAPPEN YET.
OH MY GOD.

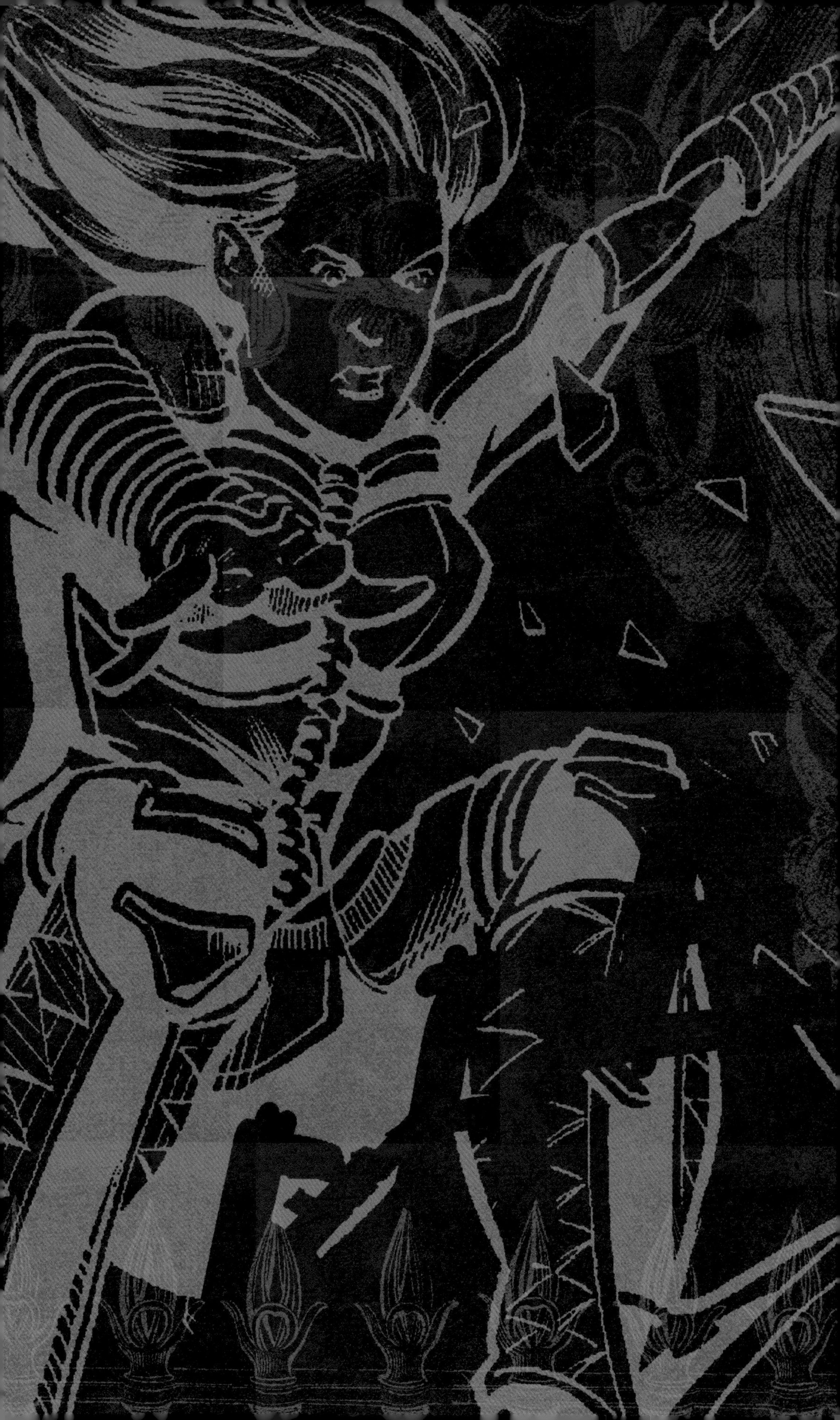

chapter
three

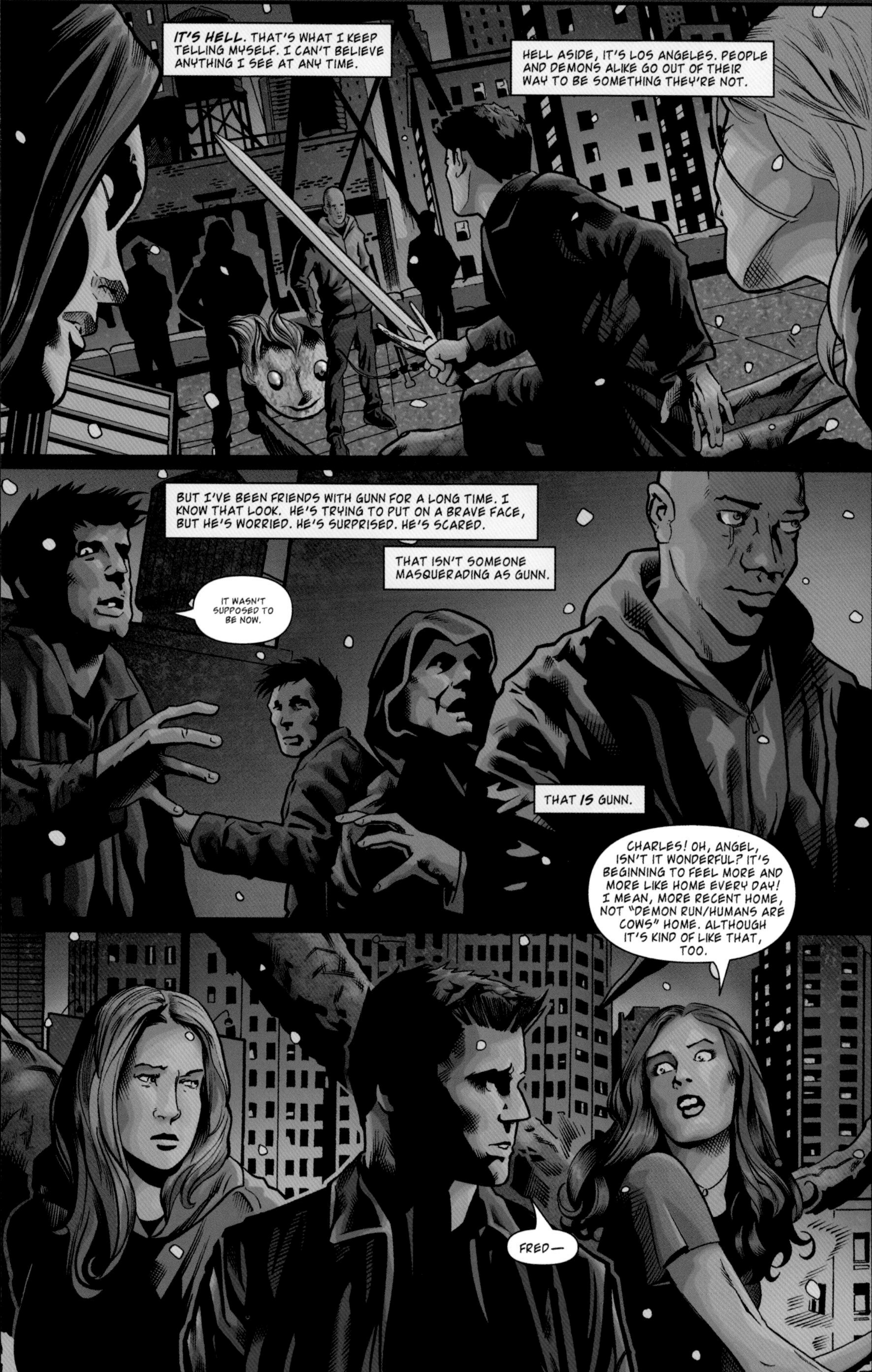
IT'S HELL. THAT'S WHAT I KEEP TELLING MYSELF. I CAN'T BELIEVE ANYTHING I SEE AT ANY TIME.
HELL ASIDE, IT'S LOS ANGELES. PEOPLE AND DEMONS ALIKE GO OUT OF THEIR WAY TO BE SOMETHING THEY'RE NOT.
BUT I'VE BEEN FRIENDS WITH GUNN FOR A LONG TIME. I KNOW THAT LOOK. HE'S TRYING TO PUT ON A BRAVE FACE, BUT HE'S WORRIED. HE'S SURPRISED. HE'S SCARED.
THAT ISN'T SOMEONE MASQUERADING AS GUNN.
IT WASN'T SUPPOSED TO BE NOW.
THAT *IS* GUNN.
CHARLES! OH, ANGEL, ISN'T IT WONDERFUL? IT'S BEGINNING TO FEEL MORE AND MORE LIKE HOME EVERY DAY! I MEAN, MORE RECENT HOME, NOT "DEMON RUN/HUMANS ARE COWS" HOME. ALTHOUGH IT'S KIND OF LIKE THAT, TOO.
FRED—

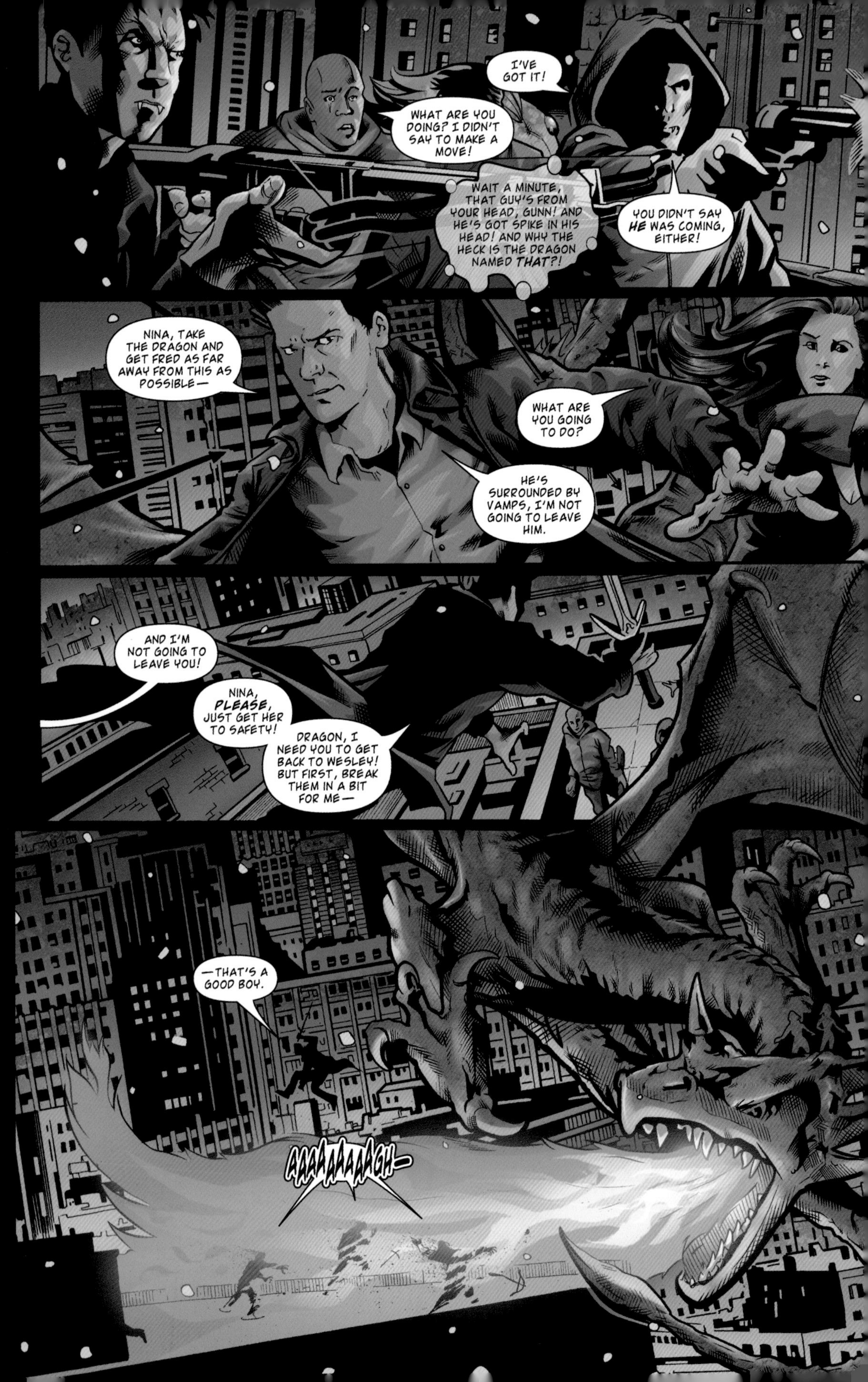

I'VE GOT IT!
WHAT ARE YOU DOING? I DIDN'T SAY TO MAKE A MOVE!
WAIT A MINUTE, THAT GUY'S FROM YOUR HEAD, GUNN! AND HE'S GOT SPIKE IN HIS HEAD! AND WHY THE HECK IS THE DRAGON NAMED THAT?!
YOU DIDN'T SAY HE WAS COMING, EITHER!
NINA, TAKE THE DRAGON AND GET FRED AS FAR AWAY FROM THIS AS POSSIBLE—
WHAT ARE YOU GOING TO DO?
HE'S SURROUNDED BY VAMPS, I'M NOT GOING TO LEAVE HIM.
AND I'M NOT GOING TO LEAVE YOU!
NINA, PLEASE, JUST GET HER TO SAFETY!
DRAGON, I NEED YOU TO GET BACK TO WESLEY! BUT FIRST, BREAK THEM IN A BIT FOR ME—
—THAT'S A GOOD BOY.
AAAAAAAAAGH—

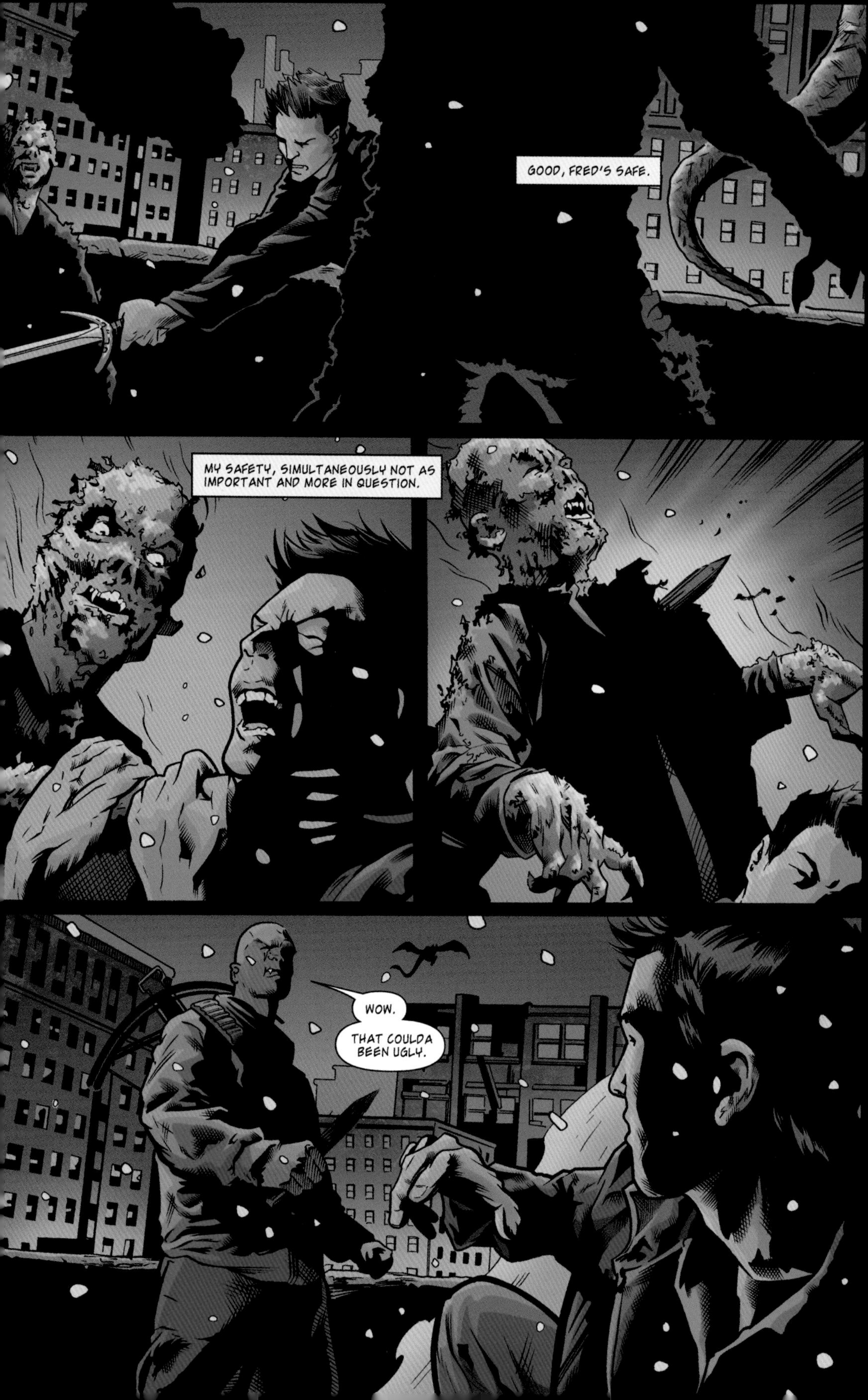
GOOD, FRED'S SAFE.
MY SAFETY, SIMULTANEOUSLY NOT AS IMPORTANT AND MORE IN QUESTION.
WOW.
THAT COULDA BEEN UGLY.

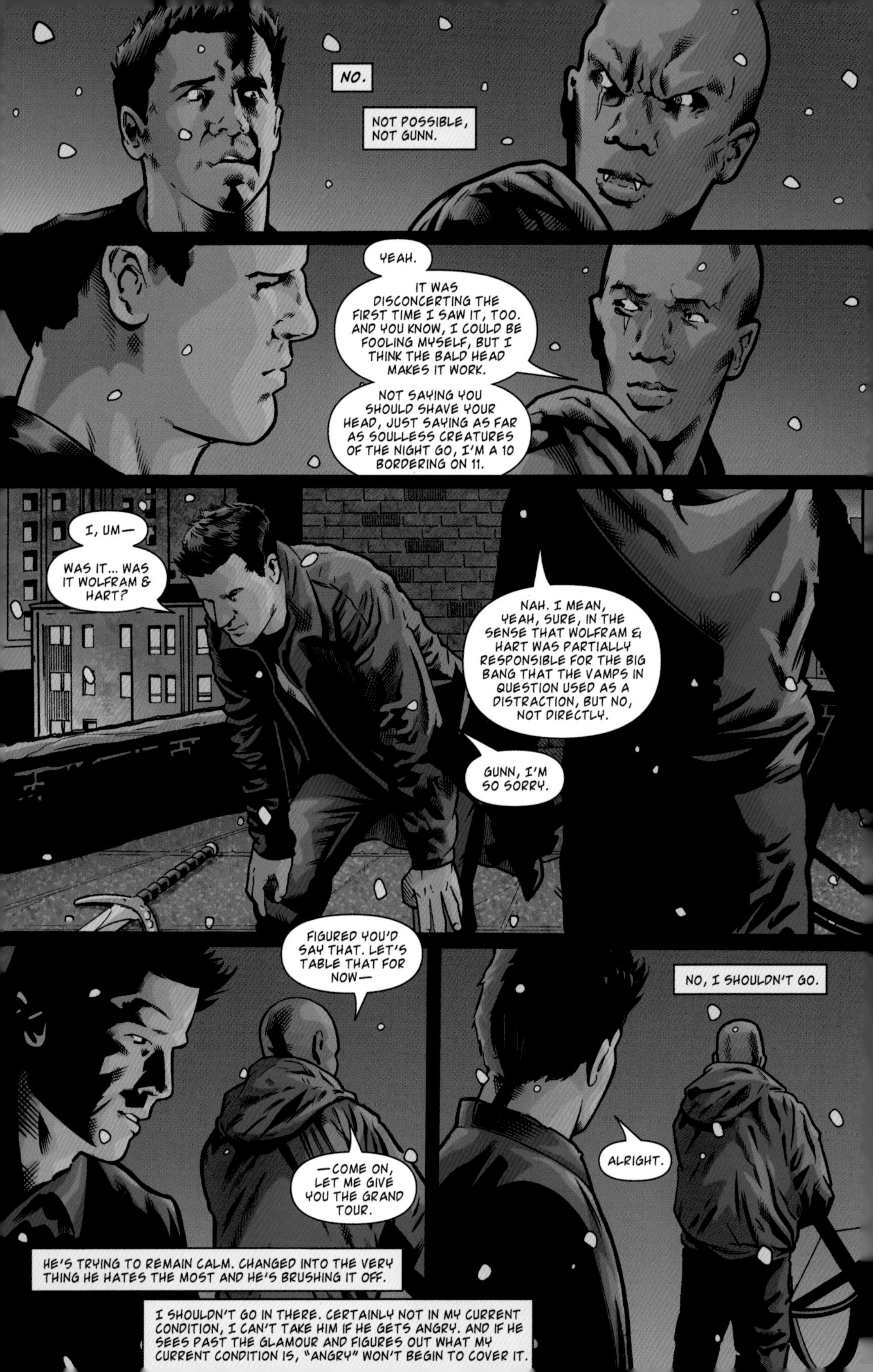
NO.
NOT POSSIBLE, NOT GUNN.
YEAH.
IT WAS DISCONCERTING THE FIRST TIME I SAW IT, TOO. AND YOU KNOW, I COULD BE FOOLING MYSELF, BUT I THINK THE BALD HEAD MAKES IT WORK.
NOT SAYING YOU SHOULD SHAVE YOUR HEAD, JUST SAYING AS FAR AS SOULLESS CREATURES OF THE NIGHT GO, I'M A 10 BORDERING ON 11.
I, UM—
WAS IT... WAS IT WOLFRAM & HART?
NAH. I MEAN, YEAH, SURE, IN THE SENSE THAT WOLFRAM & HART WAS PARTIALLY RESPONSIBLE FOR THE BIG BANG THAT THE VAMPS IN QUESTION USED AS A DISTRACTION, BUT NO, NOT DIRECTLY.
GUNN, I'M SO SORRY.
FIGURED YOU'D SAY THAT. LET'S TABLE THAT FOR NOW—
—COME ON, LET ME GIVE YOU THE GRAND TOUR.
HE'S TRYING TO REMAIN CALM. CHANGED INTO THE VERY THING HE HATES THE MOST AND HE'S BRUSHING IT OFF.
I SHOULDN'T GO IN THERE. CERTAINLY NOT IN MY CURRENT CONDITION, I CAN'T TAKE HIM IF HE GETS ANGRY. AND IF HE SEES PAST THE GLAMOUR AND FIGURES OUT WHAT MY CURRENT CONDITION IS, "ANGRY" WON'T BEGIN TO COVER IT.
NO, I SHOULDN'T GO.
ALRIGHT.

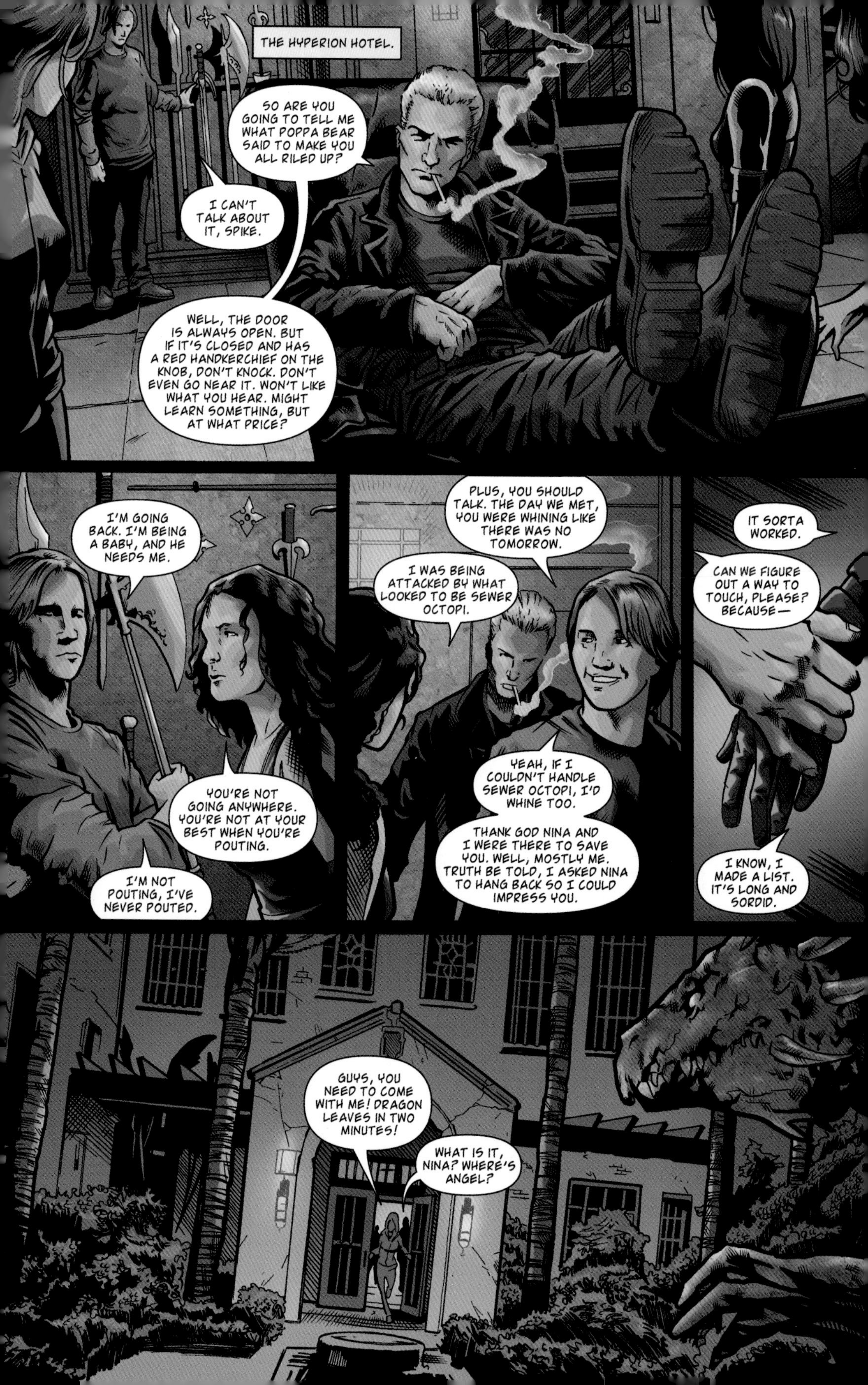
THE HYPERION HOTEL.
SO ARE YOU GOING TO TELL ME WHAT POPPA BEAR SAID TO MAKE YOU ALL RILED UP?
I CAN'T TALK ABOUT IT, SPIKE.
WELL, THE DOOR IS ALWAYS OPEN. BUT IF IT'S CLOSED AND HAS A RED HANDKERCHIEF ON THE KNOB, DON'T KNOCK. DON'T EVEN GO NEAR IT. WON'T LIKE WHAT YOU HEAR. MIGHT LEARN SOMETHING, BUT AT WHAT PRICE?
I'M GOING BACK. I'M BEING A BABY, AND HE NEEDS ME.
YOU'RE NOT GOING ANYWHERE. YOU'RE NOT AT YOUR BEST WHEN YOU'RE POUTING.
I'M NOT POUTING, I'VE NEVER POUTED.
PLUS, YOU SHOULD TALK. THE DAY WE MET, YOU WERE WHINING LIKE THERE WAS NO TOMORROW.
I WAS BEING ATTACKED BY WHAT LOOKED TO BE SEWER OCTOPI.
YEAH, IF I COULDN'T HANDLE SEWER OCTOPI, I'D WHINE TOO.
THANK GOD NINA AND I WERE THERE TO SAVE YOU. WELL, MOSTLY ME. TRUTH BE TOLD, I ASKED NINA TO HANG BACK SO I COULD IMPRESS YOU.
IT SORTA WORKED.
CAN WE FIGURE OUT A WAY TO TOUCH, PLEASE? BECAUSE—
I KNOW, I MADE A LIST. IT'S LONG AND SORDID.
GUYS, YOU NEED TO COME WITH ME! DRAGON LEAVES IN TWO MINUTES!
WHAT IS IT, NINA? WHERE'S ANGEL?

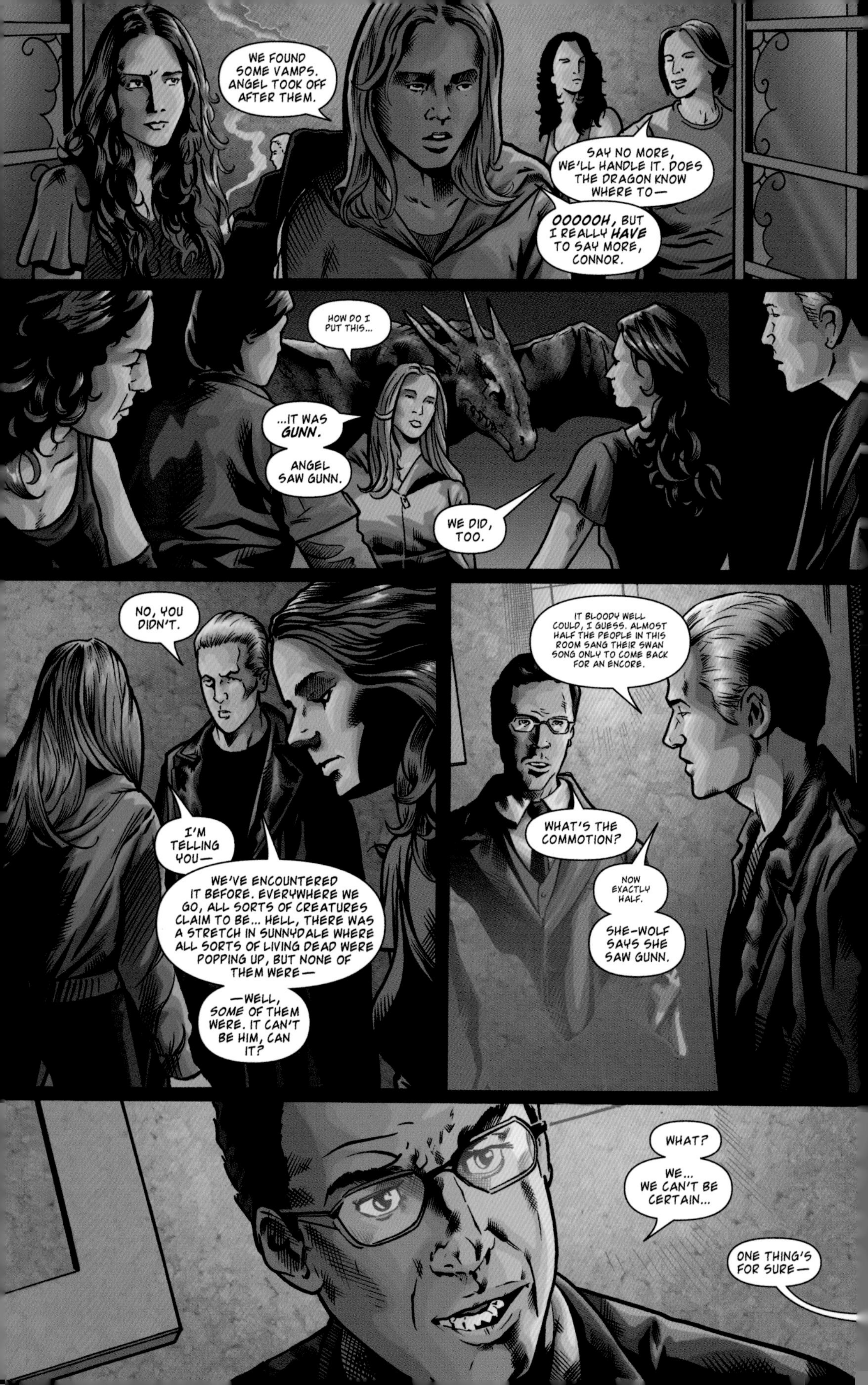
WE FOUND SOME VAMPS. ANGEL TOOK OFF AFTER THEM.
SAY NO MORE, WE'LL HANDLE IT. DOES THE DRAGON KNOW WHERE TO—
OOOOOH, BUT I REALLY HAVE TO SAY MORE, CONNOR.
HOW DO I PUT THIS...
...IT WAS GUNN.
ANGEL SAW GUNN.
WE DID, TOO.
NO, YOU DIDN'T.
I'M TELLING YOU—
WE'VE ENCOUNTERED IT BEFORE. EVERYWHERE WE GO, ALL SORTS OF CREATURES CLAIM TO BE... HELL, THERE WAS A STRETCH IN SUNNYDALE WHERE ALL SORTS OF LIVING DEAD WERE POPPING UP, BUT NONE OF THEM WERE—
—WELL, SOME OF THEM WERE. IT CAN'T BE HIM, CAN IT?
IT BLOODY WELL COULD, I GUESS. ALMOST HALF THE PEOPLE IN THIS ROOM SANG THEIR SWAN SONG ONLY TO COME BACK FOR AN ENCORE.
WHAT'S THE COMMOTION?
NOW EXACTLY HALF.
SHE-WOLF SAYS SHE SAW GUNN.
WHAT?
WE... WE CAN'T BE CERTAIN...
ONE THING'S FOR SURE—

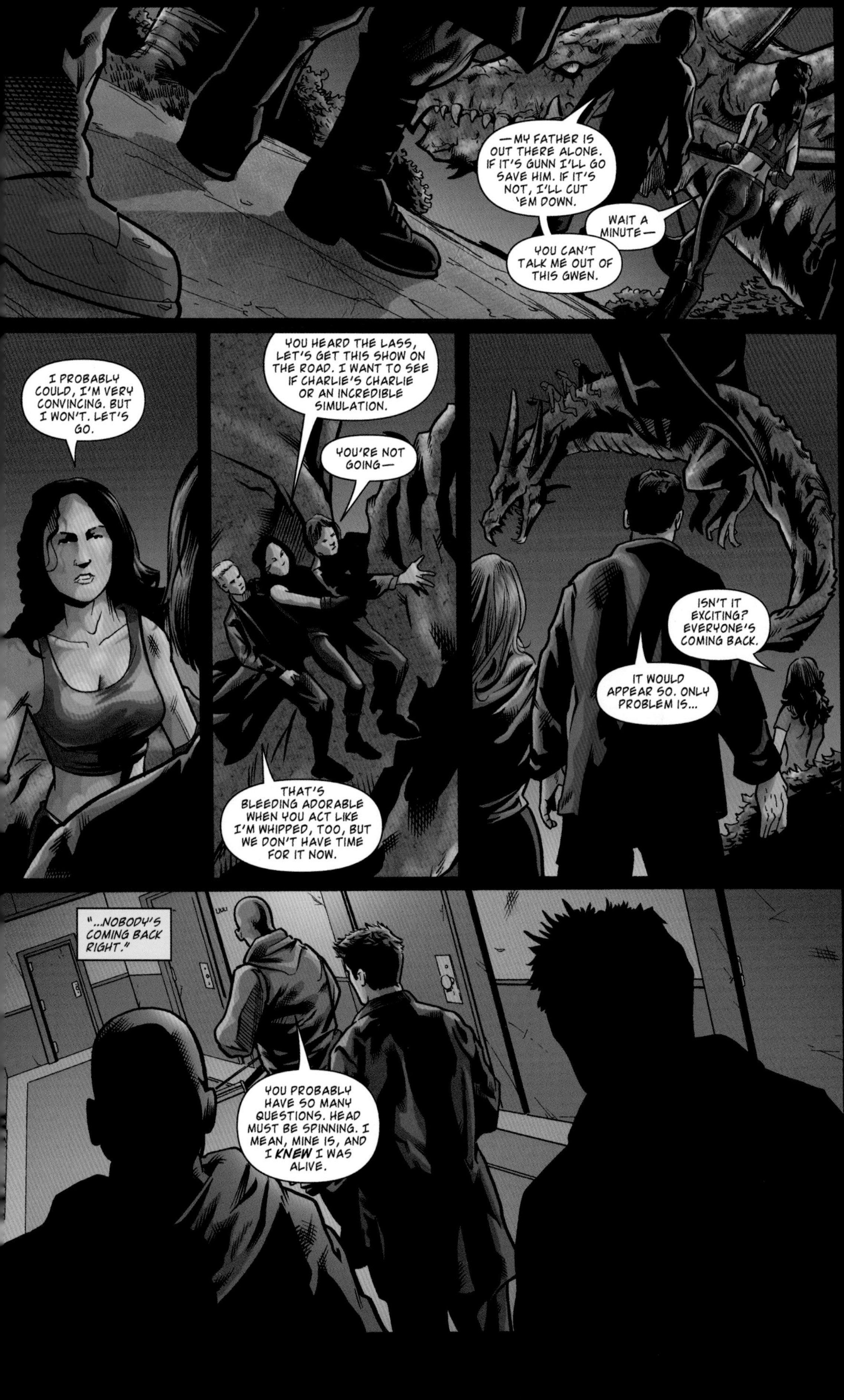
—MY FATHER IS OUT THERE ALONE. IF IT'S GUNN I'LL GO SAVE HIM. IF IT'S NOT, I'LL CUT 'EM DOWN.
WAIT A MINUTE—
YOU CAN'T TALK ME OUT OF THIS GWEN.
I PROBABLY COULD, I'M VERY CONVINCING. BUT I WON'T. LET'S GO.
YOU HEARD THE LASS, LET'S GET THIS SHOW ON THE ROAD. I WANT TO SEE IF CHARLIE'S CHARLIE OR AN INCREDIBLE SIMULATION.
YOU'RE NOT GOING—
THAT'S BLEEDING ADORABLE WHEN YOU ACT LIKE I'M WHIPPED, TOO, BUT WE DON'T HAVE TIME FOR IT NOW.
ISN'T IT EXCITING? EVERYONE'S COMING BACK.
IT WOULD APPEAR SO. ONLY PROBLEM IS...
"...NOBODY'S COMING BACK RIGHT."
YOU PROBABLY HAVE SO MANY QUESTIONS. HEAD MUST BE SPINNING. I MEAN, MINE IS, AND I KNEW I WAS ALIVE.

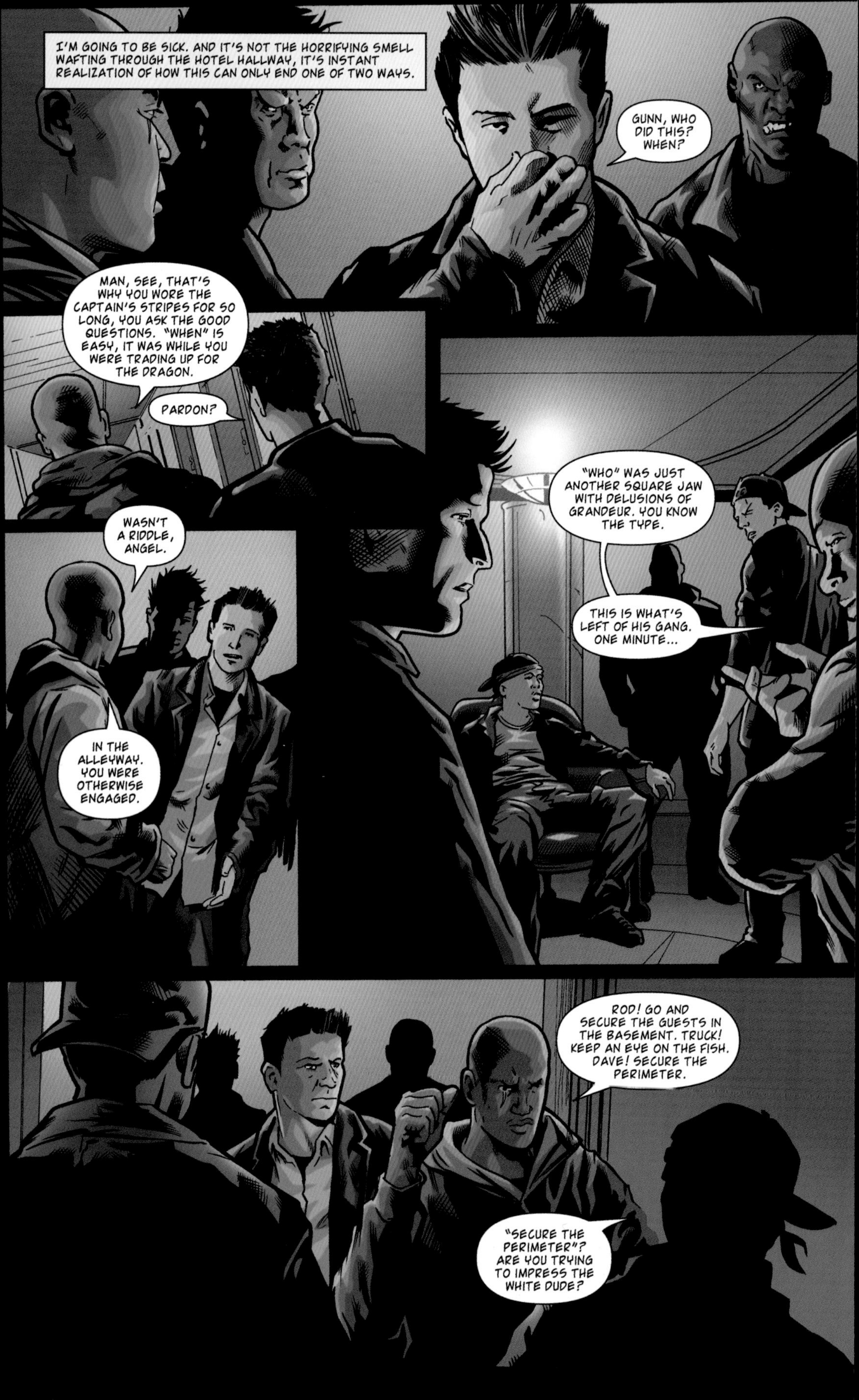
I'M GOING TO BE SICK. AND IT'S NOT THE HORRIFYING SMELL WAFTING THROUGH THE HOTEL HALLWAY, IT'S INSTANT REALIZATION OF HOW THIS CAN ONLY END ONE OF TWO WAYS.
GUNN, WHO DID THIS? WHEN?
MAN, SEE, THAT'S WHY YOU WORE THE CAPTAIN'S STRIPES FOR SO LONG, YOU ASK THE GOOD QUESTIONS. "WHEN" IS EASY, IT WAS WHILE YOU WERE TRADING UP FOR THE DRAGON.
PARDON?
WASN'T A RIDDLE, ANGEL.
IN THE ALLEYWAY. YOU WERE OTHERWISE ENGAGED.
"WHO" WAS JUST ANOTHER SQUARE JAW WITH DELUSIONS OF GRANDEUR. YOU KNOW THE TYPE.
THIS IS WHAT'S LEFT OF HIS GANG. ONE MINUTE...
ROD! GO AND SECURE THE GUESTS IN THE BASEMENT. TRUCK! KEEP AN EYE ON THE FISH. DAVE! SECURE THE PERIMETER.
"SECURE THE PERIMETER"? ARE YOU TRYING TO IMPRESS THE WHITE DUDE?

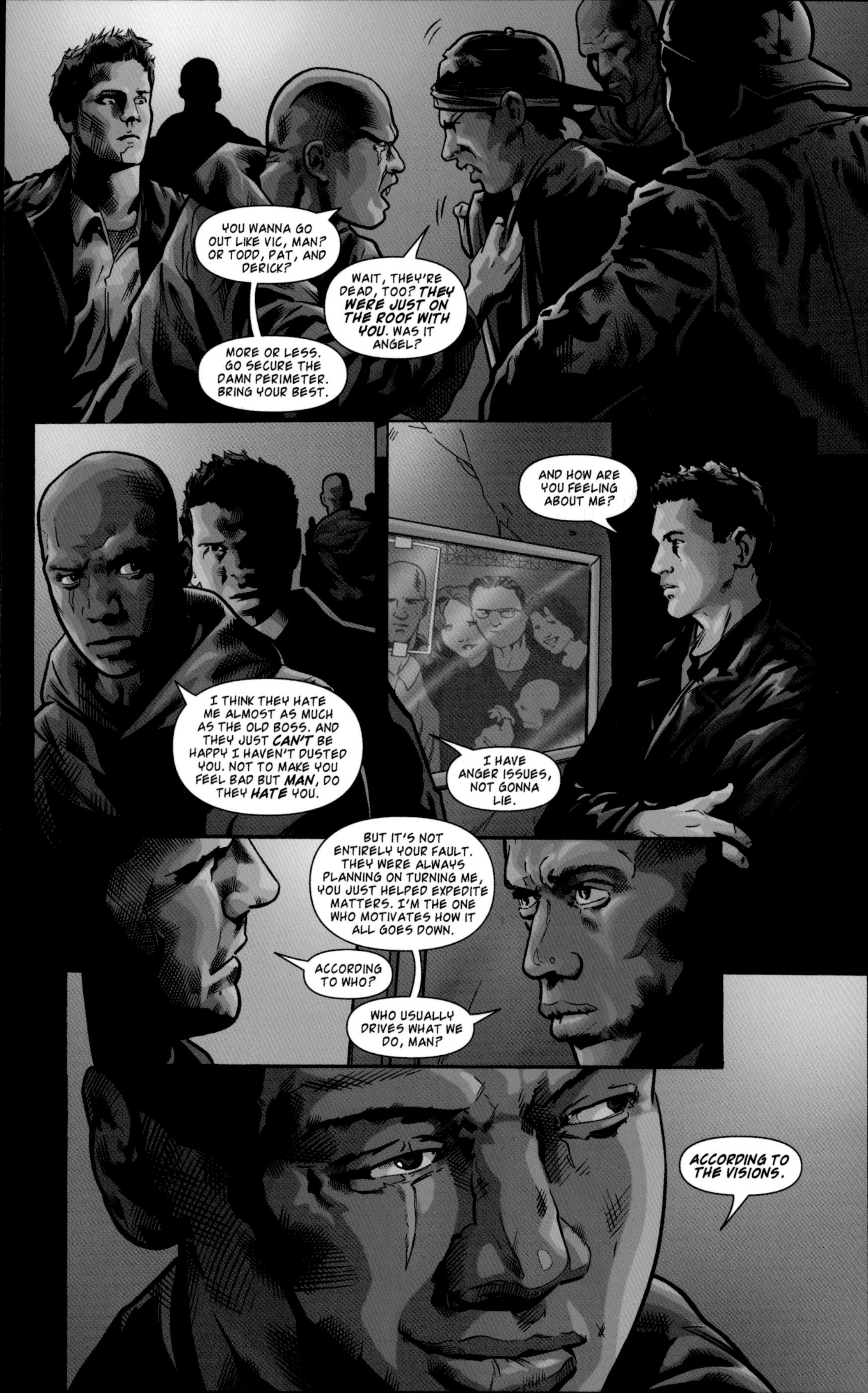
YOU WANNA GO OUT LIKE VIC, MAN? OR TODD, PAT, AND DERICK?
WAIT, THEY'RE DEAD, TOO? THEY WERE JUST ON THE ROOF WITH YOU. WAS IT ANGEL?
MORE OR LESS. GO SECURE THE DAMN PERIMETER. BRING YOUR BEST.
I THINK THEY HATE ME ALMOST AS MUCH AS THE OLD BOSS. AND THEY JUST CAN'T BE HAPPY I HAVEN'T DUSTED YOU. NOT TO MAKE YOU FEEL BAD BUT MAN, DO THEY HATE YOU.
AND HOW ARE YOU FEELING ABOUT ME?
I HAVE ANGER ISSUES, NOT GONNA LIE.
BUT IT'S NOT ENTIRELY YOUR FAULT. THEY WERE ALWAYS PLANNING ON TURNING ME, YOU JUST HELPED EXPEDITE MATTERS. I'M THE ONE WHO MOTIVATES HOW IT ALL GOES DOWN.
ACCORDING TO WHO?
WHO USUALLY DRIVES WHAT WE DO, MAN?
ACCORDING TO THE VISIONS.

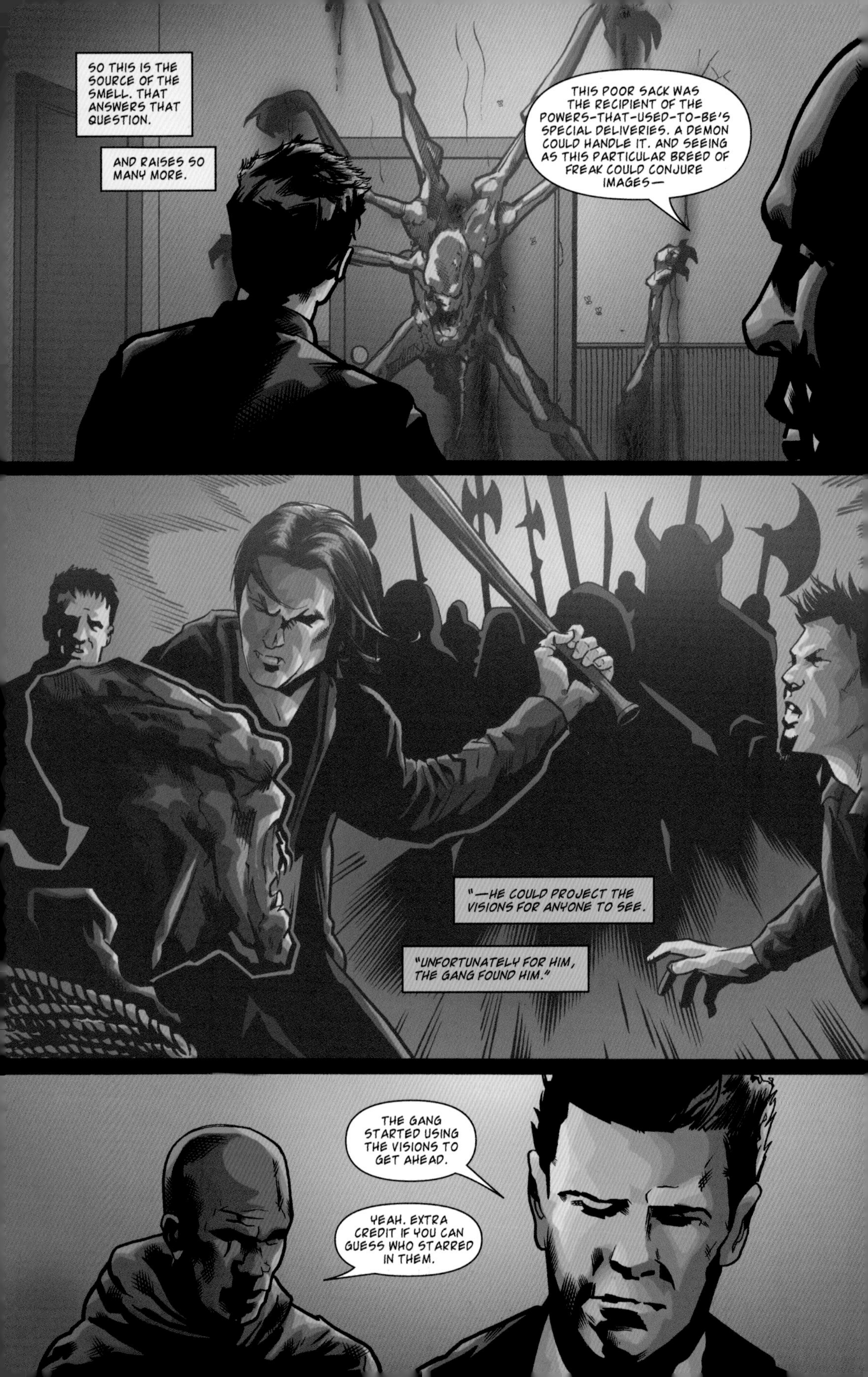
SO THIS IS THE SOURCE OF THE SMELL. THAT ANSWERS THAT QUESTION.
AND RAISES SO MANY MORE.
THIS POOR SACK WAS THE RECIPIENT OF THE POWERS-THAT-USED-TO-BE'S SPECIAL DELIVERIES. A DEMON COULD HANDLE IT. AND SEEING AS THIS PARTICULAR BREED OF FREAK COULD CONJURE IMAGES—
"—HE COULD PROJECT THE VISIONS FOR ANYONE TO SEE.
"UNFORTUNATELY FOR HIM, THE GANG FOUND HIM."
THE GANG STARTED USING THE VISIONS TO GET AHEAD.
YEAH. EXTRA CREDIT IF YOU CAN GUESS WHO STARRED IN THEM.

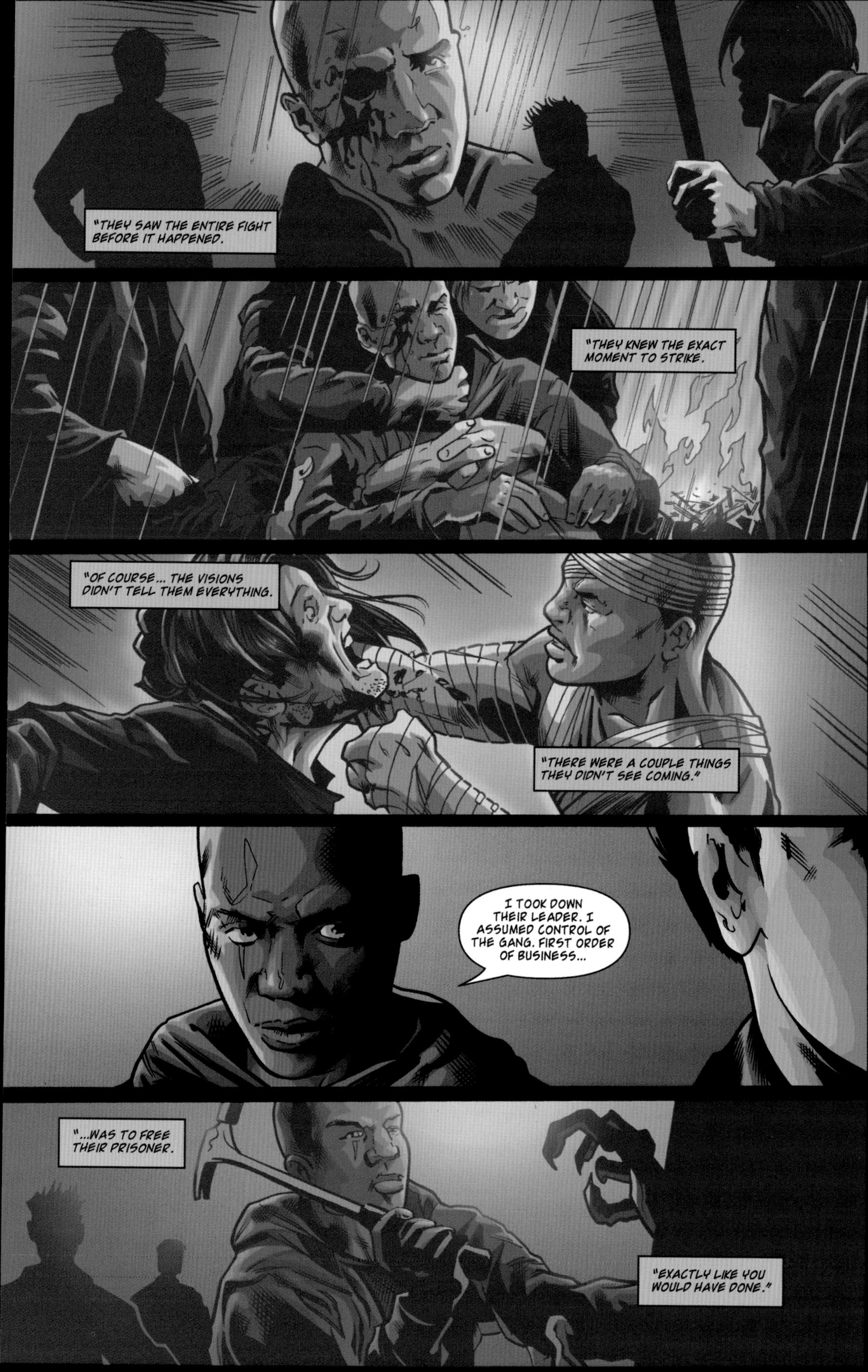
"THEY SAW THE ENTIRE FIGHT BEFORE IT HAPPENED.
"THEY KNEW THE EXACT MOMENT TO STRIKE.
"OF COURSE... THE VISIONS DIDN'T TELL THEM EVERYTHING.
"THERE WERE A COUPLE THINGS THEY DIDN'T SEE COMING."
I TOOK DOWN THEIR LEADER. I ASSUMED CONTROL OF THE GANG. FIRST ORDER OF BUSINESS...
"...WAS TO FREE THEIR PRISONER.
"EXACTLY LIKE YOU WOULD HAVE DONE."

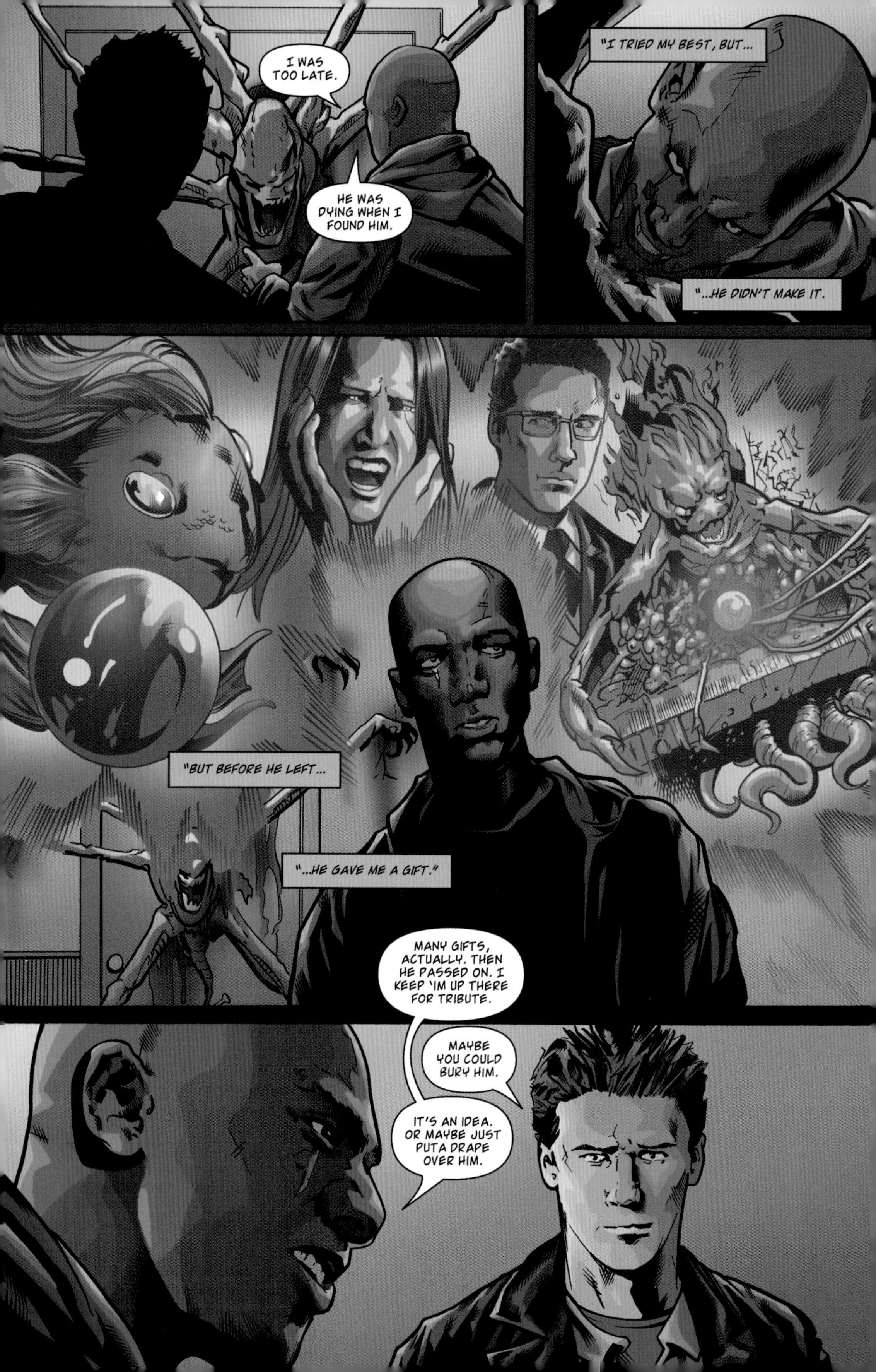
I WAS TOO LATE.
HE WAS DYING WHEN I FOUND HIM.
"I TRIED MY BEST, BUT...
"...HE DIDN'T MAKE IT.
"BUT BEFORE HE LEFT...
"...HE GAVE ME A GIFT."
MANY GIFTS, ACTUALLY. THEN HE PASSED ON. I KEEP 'IM UP THERE FOR TRIBUTE.
MAYBE YOU COULD BURY HIM.
IT'S AN IDEA. OR MAYBE JUST PUTA DRAPE OVER HIM.

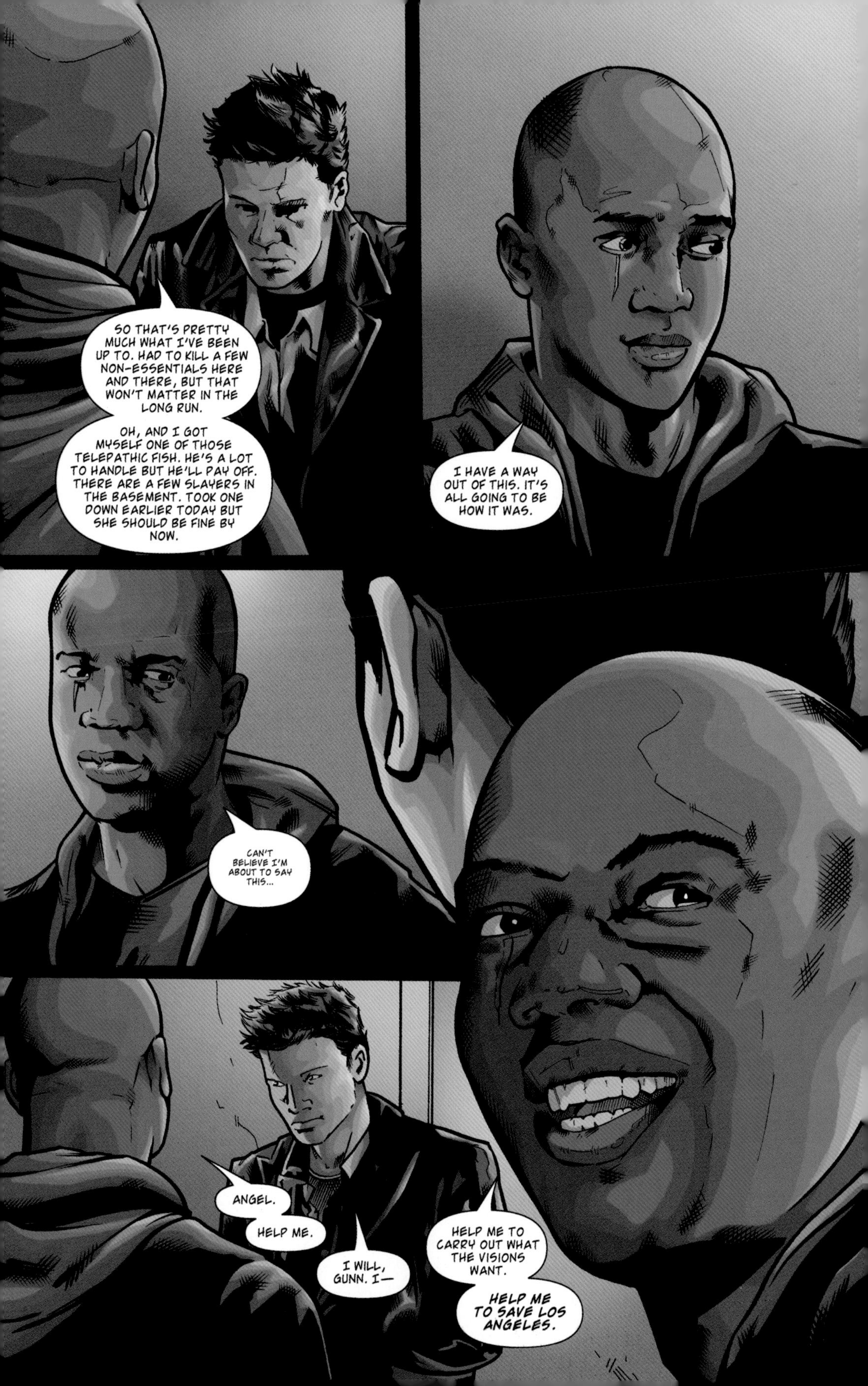
SO THAT'S PRETTY MUCH WHAT I'VE BEEN UP TO. HAD TO KILL A FEW NON-ESSENTIALS HERE AND THERE, BUT THAT WON'T MATTER IN THE LONG RUN.
OH, AND I GOT MYSELF ONE OF THOSE TELEPATHIC FISH. HE'S A LOT TO HANDLE BUT HE'LL PAY OFF. THERE ARE A FEW SLAYERS IN THE BASEMENT. TOOK ONE DOWN EARLIER TODAY BUT SHE SHOULD BE FINE BY NOW.
I HAVE A WAY OUT OF THIS. IT'S ALL GOING TO BE HOW IT WAS.
CAN'T BELIEVE I'M ABOUT TO SAY THIS...
ANGEL.
HELP ME.
I WILL, GUNN. I—
HELP ME TO CARRY OUT WHAT THE VISIONS WANT.
HELP ME TO SAVE LOS ANGELES.

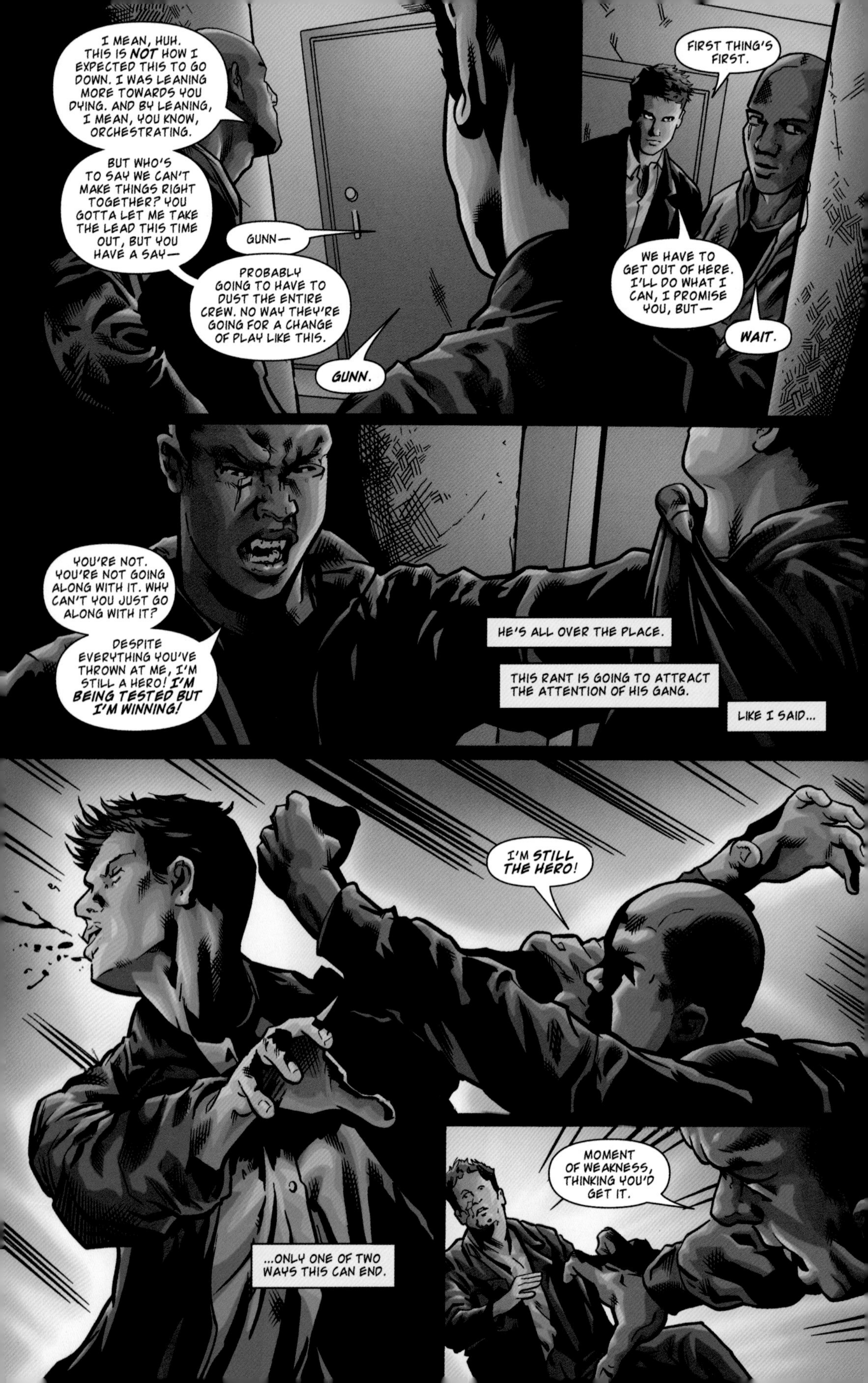
I MEAN, HUH. THIS IS NOT HOW I EXPECTED THIS TO GO DOWN. I WAS LEANING MORE TOWARDS YOU DYING. AND BY LEANING, I MEAN, YOU KNOW, ORCHESTRATING.
BUT WHO'S TO SAY WE CAN'T MAKE THINGS RIGHT TOGETHER? YOU GOTTA LET ME TAKE THE LEAD THIS TIME OUT, BUT YOU HAVE A SAY—
GUNN—
PROBABLY GOING TO HAVE TO DUST THE ENTIRE CREW. NO WAY THEY'RE GOING FOR A CHANGE OF PLAY LIKE THIS.
GUNN.
FIRST THING'S FIRST.
WE HAVE TO GET OUT OF HERE. I'LL DO WHAT I CAN, I PROMISE YOU, BUT—
WAIT.
YOU'RE NOT. YOU'RE NOT GOING ALONG WITH IT. WHY CAN'T YOU JUST GO ALONG WITH IT?
DESPITE EVERYTHING YOU'VE THROWN AT ME, I'M STILL A HERO! I'M BEING TESTED BUT I'M WINNING!
HE'S ALL OVER THE PLACE.
THIS RANT IS GOING TO ATTRACT THE ATTENTION OF HIS GANG.
LIKE I SAID...
I'M STILL THE HERO!
...ONLY ONE OF TWO WAYS THIS CAN END.
MOMENT OF WEAKNESS, THINKING YOU'D GET IT.

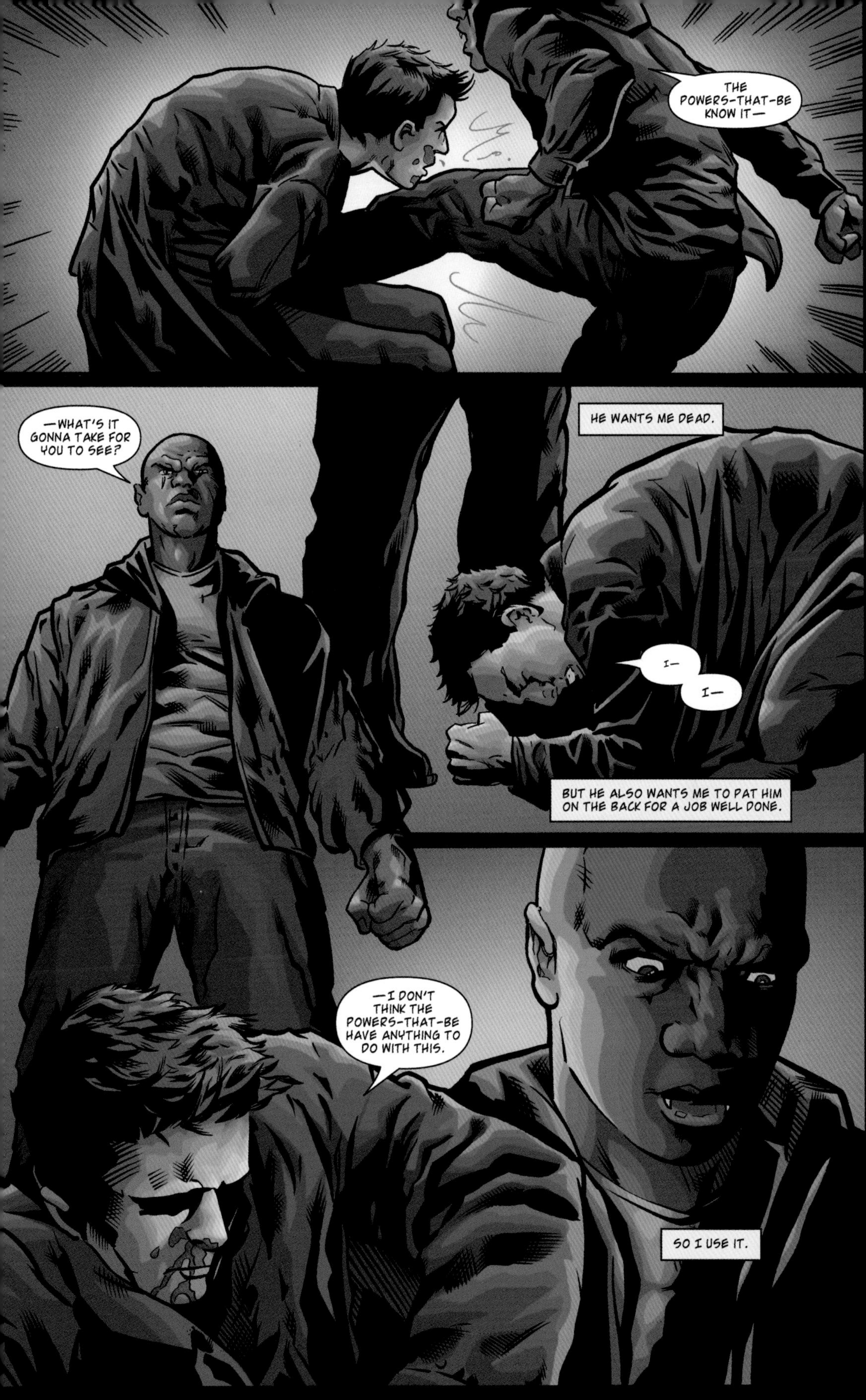
THE POWERS-THAT-BE KNOW IT—
—WHAT'S IT GONNA TAKE FOR YOU TO SEE?
HE WANTS ME DEAD.
I—
I—
BUT HE ALSO WANTS ME TO PAT HIM ON THE BACK FOR A JOB WELL DONE.
—I DON'T THINK THE POWERS-THAT-BE HAVE ANYTHING TO DO WITH THIS.
SO I USE IT.

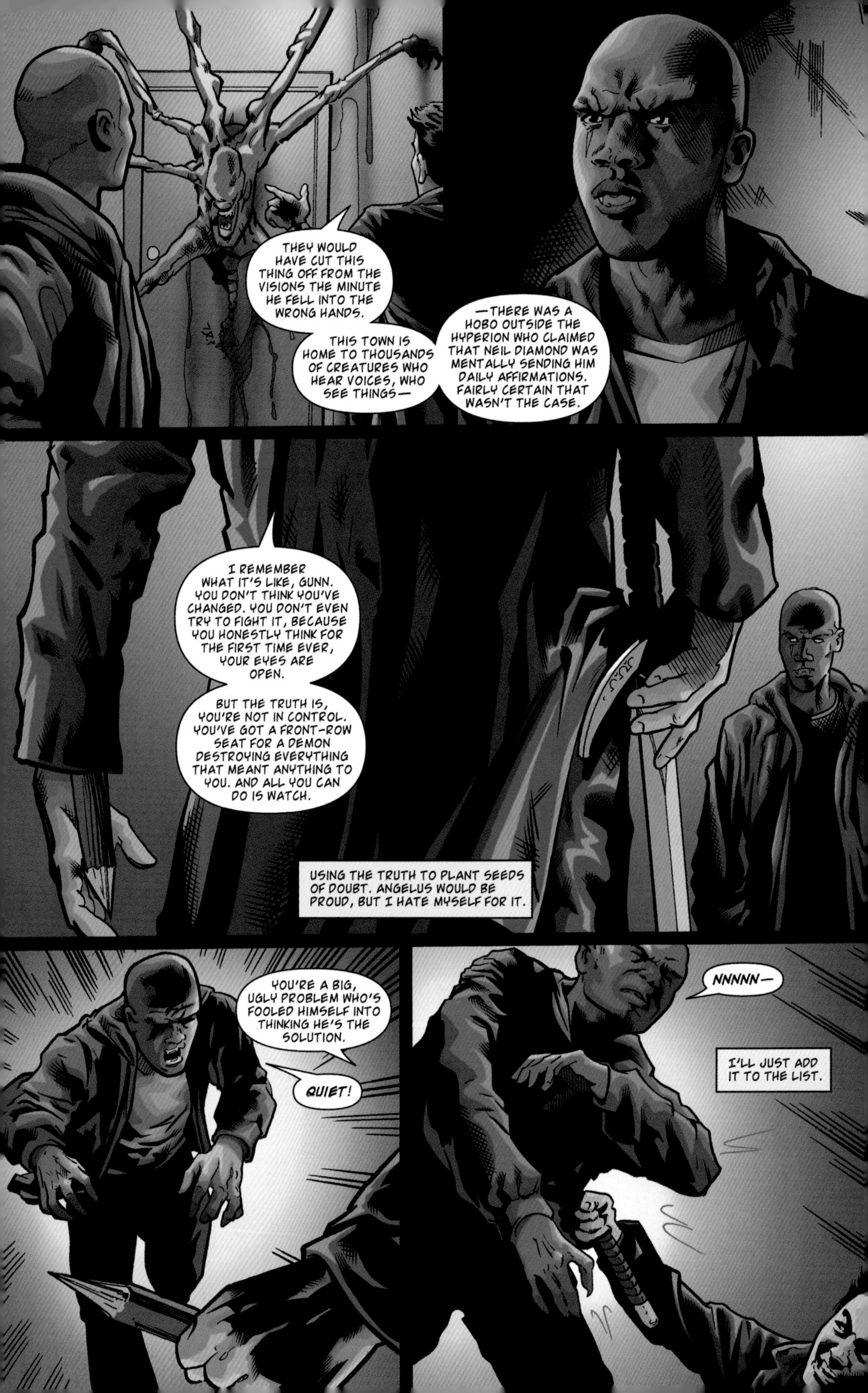
THEY WOULD HAVE CUT THIS THING OFF FROM THE VISIONS THE MINUTE HE FELL INTO THE WRONG HANDS.
THIS TOWN IS HOME TO THOUSANDS OF CREATURES WHO HEAR VOICES, WHO SEE THINGS—
—THERE WAS A HOBO OUTSIDE THE HYPERION WHO CLAIMED THAT NEIL DIAMOND WAS MENTALLY SENDING HIM DAILY AFFIRMATIONS. FAIRLY CERTAIN THAT WASN'T THE CASE.
I REMEMBER WHAT IT'S LIKE, GUNN. YOU DON'T THINK YOU'VE CHANGED. YOU DON'T EVEN TRY TO FIGHT IT, BECAUSE YOU HONESTLY THINK FOR THE FIRST TIME EVER, YOUR EYES ARE OPEN.
BUT THE TRUTH IS, YOU'RE NOT IN CONTROL. YOU'VE GOT A FRONT-ROW SEAT FOR A DEMON DESTROYING EVERYTHING THAT MEANT ANYTHING TO YOU. AND ALL YOU CAN DO IS WATCH.
USING THE TRUTH TO PLANT SEEDS OF DOUBT. ANGELUS WOULD BE PROUD, BUT I HATE MYSELF FOR IT.
YOU'RE A BIG, UGLY PROBLEM WHO'S FOOLED HIMSELF INTO THINKING HE'S THE SOLUTION.
QUIET!
NNNNN—
I'LL JUST ADD IT TO THE LIST.

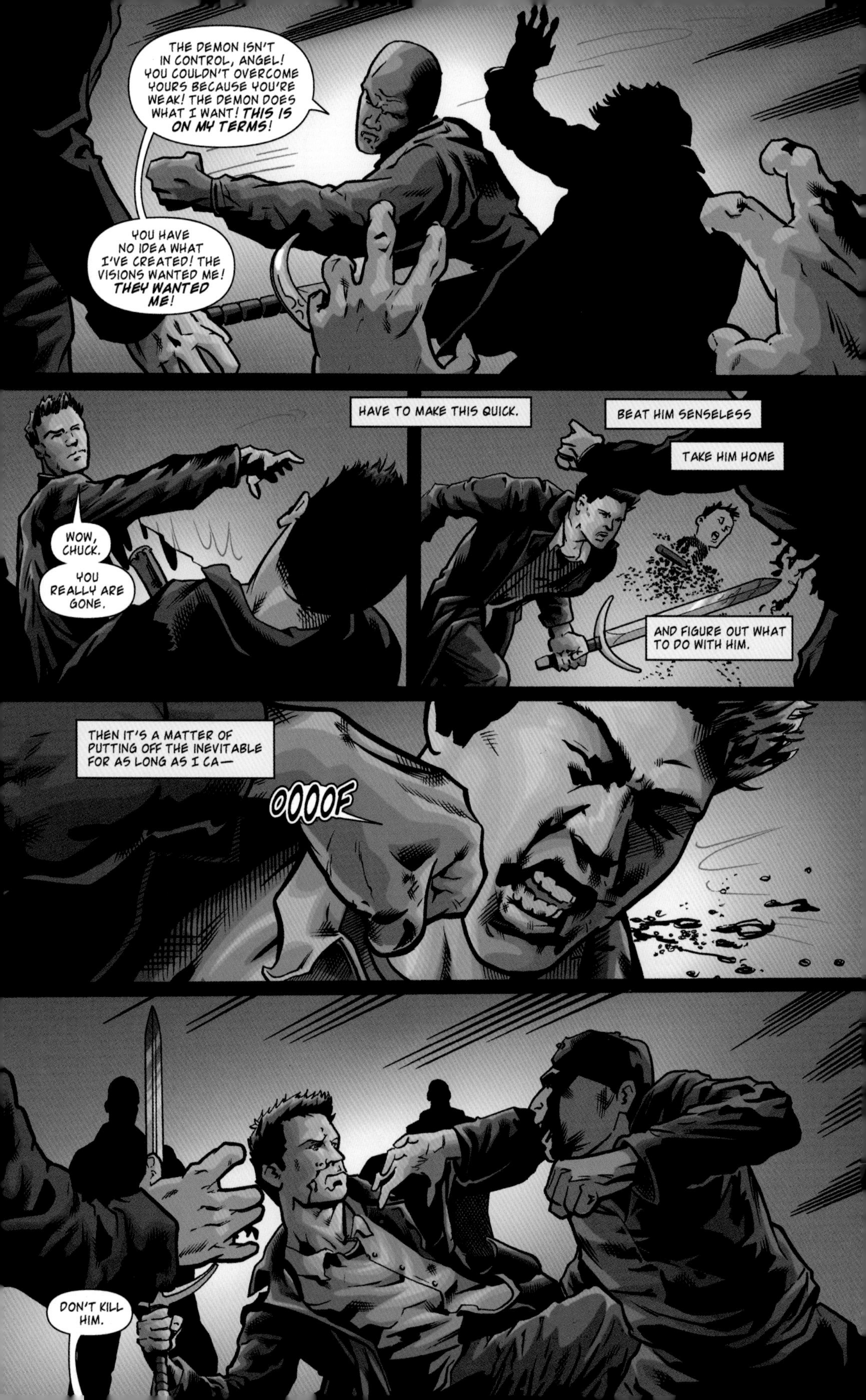
THE DEMON ISN'T IN CONTROL, ANGEL! YOU COULDN'T OVERCOME YOURS BECAUSE YOU'RE WEAK! THE DEMON DOES WHAT I WANT! THIS IS ON MY TERMS!
YOU HAVE NO IDEA WHAT I'VE CREATED! THE VISIONS WANTED ME! THEY WANTED ME!
HAVE TO MAKE THIS QUICK.
WOW, CHUCK.
YOU REALLY ARE GONE.
BEAT HIM SENSELESS
TAKE HIM HOME
AND FIGURE OUT WHAT TO DO WITH HIM.
THEN IT'S A MATTER OF PUTTING OFF THE INEVITABLE FOR AS LONG AS I CA—
OOOOF
DON'T KILL HIM.

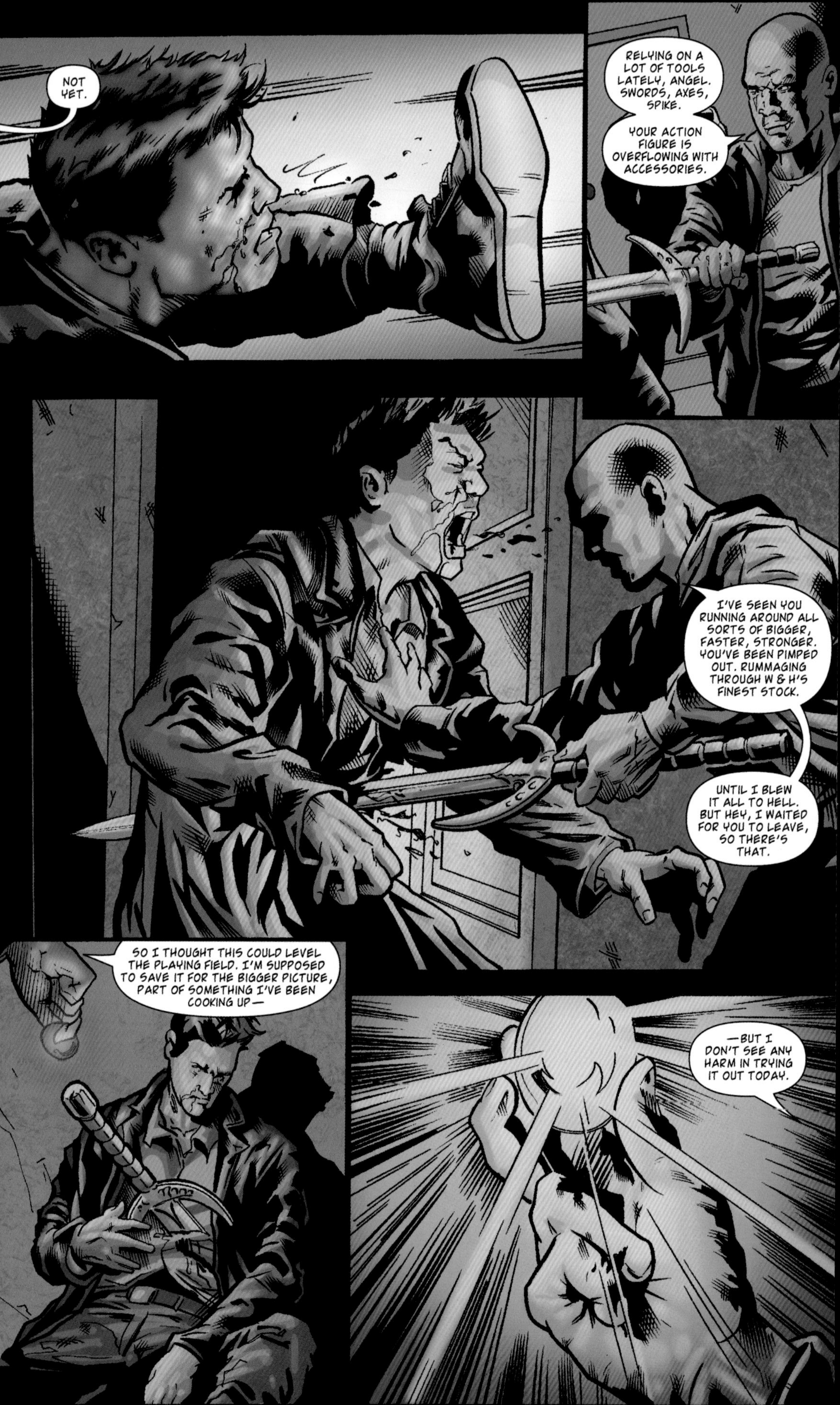
NOT YET.
RELYING ON A LOT OF TOOLS LATELY, ANGEL. SWORDS, AXES, SPIKE.
YOUR ACTION FIGURE IS OVERFLOWING WITH ACCESSORIES.
I'VE SEEN YOU RUNNING AROUND ALL SORTS OF BIGGER, FASTER, STRONGER. YOU'VE BEEN PIMPED OUT. RUMMAGING THROUGH W & H'S FINEST STOCK.
UNTIL I BLEW IT ALL TO HELL. BUT HEY, I WAITED FOR YOU TO LEAVE, SO THERE'S THAT.
SO I THOUGHT THIS COULD LEVEL THE PLAYING FIELD. I'M SUPPOSED TO SAVE IT FOR THE BIGGER PICTURE, PART OF SOMETHING I'VE BEEN COOKING UP—
—BUT I DON'T SEE ANY HARM IN TRYING IT OUT TODAY.

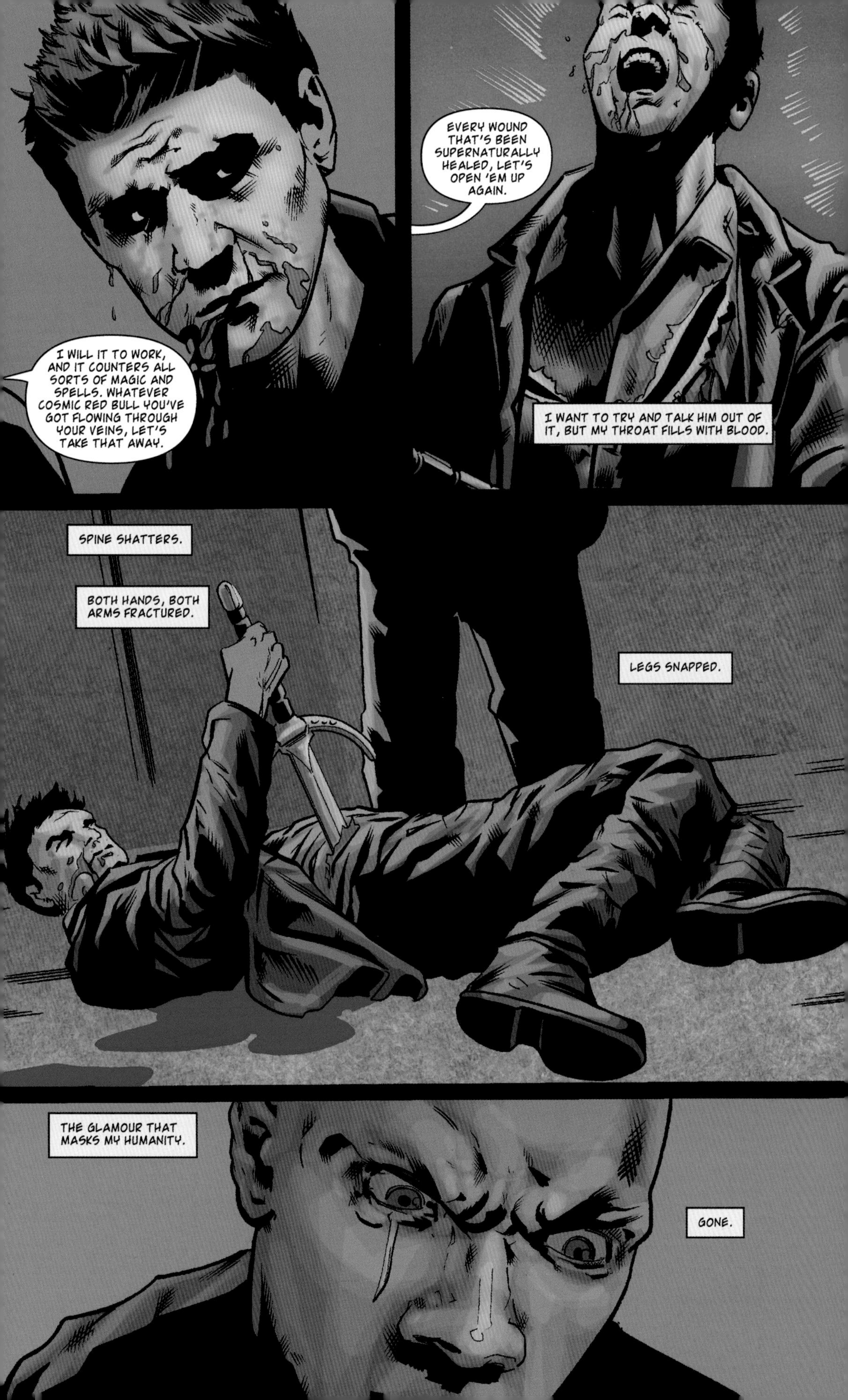
I WILL IT TO WORK, AND IT COUNTERS ALL SORTS OF MAGIC AND SPELLS. WHATEVER COSMIC RED BULL YOU'VE GOT FLOWING THROUGH YOUR VEINS, LET'S TAKE THAT AWAY.
EVERY WOUND THAT'S BEEN SUPERNATURALLY HEALED, LET'S OPEN 'EM UP AGAIN.
I WANT TO TRY AND TALK HIM OUT OF IT, BUT MY THROAT FILLS WITH BLOOD.
SPINE SHATTERS.
BOTH HANDS, BOTH ARMS FRACTURED.
LEGS SNAPPED.
THE GLAMOUR THAT MASKS MY HUMANITY.
GONE.

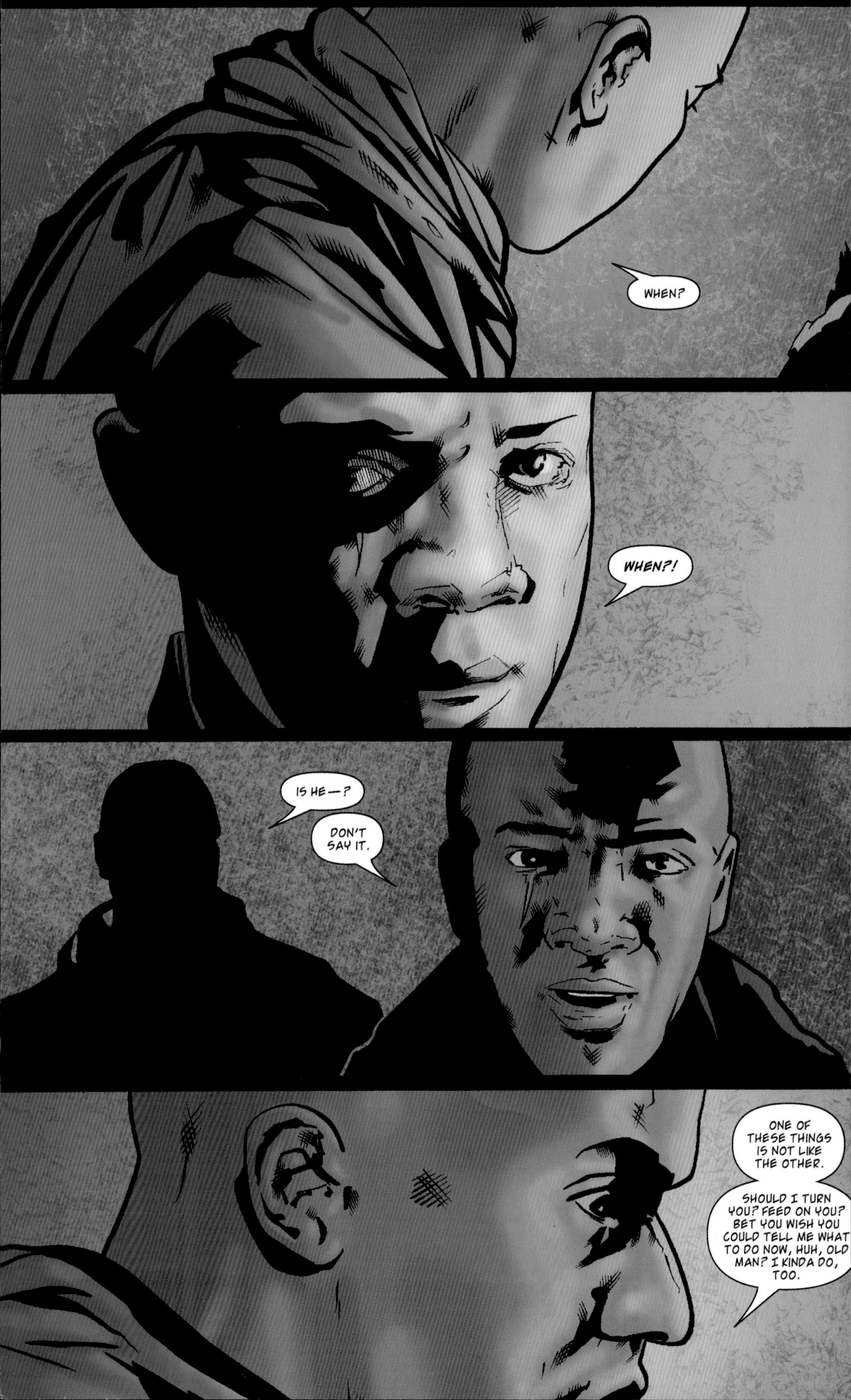
WHEN?
WHEN?!
IS HE—?
DON'T SAY IT.
ONE OF THESE THINGS IS NOT LIKE THE OTHER.
SHOULD I TURN YOU? FEED ON YOU? BET YOU WISH YOU COULD TELL ME WHAT TO DO NOW, HUH, OLD MAN? I KINDA DO, TOO.

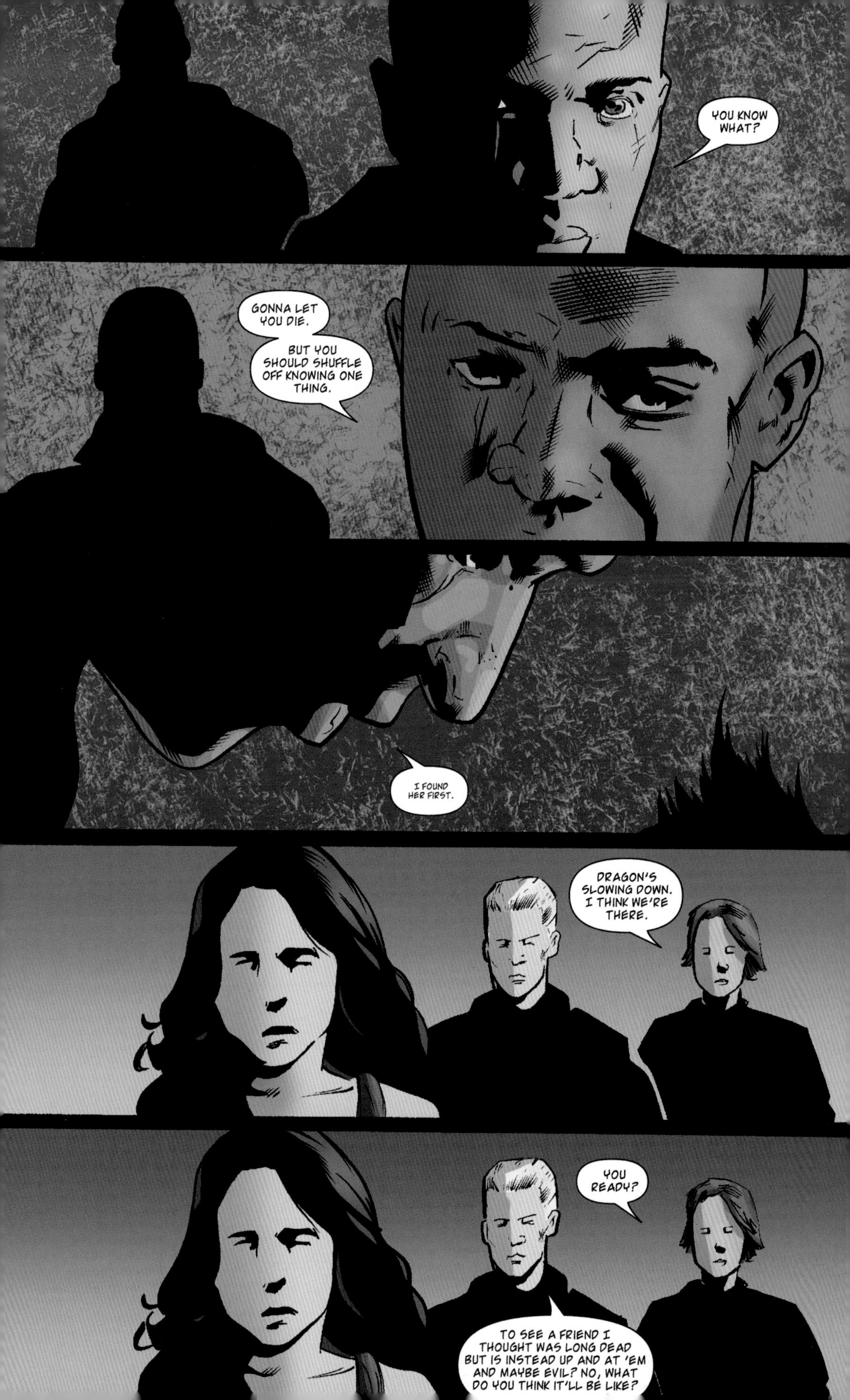
YOU KNOW WHAT?
GONNA LET YOU DIE.
BUT YOU SHOULD SHUFFLE OFF KNOWING ONE THING.
I FOUND HER FIRST.
DRAGON'S SLOWING DOWN. I THINK WE'RE THERE.
YOU READY?
TO SEE A FRIEND I THOUGHT WAS LONG DEAD BUT IS INSTEAD UP AND AT 'EM AND MAYBE EVIL? NO, WHAT DO YOU THINK IT'LL BE LIKE?

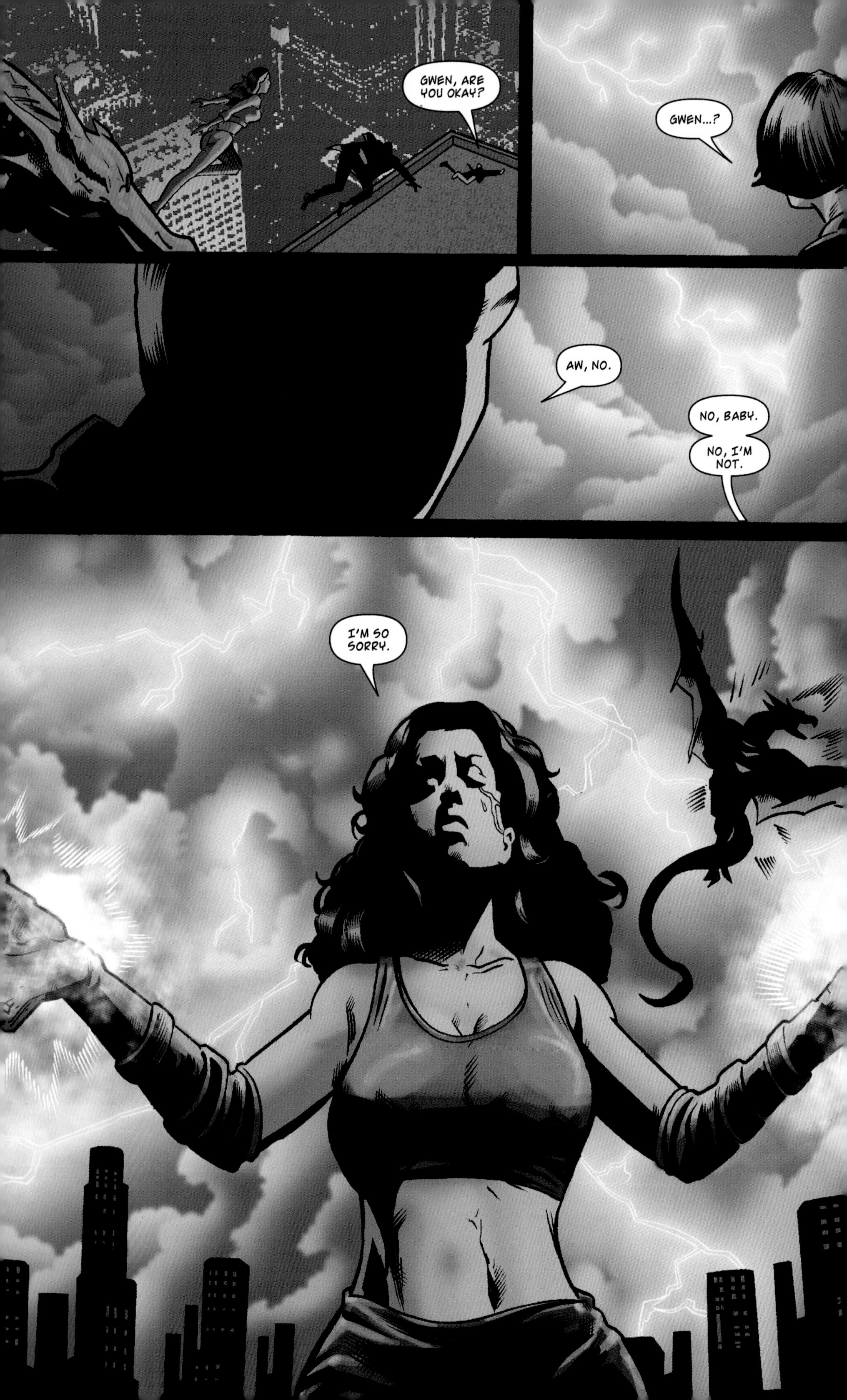
GWEN, ARE YOU OKAY?
GWEN...?
AW, NO.
NO, BABY.
NO, I'M NOT.
I'M SO SORRY.

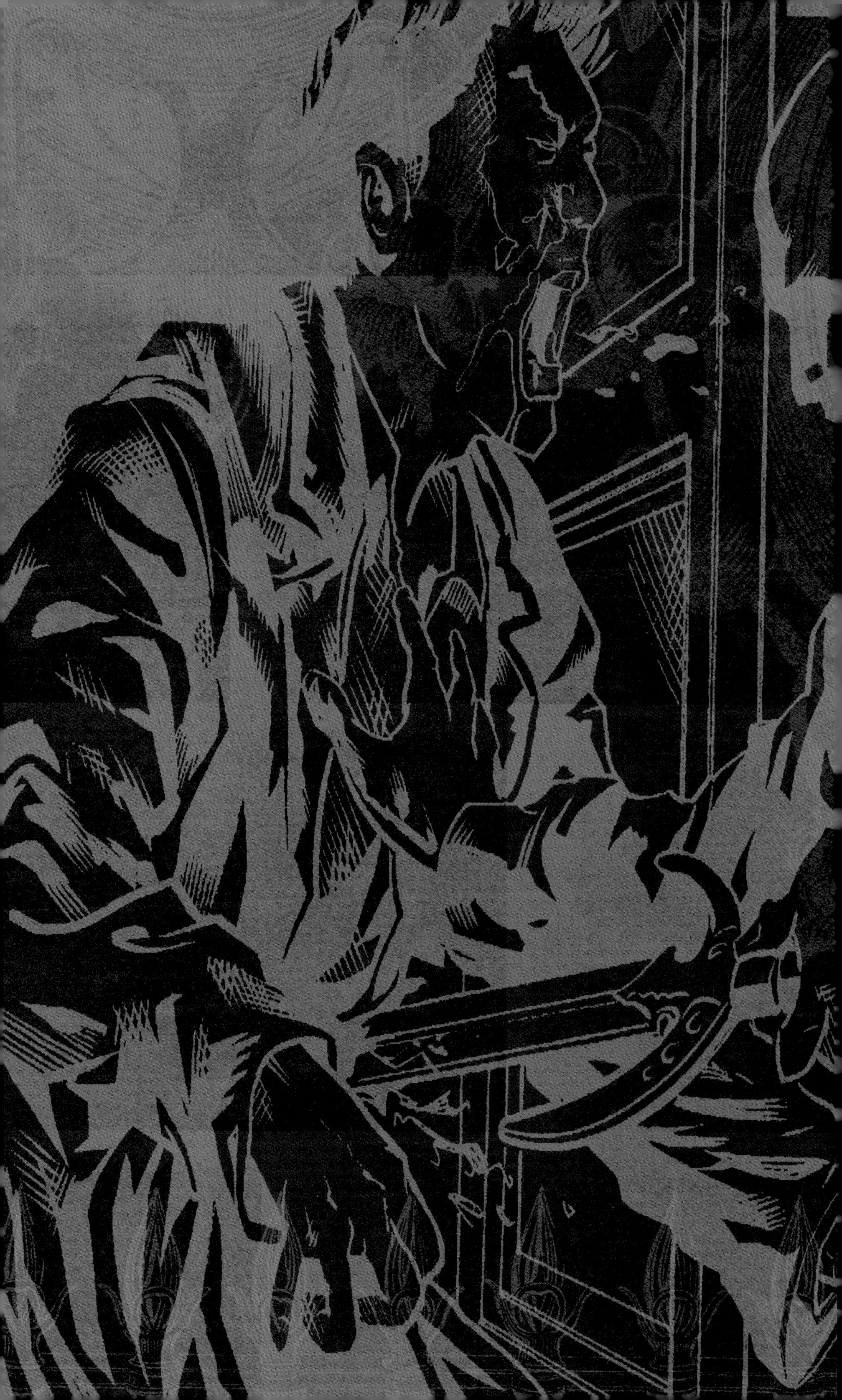

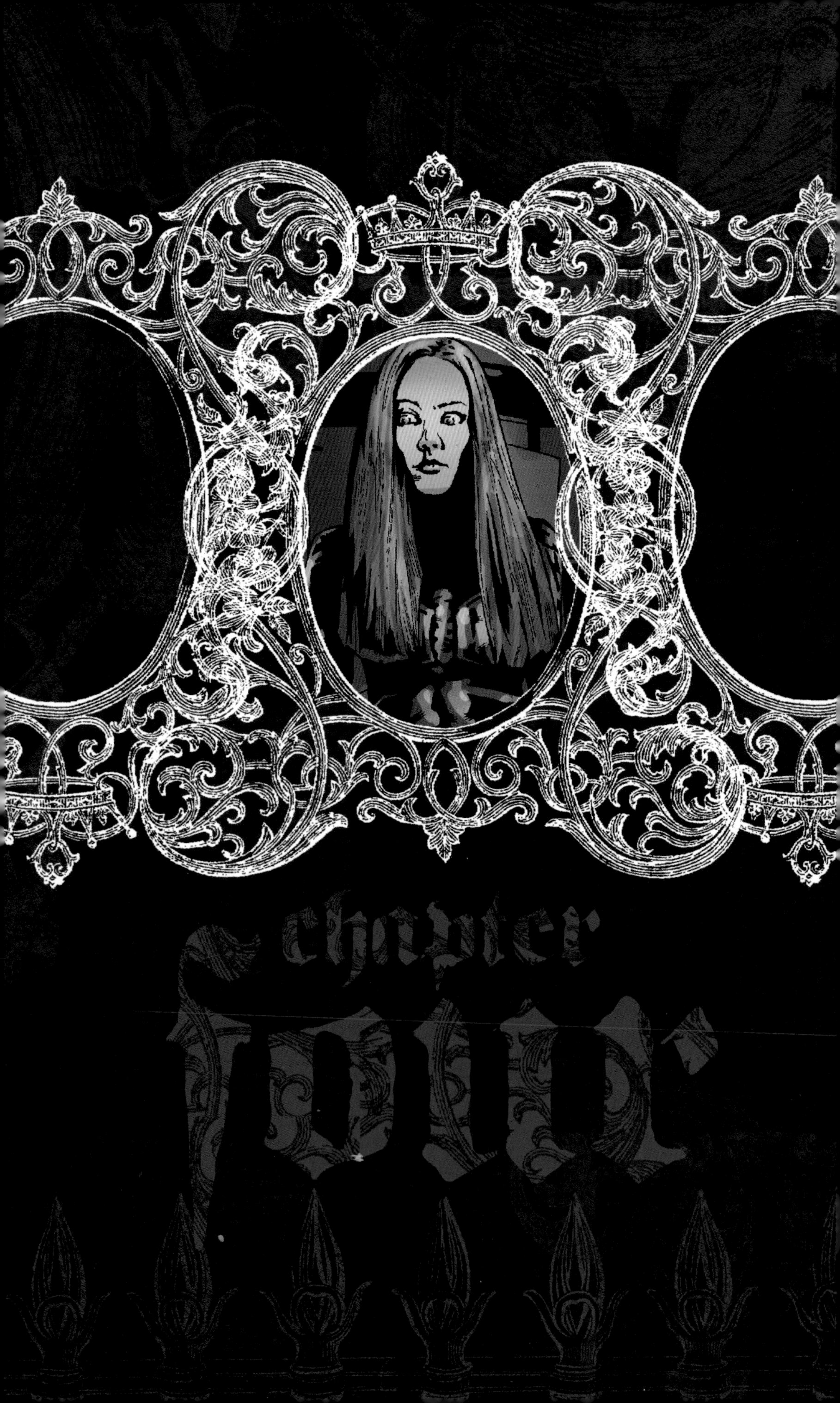

chapter four

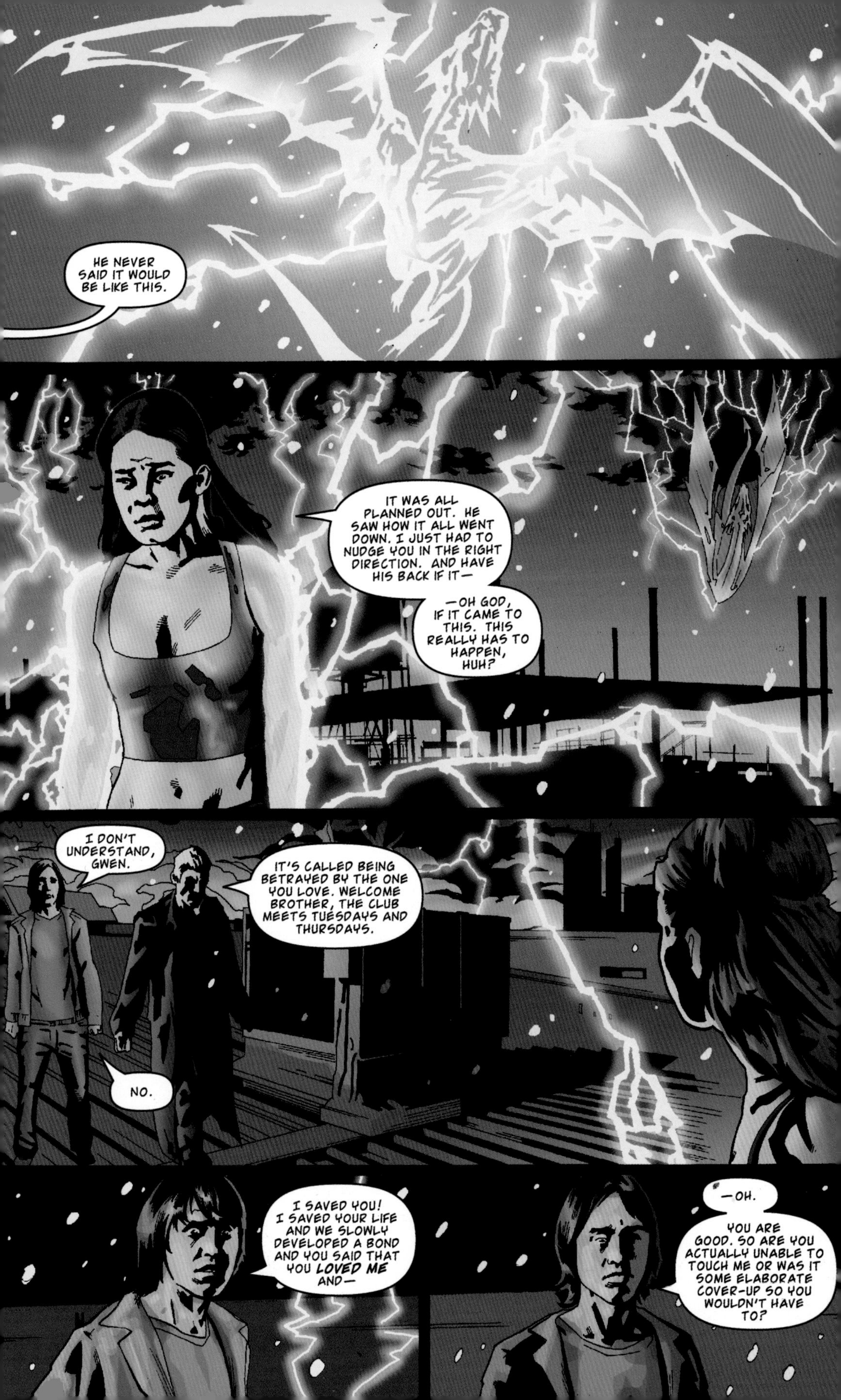
HE NEVER SAID IT WOULD BE LIKE THIS.
IT WAS ALL PLANNED OUT. HE SAW HOW IT ALL WENT DOWN. I JUST HAD TO NUDGE YOU IN THE RIGHT DIRECTION. AND HAVE HIS BACK IF IT—
—OH GOD, IF IT CAME TO THIS. THIS REALLY HAS TO HAPPEN, HUH?
I DON'T UNDERSTAND, GWEN.
IT'S CALLED BEING BETRAYED BY THE ONE YOU LOVE. WELCOME BROTHER, THE CLUB MEETS TUESDAYS AND THURSDAYS.
NO.
I SAVED YOU! I SAVED YOUR LIFE AND WE SLOWLY DEVELOPED A BOND AND YOU SAID THAT YOU ***LOVED ME*** AND—
—OH.
YOU ARE GOOD. SO ARE YOU ACTUALLY UNABLE TO TOUCH ME OR WAS IT SOME ELABORATE COVER-UP SO YOU WOULDN'T HAVE TO?

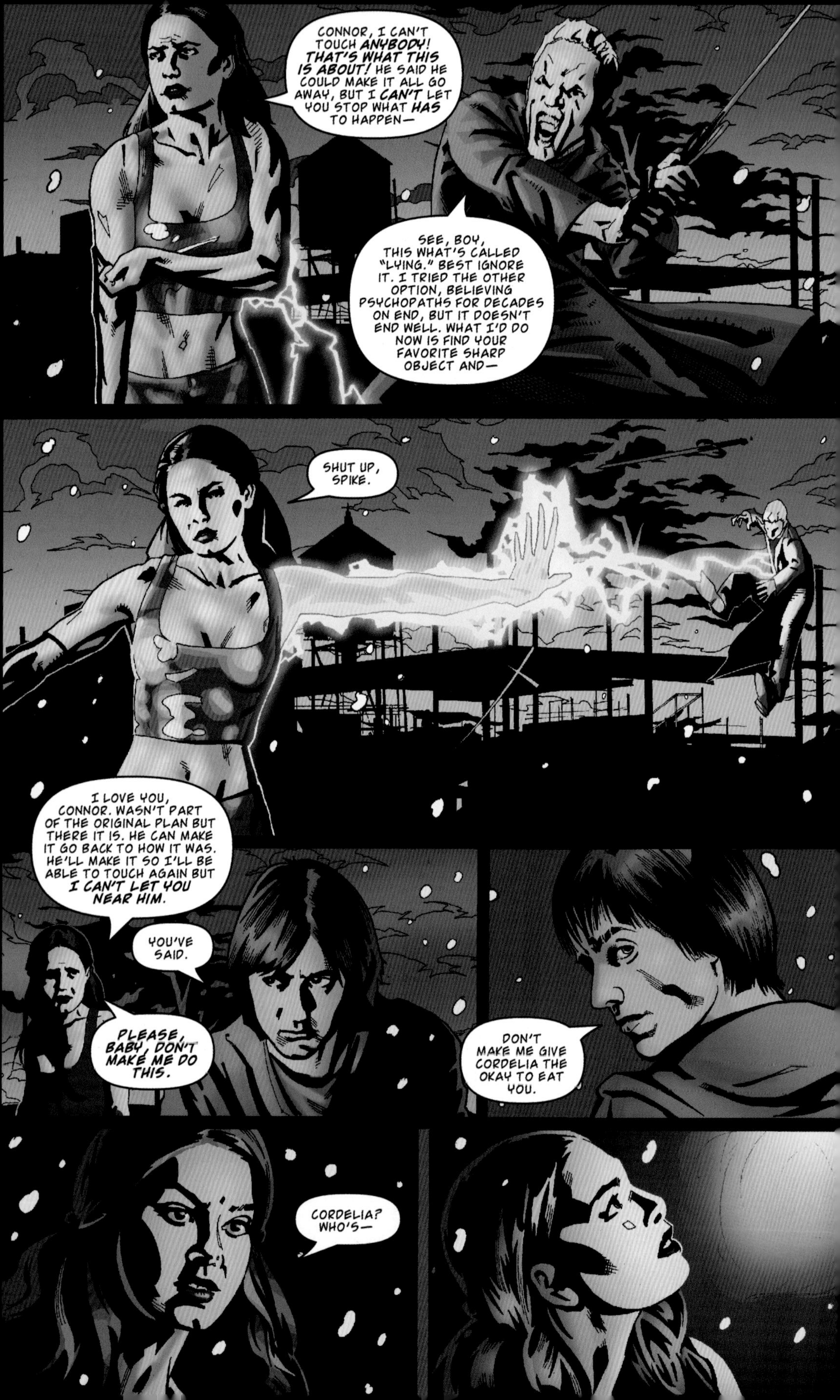
CONNOR, I CAN'T TOUCH ANYBODY! THAT'S WHAT THIS IS ABOUT! HE SAID HE COULD MAKE IT ALL GO AWAY, BUT I CAN'T LET YOU STOP WHAT HAS TO HAPPEN—
SEE, BOY, THIS WHAT'S CALLED "LYING." BEST IGNORE IT. I TRIED THE OTHER OPTION, BELIEVING PSYCHOPATHS FOR DECADES ON END, BUT IT DOESN'T END WELL. WHAT I'D DO NOW IS FIND YOUR FAVORITE SHARP OBJECT AND—
SHUT UP, SPIKE.
I LOVE YOU, CONNOR. WASN'T PART OF THE ORIGINAL PLAN BUT THERE IT IS. HE CAN MAKE IT GO BACK TO HOW IT WAS. HE'LL MAKE IT SO I'LL BE ABLE TO TOUCH AGAIN BUT I CAN'T LET YOU NEAR HIM.
YOU'VE SAID.
PLEASE, BABY, DON'T MAKE ME DO THIS.
DON'T MAKE ME GIVE CORDELIA THE OKAY TO EAT YOU.
CORDELIA? WHO'S—

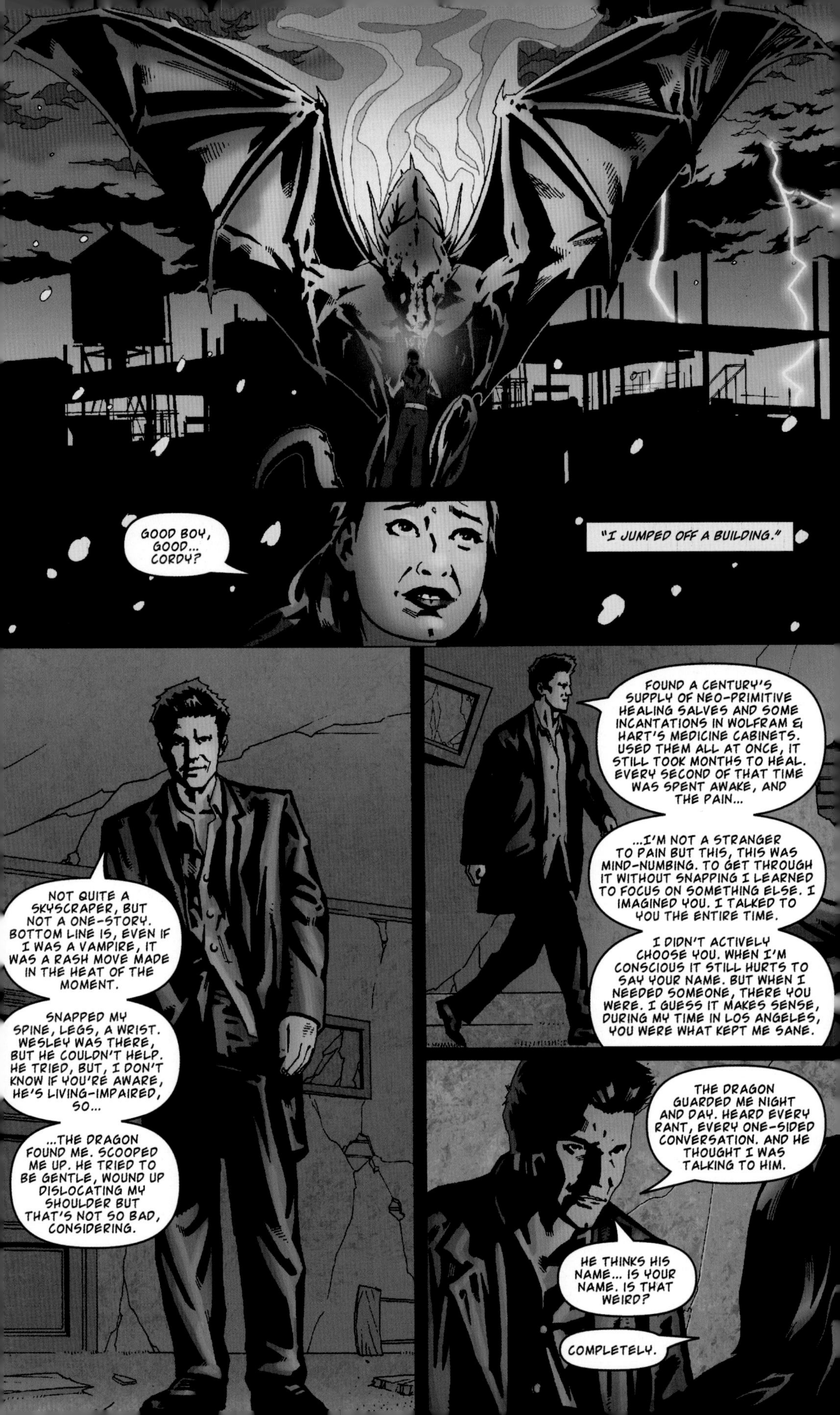
GOOD BOY, GOOD... CORDY?
"I JUMPED OFF A BUILDING."
NOT QUITE A SKYSCRAPER, BUT NOT A ONE-STORY. BOTTOM LINE IS, EVEN IF I WAS A VAMPIRE, IT WAS A RASH MOVE MADE IN THE HEAT OF THE MOMENT.
SNAPPED MY SPINE, LEGS, A WRIST. WESLEY WAS THERE, BUT HE COULDN'T HELP. HE TRIED, BUT, I DON'T KNOW IF YOU'RE AWARE, HE'S LIVING-IMPAIRED, SO...
...THE DRAGON FOUND ME. SCOOPED ME UP. HE TRIED TO BE GENTLE, WOUND UP DISLOCATING MY SHOULDER BUT THAT'S NOT SO BAD, CONSIDERING.
FOUND A CENTURY'S SUPPLY OF NEO-PRIMITIVE HEALING SALVES AND SOME INCANTATIONS IN WOLFRAM & HART'S MEDICINE CABINETS. USED THEM ALL AT ONCE, IT STILL TOOK MONTHS TO HEAL. EVERY SECOND OF THAT TIME WAS SPENT AWAKE, AND THE PAIN...
...I'M NOT A STRANGER TO PAIN BUT THIS, THIS WAS MIND-NUMBING. TO GET THROUGH IT WITHOUT SNAPPING I LEARNED TO FOCUS ON SOMETHING ELSE. I IMAGINED YOU. I TALKED TO YOU THE ENTIRE TIME.
I DIDN'T ACTIVELY CHOOSE YOU. WHEN I'M CONSCIOUS IT STILL HURTS TO SAY YOUR NAME. BUT WHEN I NEEDED SOMEONE, THERE YOU WERE. I GUESS IT MAKES SENSE, DURING MY TIME IN LOS ANGELES, YOU WERE WHAT KEPT ME SANE.
THE DRAGON GUARDED ME NIGHT AND DAY. HEARD EVERY RANT, EVERY ONE-SIDED CONVERSATION. AND HE THOUGHT I WAS TALKING TO HIM.
HE THINKS HIS NAME... IS YOUR NAME. IS THAT WEIRD?
COMPLETELY.

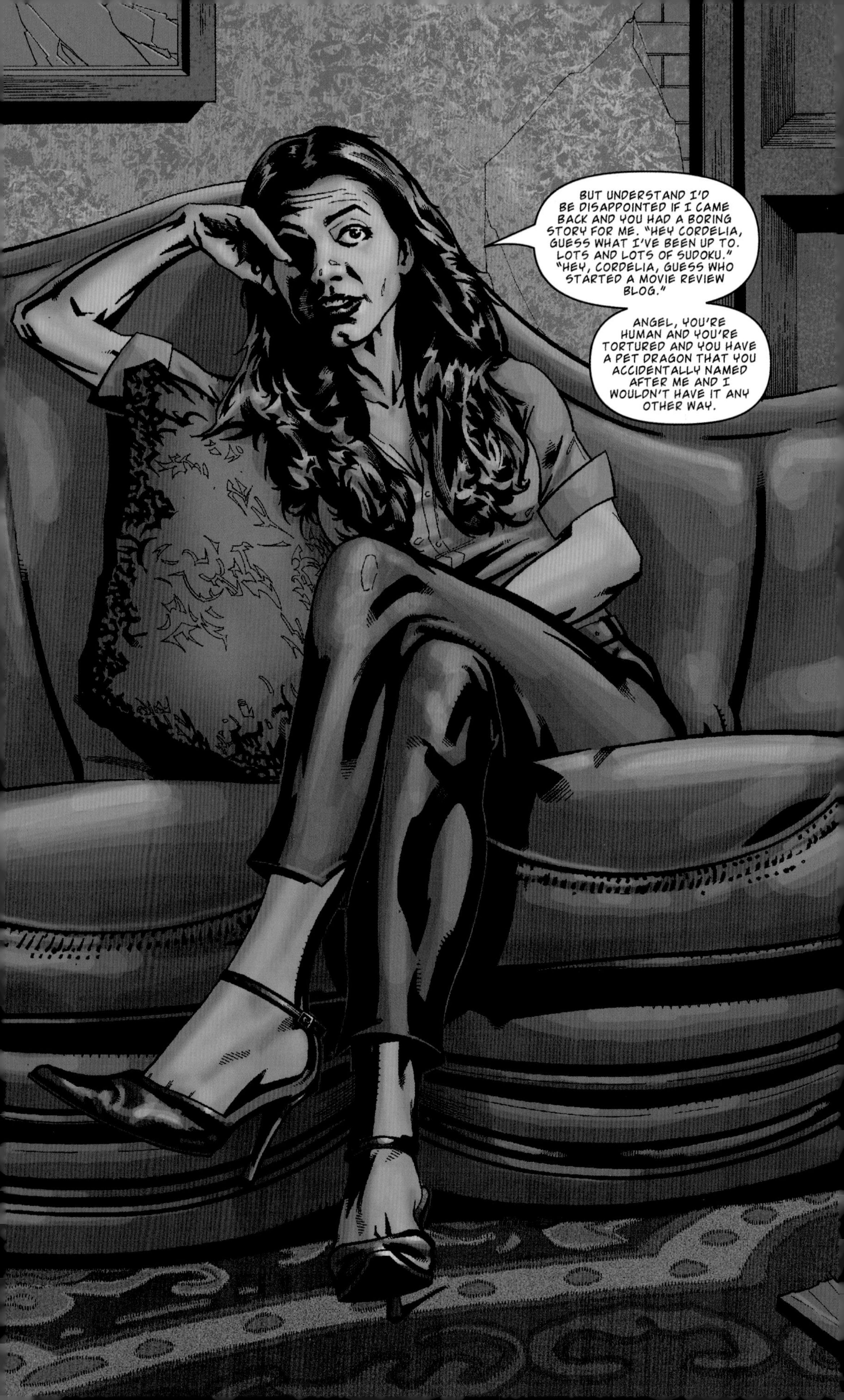
BUT UNDERSTAND I'D BE DISAPPOINTED IF I CAME BACK AND YOU HAD A BORING STORY FOR ME. "HEY CORDELIA, GUESS WHAT I'VE BEEN UP TO. LOTS AND LOTS OF SUDOKU." "HEY, CORDELIA, GUESS WHO STARTED A MOVIE REVIEW BLOG."
ANGEL, YOU'RE HUMAN AND YOU'RE TORTURED AND YOU HAVE A PET DRAGON THAT YOU ACCIDENTALLY NAMED AFTER ME AND I WOULDN'T HAVE IT ANY OTHER WAY.

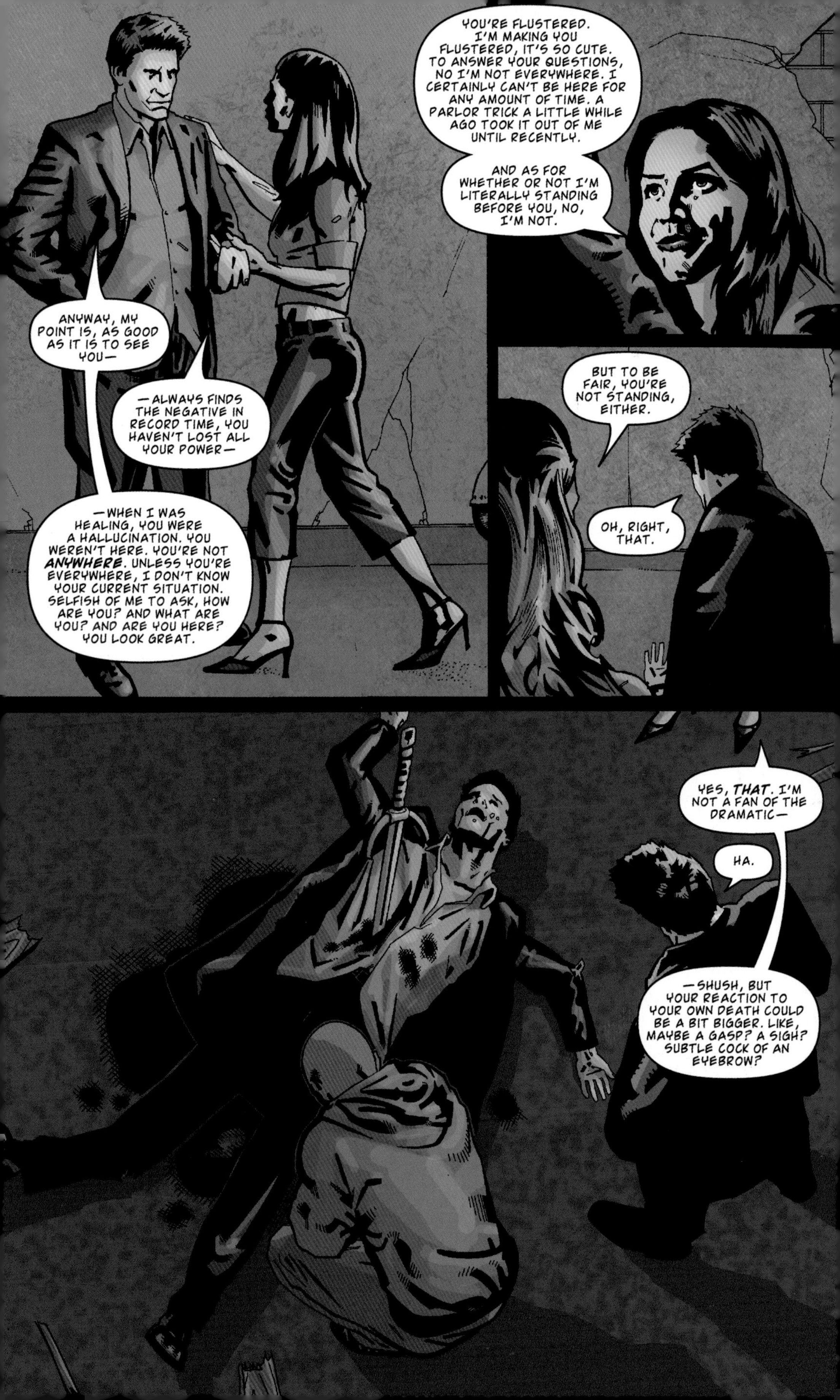
ANYWAY, MY POINT IS, AS GOOD AS IT IS TO SEE YOU—
—ALWAYS FINDS THE NEGATIVE IN RECORD TIME, YOU HAVEN'T LOST ALL YOUR POWER—
—WHEN I WAS HEALING, YOU WERE A HALLUCINATION. YOU WEREN'T HERE. YOU'RE NOT ANYWHERE. UNLESS YOU'RE EVERYWHERE, I DON'T KNOW YOUR CURRENT SITUATION. SELFISH OF ME TO ASK, HOW ARE YOU? AND WHAT ARE YOU? AND ARE YOU HERE? YOU LOOK GREAT.
YOU'RE FLUSTERED. I'M MAKING YOU FLUSTERED, IT'S SO CUTE. TO ANSWER YOUR QUESTIONS, NO I'M NOT EVERYWHERE. I CERTAINLY CAN'T BE HERE FOR ANY AMOUNT OF TIME. A PARLOR TRICK A LITTLE WHILE AGO TOOK IT OUT OF ME UNTIL RECENTLY.
AND AS FOR WHETHER OR NOT I'M LITERALLY STANDING BEFORE YOU, NO, I'M NOT.
BUT TO BE FAIR, YOU'RE NOT STANDING, EITHER.
OH, RIGHT, THAT.
YES, THAT. I'M NOT A FAN OF THE DRAMATIC—
HA.
—SHUSH, BUT YOUR REACTION TO YOUR OWN DEATH COULD BE A BIT BIGGER. LIKE, MAYBE A GASP? A SIGH? SUBTLE COCK OF AN EYEBROW?

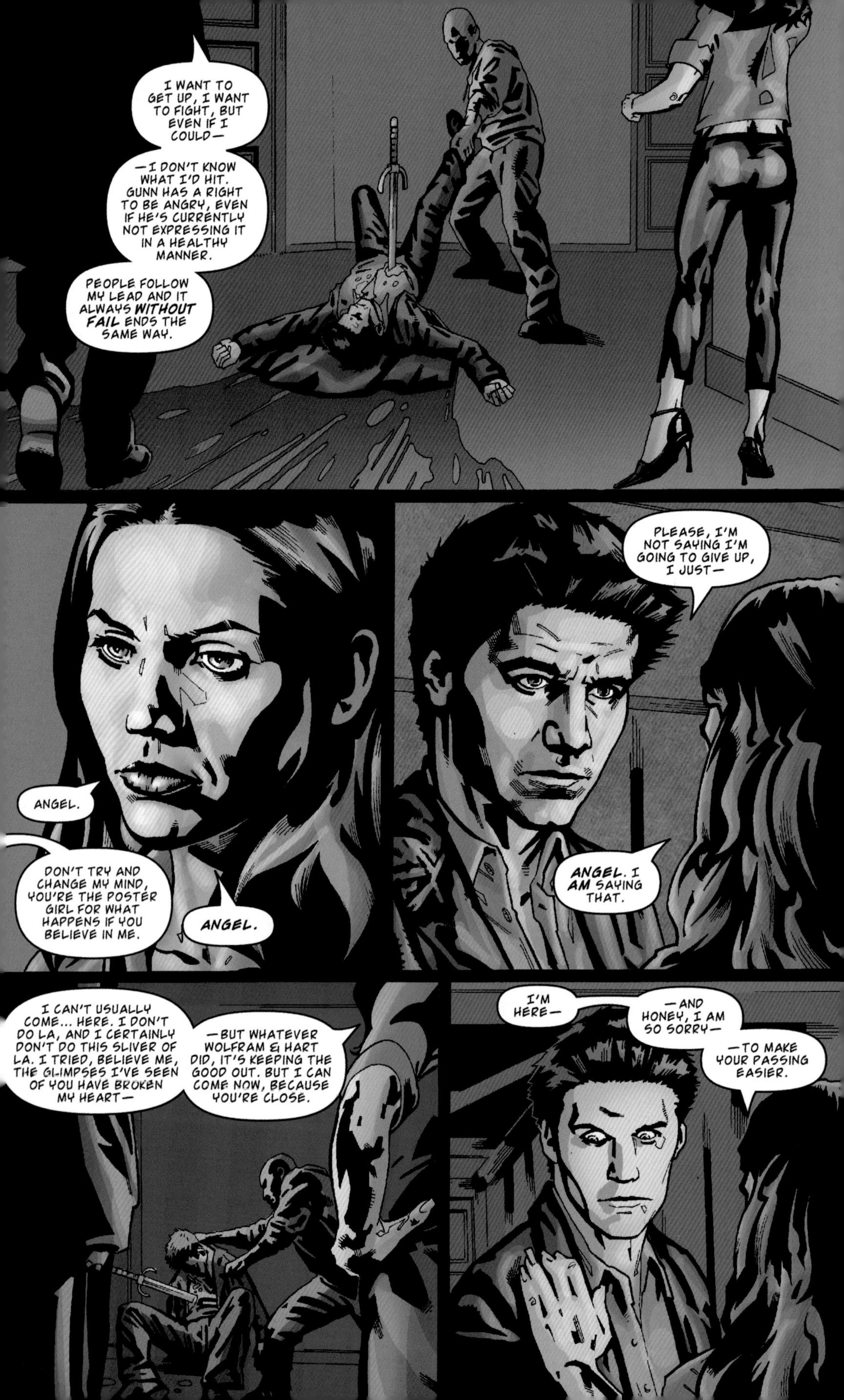
I WANT TO GET UP, I WANT TO FIGHT, BUT EVEN IF I COULD—
—I DON'T KNOW WHAT I'D HIT. GUNN HAS A RIGHT TO BE ANGRY, EVEN IF HE'S CURRENTLY NOT EXPRESSING IT IN A HEALTHY MANNER.
PEOPLE FOLLOW MY LEAD AND IT ALWAYS WITHOUT FAIL ENDS THE SAME WAY.
ANGEL.
DON'T TRY AND CHANGE MY MIND, YOU'RE THE POSTER GIRL FOR WHAT HAPPENS IF YOU BELIEVE IN ME.
ANGEL.
PLEASE, I'M NOT SAYING I'M GOING TO GIVE UP, I JUST—
ANGEL. I AM SAYING THAT.
I CAN'T USUALLY COME... HERE. I DON'T DO LA, AND I CERTAINLY DON'T DO THIS SLIVER OF LA. I TRIED, BELIEVE ME, THE GLIMPSES I'VE SEEN OF YOU HAVE BROKEN MY HEART—
—BUT WHATEVER WOLFRAM & HART DID, IT'S KEEPING THE GOOD OUT. BUT I CAN COME NOW, BECAUSE YOU'RE CLOSE.
I'M HERE—
—AND HONEY, I AM SO SORRY—
—TO MAKE YOUR PASSING EASIER.

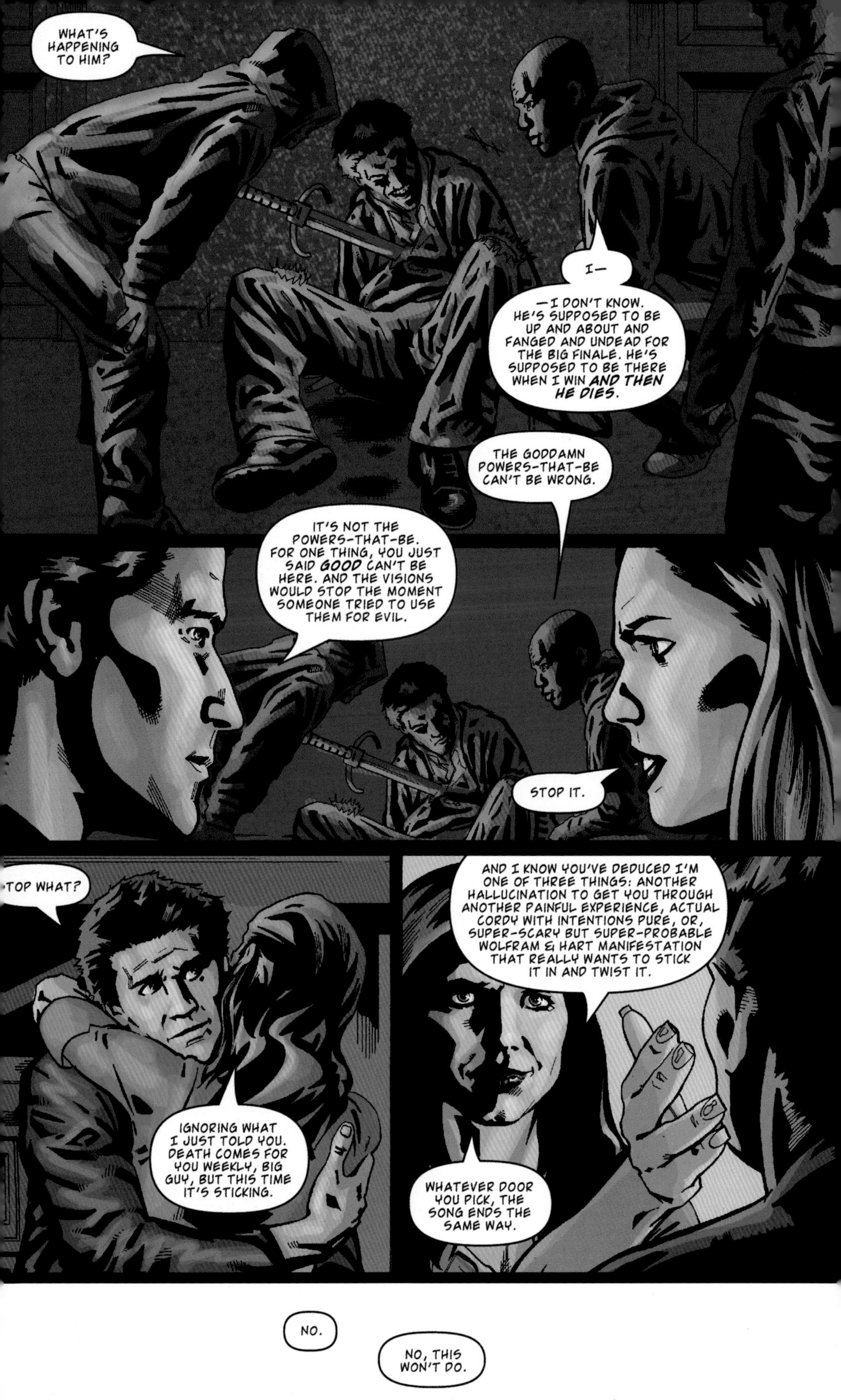
WHAT'S HAPPENING TO HIM?
I—
—I DON'T KNOW. HE'S SUPPOSED TO BE UP AND ABOUT AND FANGED AND UNDEAD FOR THE BIG FINALE. HE'S SUPPOSED TO BE THERE WHEN I WIN AND THEN HE DIES.
THE GODDAMN POWERS-THAT-BE CAN'T BE WRONG.
IT'S NOT THE POWERS-THAT-BE. FOR ONE THING, YOU JUST SAID GOOD CAN'T BE HERE. AND THE VISIONS WOULD STOP THE MOMENT SOMEONE TRIED TO USE THEM FOR EVIL.
STOP IT.
TOP WHAT?
IGNORING WHAT I JUST TOLD YOU. DEATH COMES FOR YOU WEEKLY, BIG GUY, BUT THIS TIME IT'S STICKING.
AND I KNOW YOU'VE DEDUCED I'M ONE OF THREE THINGS: ANOTHER HALLUCINATION TO GET YOU THROUGH ANOTHER PAINFUL EXPERIENCE, ACTUAL CORDY WITH INTENTIONS PURE, OR, SUPER-SCARY BUT SUPER-PROBABLE WOLFRAM & HART MANIFESTATION THAT REALLY WANTS TO STICK IT IN AND TWIST IT.
WHATEVER DOOR YOU PICK, THE SONG ENDS THE SAME WAY.
NO.
NO, THIS WON'T DO.

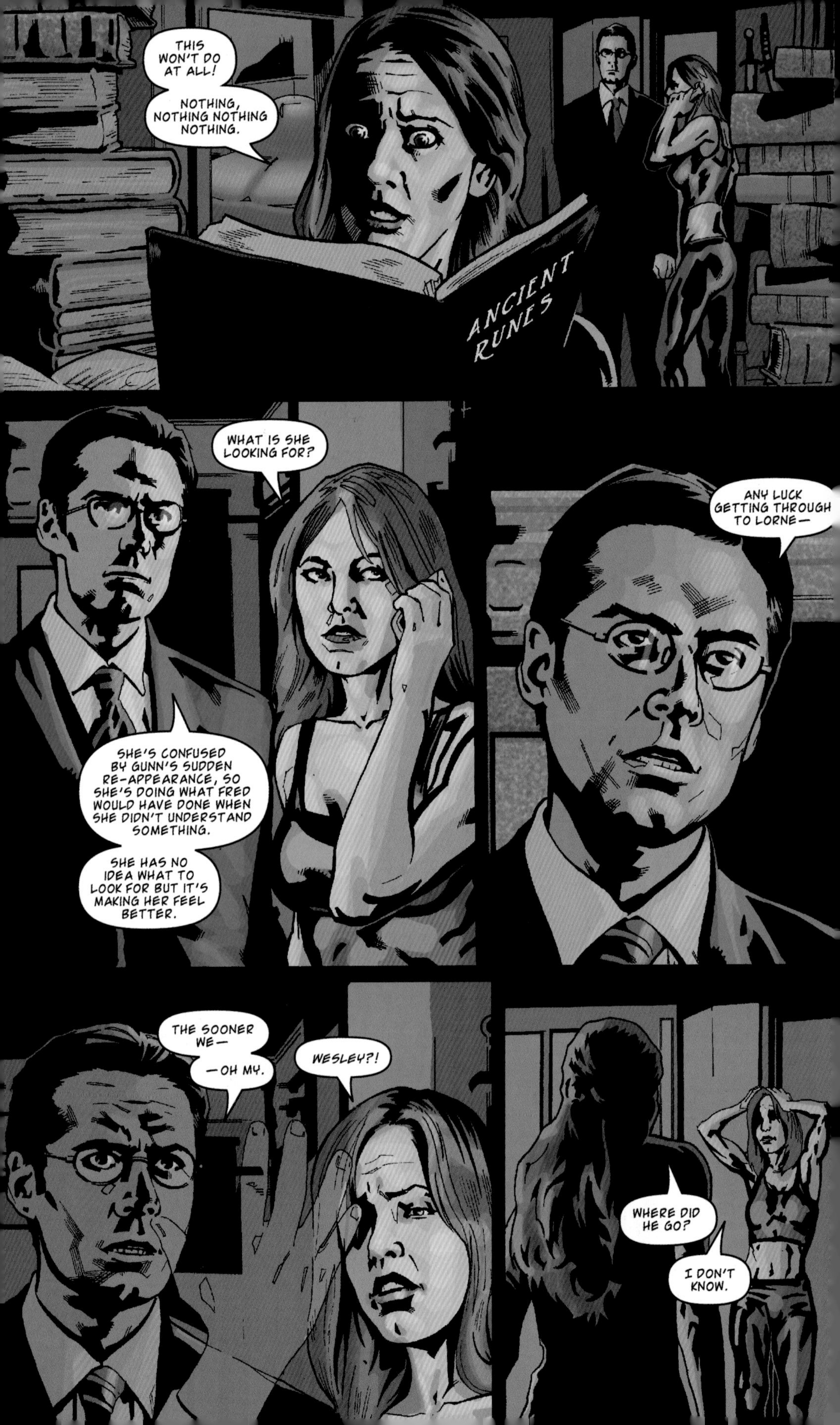
THIS WON'T DO AT ALL!
NOTHING, NOTHING NOTHING NOTHING.
ANCIENT RUNES
WHAT IS SHE LOOKING FOR?
SHE'S CONFUSED BY GUNN'S SUDDEN RE-APPEARANCE, SO SHE'S DOING WHAT FRED WOULD HAVE DONE WHEN SHE DIDN'T UNDERSTAND SOMETHING.
SHE HAS NO IDEA WHAT TO LOOK FOR BUT IT'S MAKING HER FEEL BETTER.
ANY LUCK GETTING THROUGH TO LORNE—
THE SOONER WE—
—OH MY.
WESLEY?!
WHERE DID HE GO?
I DON'T KNOW.

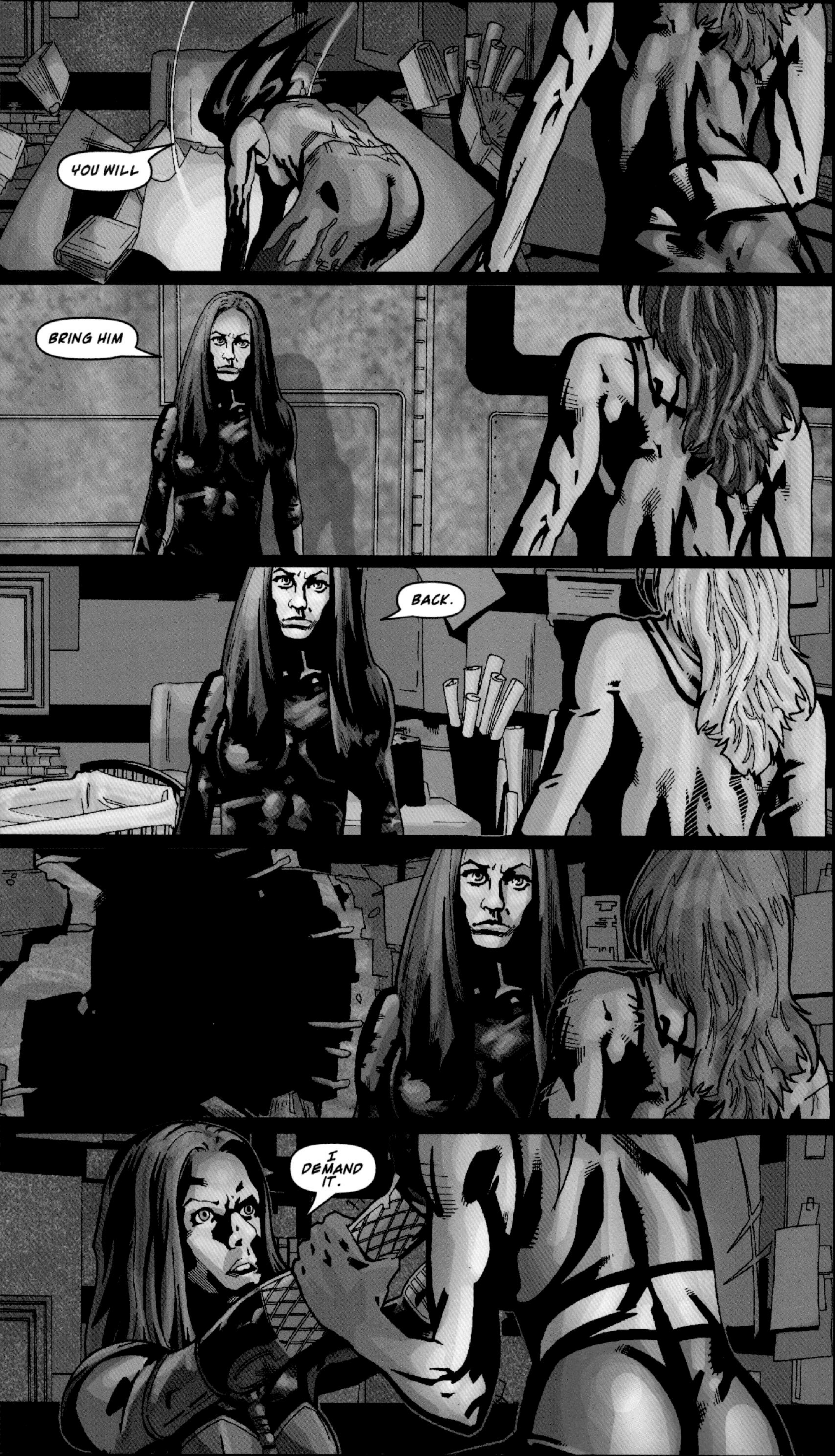
YOU WILL
BRING HIM
BACK.
I DEMAND IT.

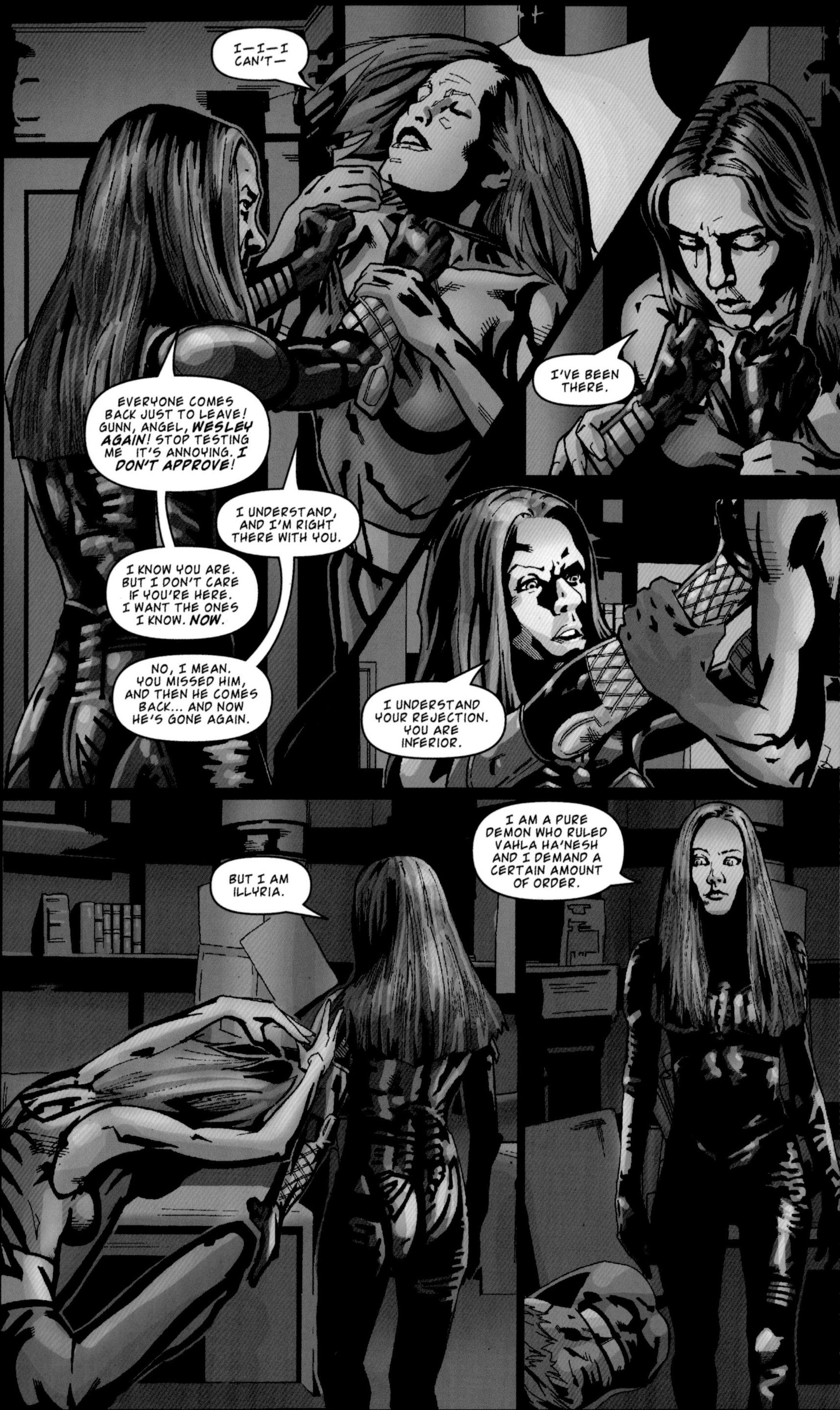

I—I—I CAN'T—
EVERYONE COMES BACK JUST TO LEAVE! GUNN, ANGEL, WESLEY AGAIN! STOP TESTING ME IT'S ANNOYING. I DON'T APPROVE!
I'VE BEEN THERE.
I UNDERSTAND, AND I'M RIGHT THERE WITH YOU.
I KNOW YOU ARE. BUT I DON'T CARE IF YOU'RE HERE. I WANT THE ONES I KNOW. NOW.
NO, I MEAN. YOU MISSED HIM, AND THEN HE COMES BACK... AND NOW HE'S GONE AGAIN.
I UNDERSTAND YOUR REJECTION. YOU ARE INFERIOR.
BUT I AM ILLYRIA.
I AM A PURE DEMON WHO RULED VAHLA HA'NESH AND I DEMAND A CERTAIN AMOUNT OF ORDER.

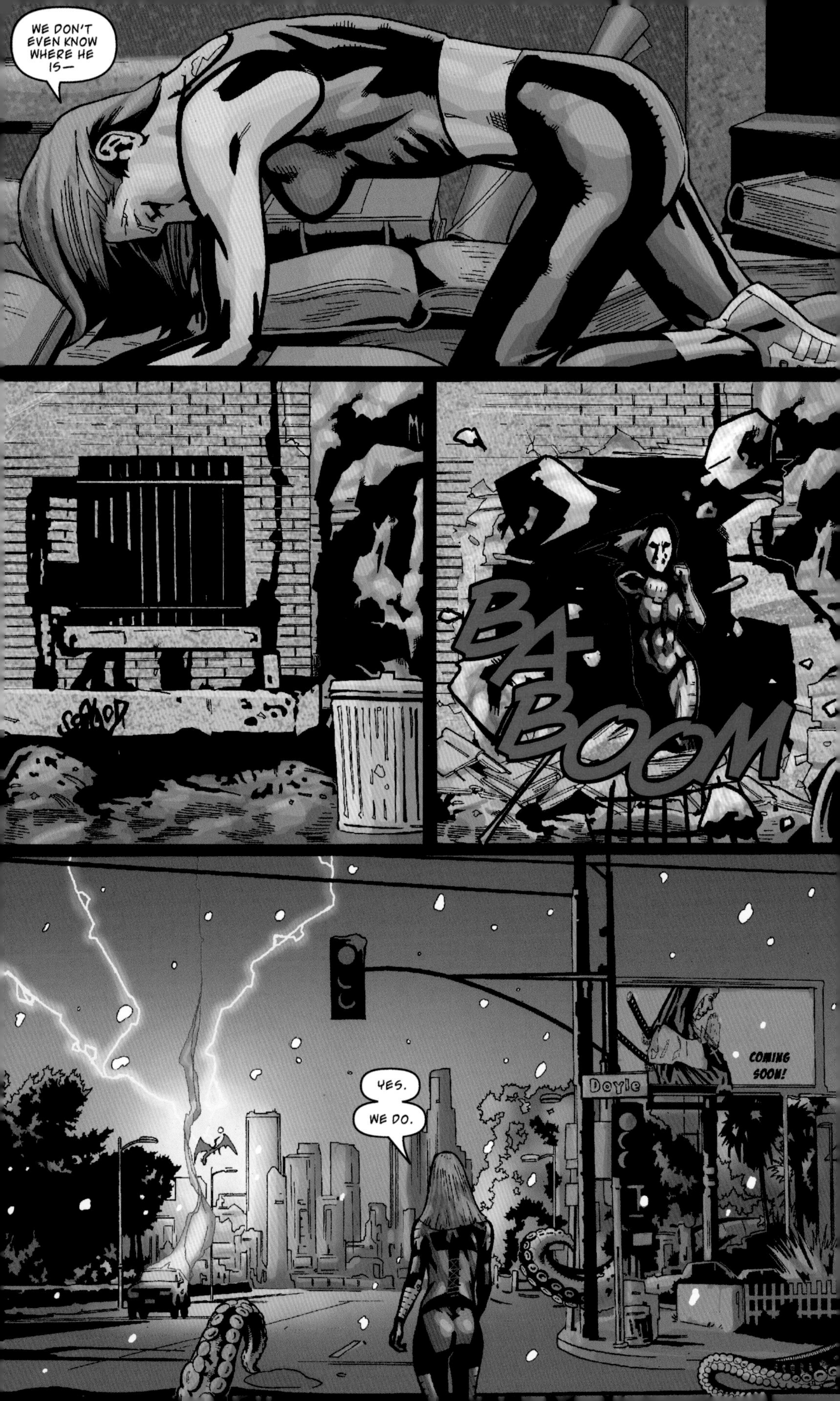
WE DON'T EVEN KNOW WHERE HE IS—
BA-BOOM
COMING SOON!
Doyle
YES.
WE DO.

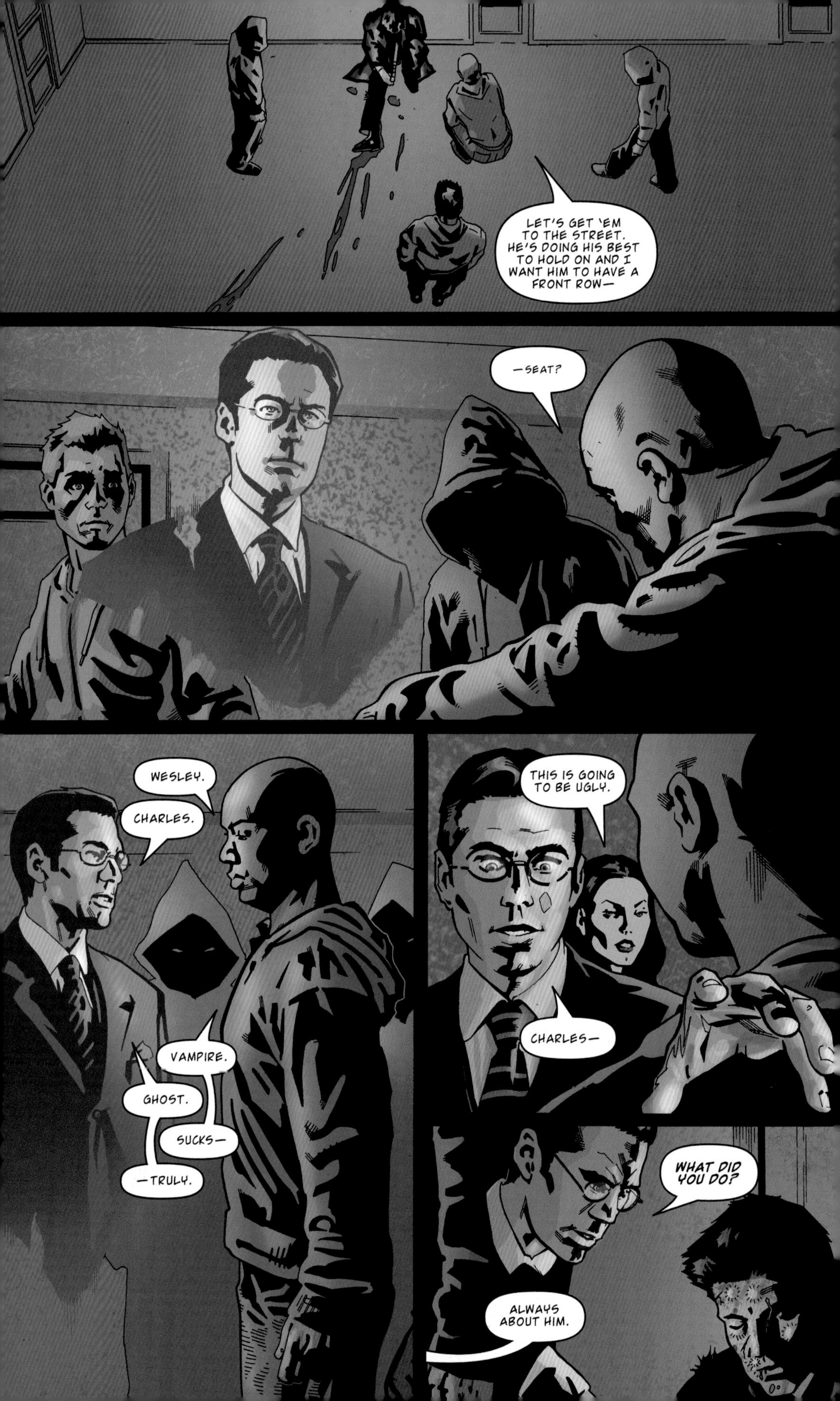
LET'S GET 'EM TO THE STREET. HE'S DOING HIS BEST TO HOLD ON AND I WANT HIM TO HAVE A FRONT ROW—
—SEAT?
WESLEY.
CHARLES.
VAMPIRE.
GHOST.
SUCKS—
—TRULY.
THIS IS GOING TO BE UGLY.
CHARLES—
WHAT DID YOU DO?
ALWAYS ABOUT HIM.

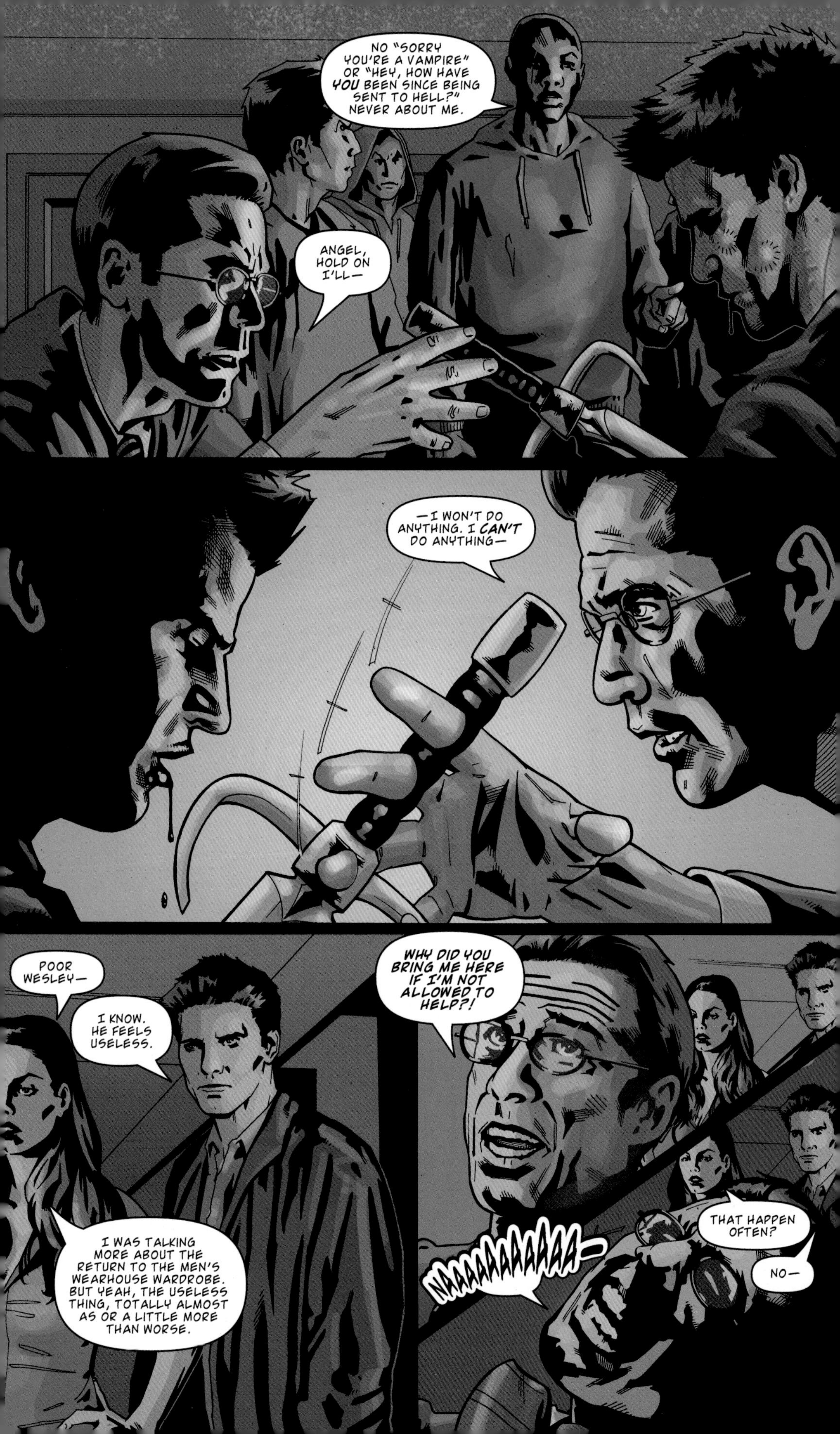
NO "SORRY YOU'RE A VAMPIRE" OR "HEY, HOW HAVE YOU BEEN SINCE BEING SENT TO HELL?" NEVER ABOUT ME.
ANGEL, HOLD ON I'LL—
—I WON'T DO ANYTHING. I CAN'T DO ANYTHING—
POOR WESLEY—
I KNOW. HE FEELS USELESS.
I WAS TALKING MORE ABOUT THE RETURN TO THE MEN'S WEARHOUSE WARDROBE. BUT YEAH, THE USELESS THING, TOTALLY ALMOST AS OR A LITTLE MORE THAN WORSE.
WHY DID YOU BRING ME HERE IF I'M NOT ALLOWED TO HELP?!
NAAAAAAAAAAA—
THAT HAPPEN OFTEN?
NO—

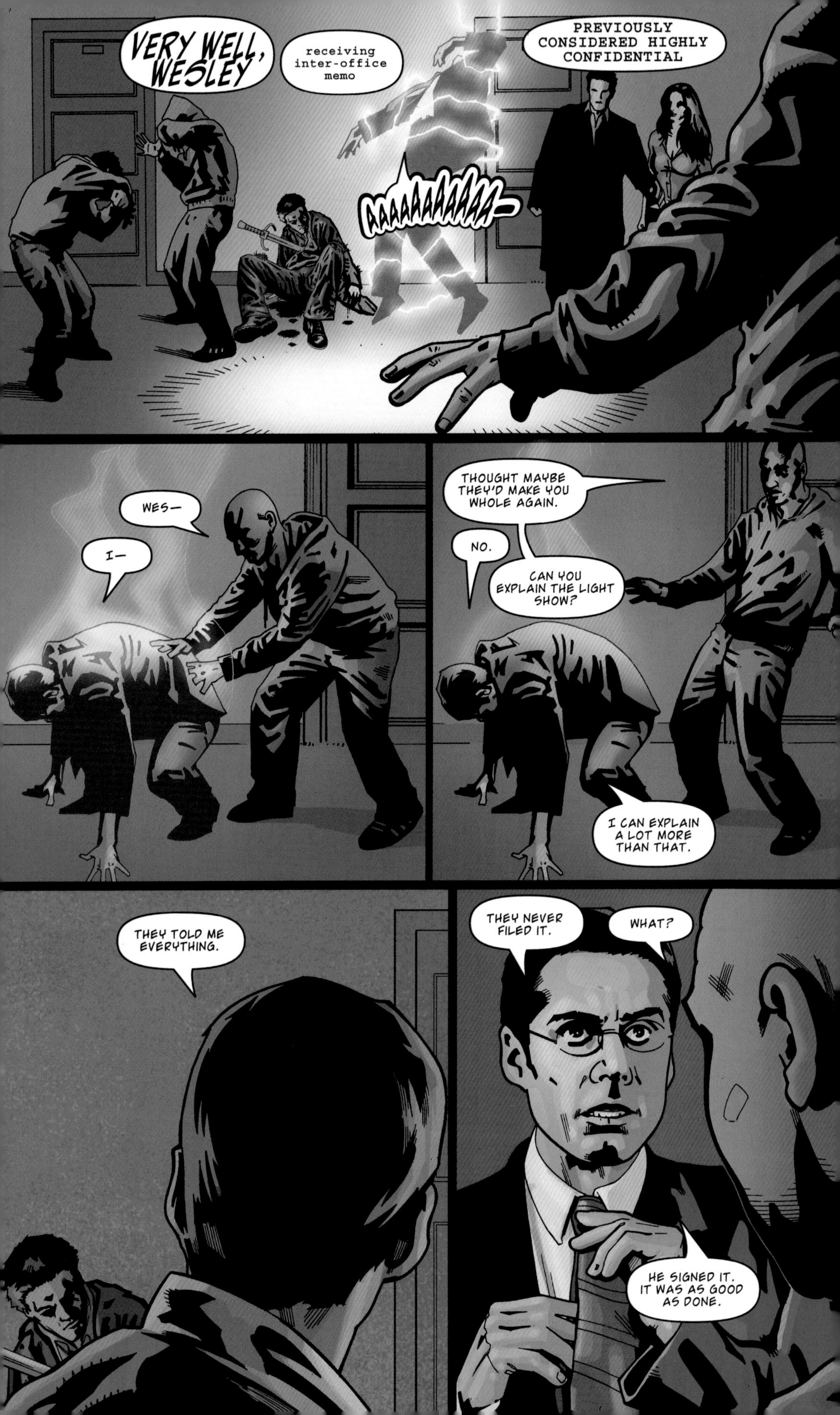
VERY WELL, WESLEY
receiving inter-office memo
PREVIOUSLY CONSIDERED HIGHLY CONFIDENTIAL
AAAAAAAAAAA—
WES—
I—
THOUGHT MAYBE THEY'D MAKE YOU WHOLE AGAIN.
NO.
CAN YOU EXPLAIN THE LIGHT SHOW?
I CAN EXPLAIN A LOT MORE THAN THAT.
THEY TOLD ME EVERYTHING.
THEY NEVER FILED IT.
WHAT?
HE SIGNED IT. IT WAS AS GOOD AS DONE.

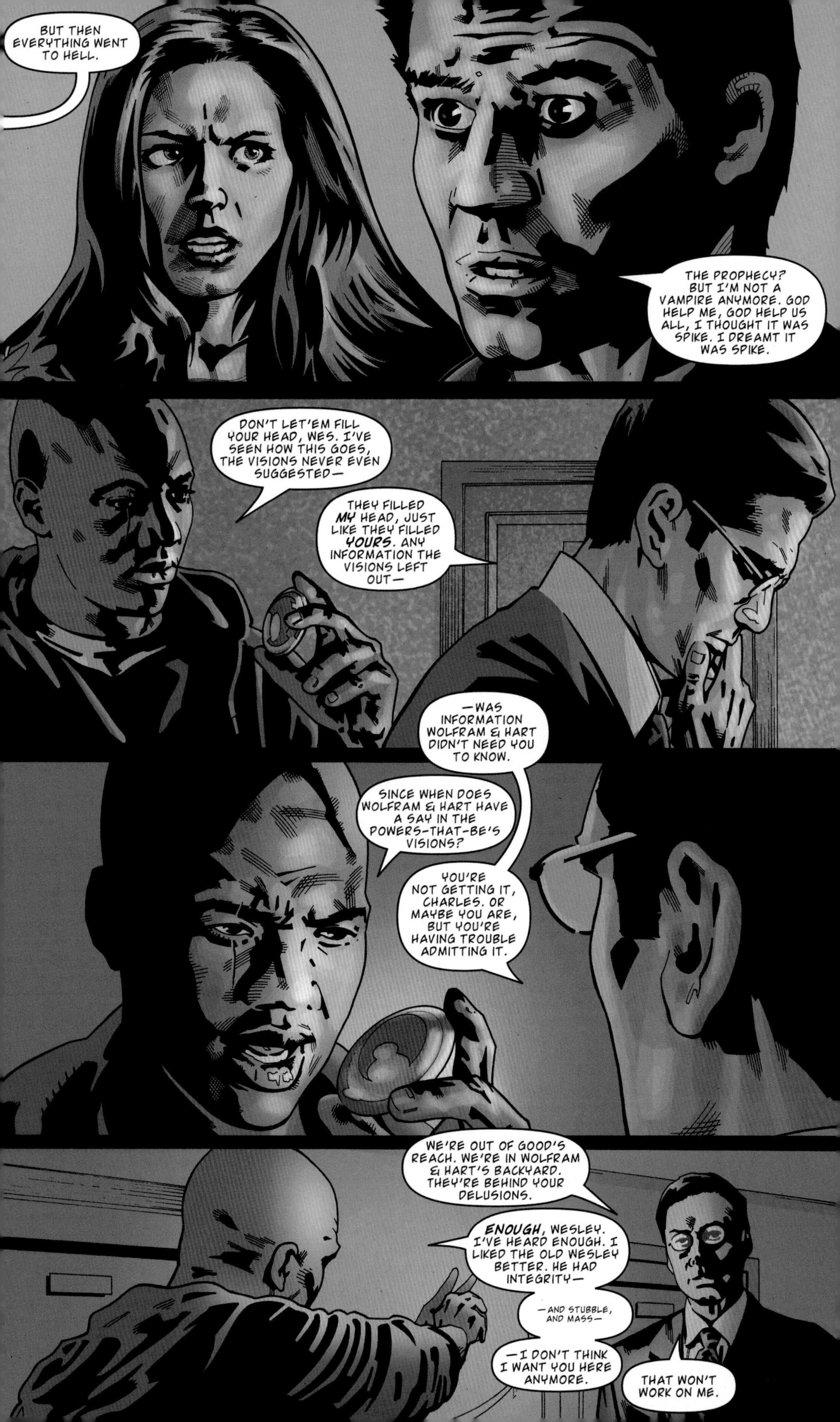
BUT THEN EVERYTHING WENT TO HELL.
THE PROPHECY? BUT I'M NOT A VAMPIRE ANYMORE. GOD HELP ME, GOD HELP US ALL, I THOUGHT IT WAS SPIKE. I DREAMT IT WAS SPIKE.
DON'T LET'EM FILL YOUR HEAD, WES. I'VE SEEN HOW THIS GOES, THE VISIONS NEVER EVEN SUGGESTED—
THEY FILLED ***MY*** HEAD, JUST LIKE THEY FILLED ***YOURS***. ANY INFORMATION THE VISIONS LEFT OUT—
—WAS INFORMATION WOLFRAM & HART DIDN'T NEED YOU TO KNOW.
SINCE WHEN DOES WOLFRAM & HART HAVE A SAY IN THE POWERS-THAT-BE'S VISIONS?
YOU'RE NOT GETTING IT, CHARLES. OR MAYBE YOU ARE, BUT YOU'RE HAVING TROUBLE ADMITTING IT.
WE'RE OUT OF GOOD'S REACH. WE'RE IN WOLFRAM & HART'S BACKYARD. THEY'RE BEHIND YOUR DELUSIONS.
ENOUGH, WESLEY. I'VE HEARD ENOUGH. I LIKED THE OLD WESLEY BETTER. HE HAD INTEGRITY—
—AND STUBBLE, AND MASS—
—I DON'T THINK I WANT YOU HERE ANYMORE.
THAT WON'T WORK ON ME.

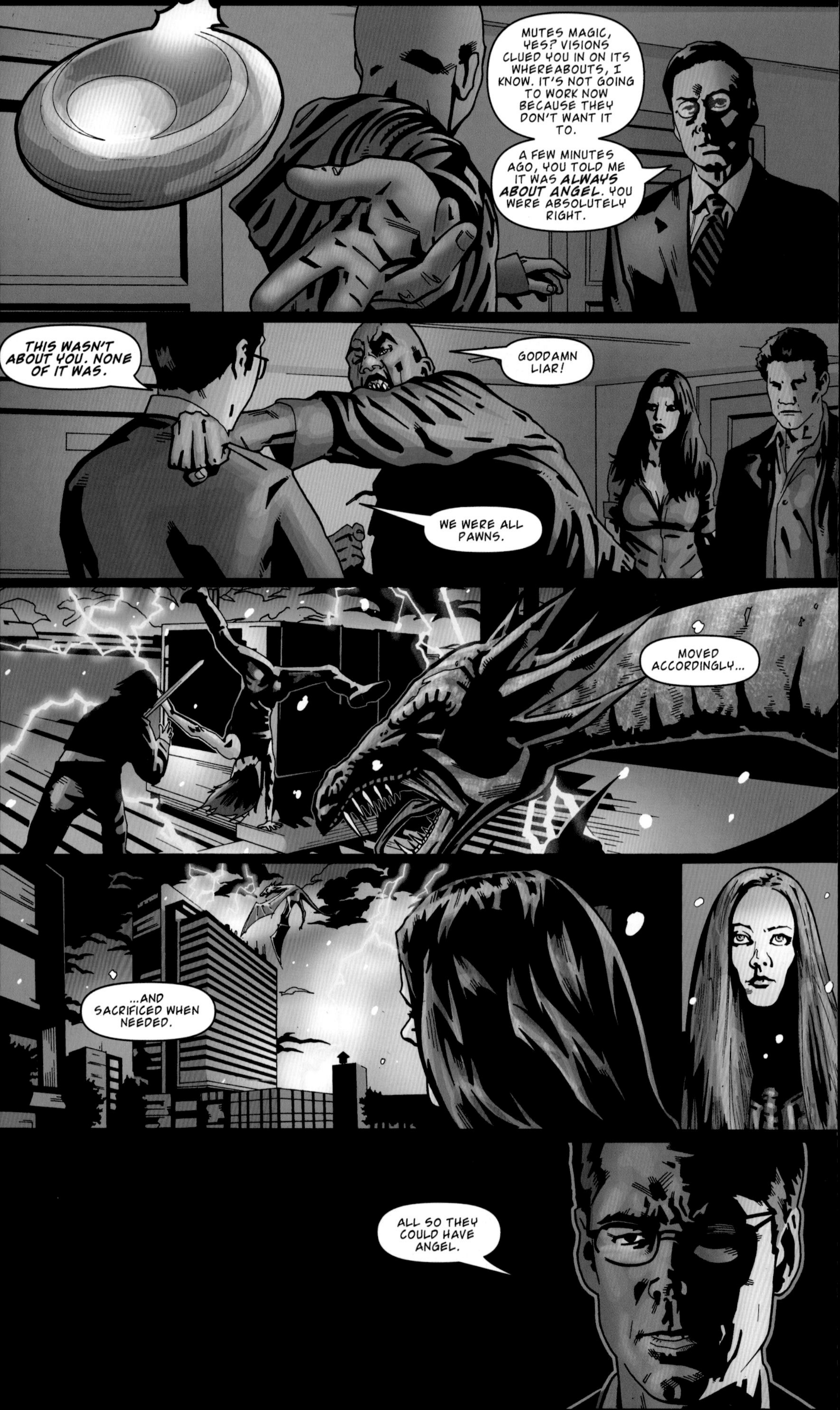
MUTES MAGIC, YES? VISIONS CLUED YOU IN ON ITS WHEREABOUTS, I KNOW. IT'S NOT GOING TO WORK NOW BECAUSE THEY DON'T WANT IT TO.
A FEW MINUTES AGO, YOU TOLD ME IT WAS ALWAYS ABOUT ANGEL. YOU WERE ABSOLUTELY RIGHT.
THIS WASN'T ABOUT YOU. NONE OF IT WAS.
GODDAMN LIAR!
WE WERE ALL PAWNS.
MOVED ACCORDINGLY...
...AND SACRIFICED WHEN NEEDED.
ALL SO THEY COULD HAVE ANGEL.

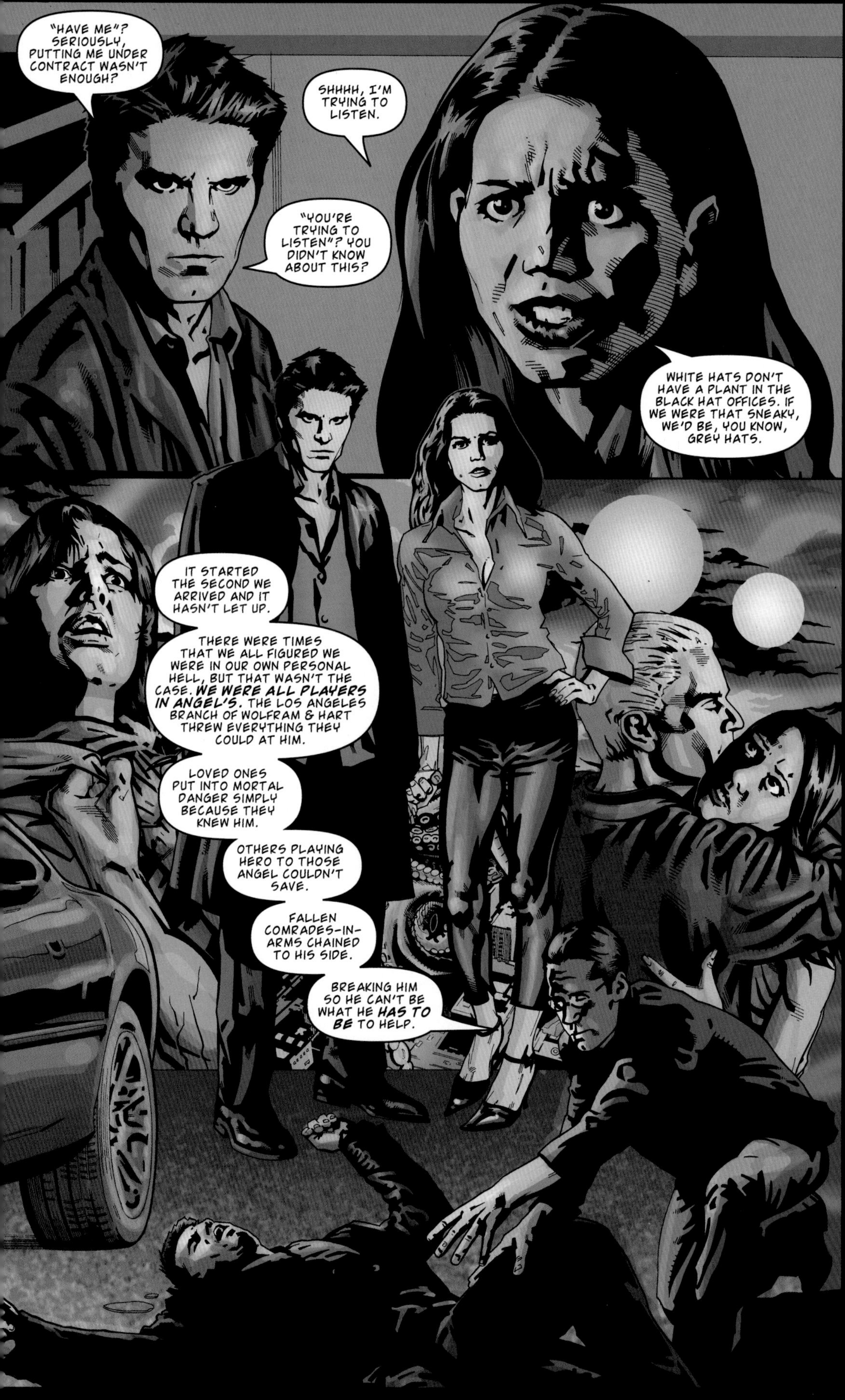
"HAVE ME"? SERIOUSLY, PUTTING ME UNDER CONTRACT WASN'T ENOUGH?
SHHHH, I'M TRYING TO LISTEN.
"YOU'RE TRYING TO LISTEN"? YOU DIDN'T KNOW ABOUT THIS?
WHITE HATS DON'T HAVE A PLANT IN THE BLACK HAT OFFICES. IF WE WERE THAT SNEAKY, WE'D BE, YOU KNOW, GREY HATS.
IT STARTED THE SECOND WE ARRIVED AND IT HASN'T LET UP.
THERE WERE TIMES THAT WE ALL FIGURED WE WERE IN OUR OWN PERSONAL HELL, BUT THAT WASN'T THE CASE. ***WE WERE ALL PLAYERS IN ANGEL'S.*** THE LOS ANGELES BRANCH OF WOLFRAM & HART THREW EVERYTHING THEY COULD AT HIM.
LOVED ONES PUT INTO MORTAL DANGER SIMPLY BECAUSE THEY KNEW HIM.
OTHERS PLAYING HERO TO THOSE ANGEL COULDN'T SAVE.
FALLEN COMRADES-IN-ARMS CHAINED TO HIS SIDE.
BREAKING HIM SO HE CAN'T BE WHAT HE ***HAS TO BE*** TO HELP.

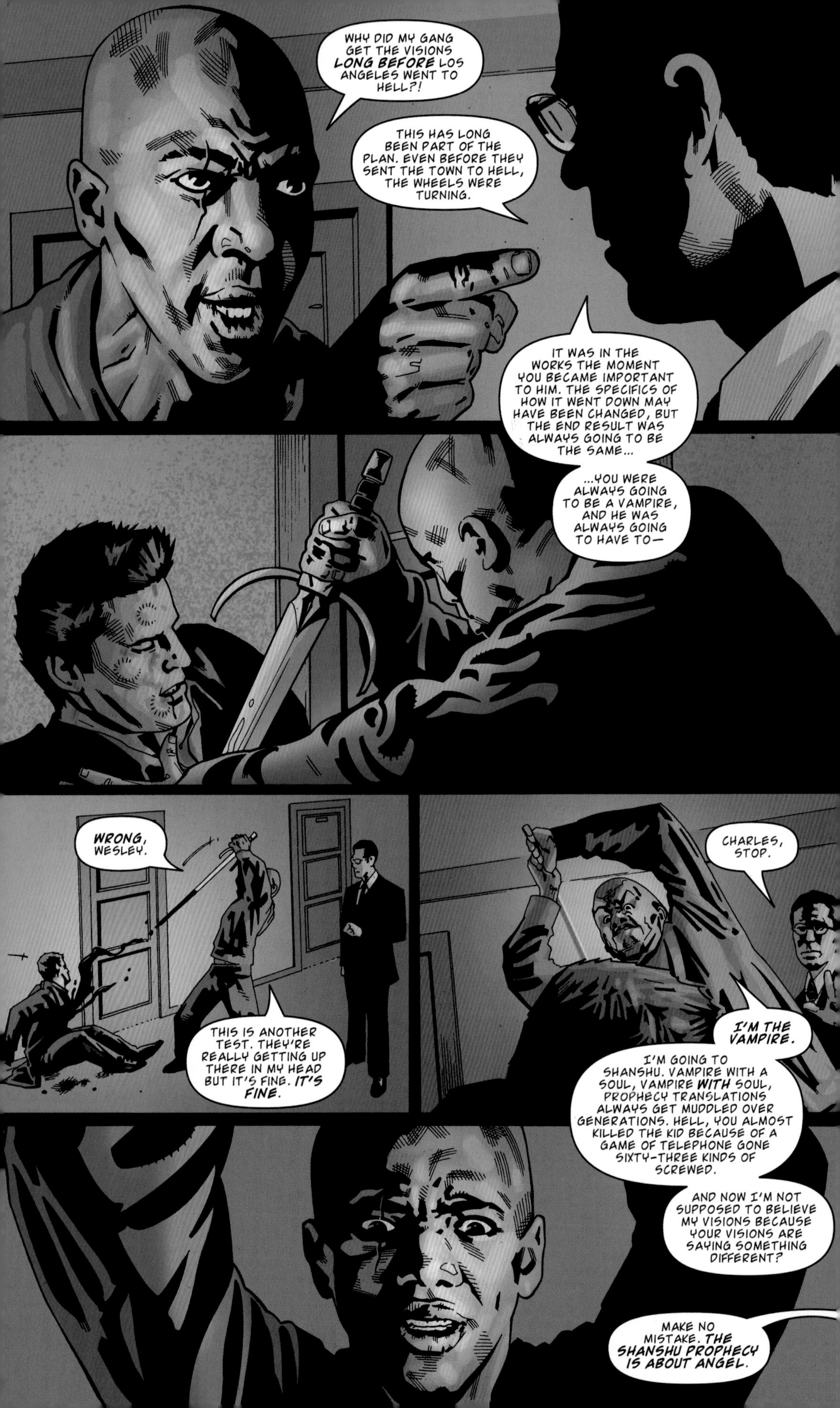
WHY DID MY GANG GET THE VISIONS LONG BEFORE LOS ANGELES WENT TO HELL?!
THIS HAS LONG BEEN PART OF THE PLAN. EVEN BEFORE THEY SENT THE TOWN TO HELL, THE WHEELS WERE TURNING.
IT WAS IN THE WORKS THE MOMENT YOU BECAME IMPORTANT TO HIM. THE SPECIFICS OF HOW IT WENT DOWN MAY HAVE BEEN CHANGED, BUT THE END RESULT WAS ALWAYS GOING TO BE THE SAME...
...YOU WERE ALWAYS GOING TO BE A VAMPIRE, AND HE WAS ALWAYS GOING TO HAVE TO—
WRONG, WESLEY.
THIS IS ANOTHER TEST. THEY'RE REALLY GETTING UP THERE IN MY HEAD BUT IT'S FINE. IT'S FINE.
CHARLES, STOP.
I'M THE VAMPIRE.
I'M GOING TO SHANSHU. VAMPIRE WITH A SOUL, VAMPIRE WITH SOUL, PROPHECY TRANSLATIONS ALWAYS GET MUDDLED OVER GENERATIONS. HELL, YOU ALMOST KILLED THE KID BECAUSE OF A GAME OF TELEPHONE GONE SIXTY-THREE KINDS OF SCREWED.
AND NOW I'M NOT SUPPOSED TO BELIEVE MY VISIONS BECAUSE YOUR VISIONS ARE SAYING SOMETHING DIFFERENT?
MAKE NO MISTAKE. THE SHANSHU PROPHECY IS ABOUT ANGEL.

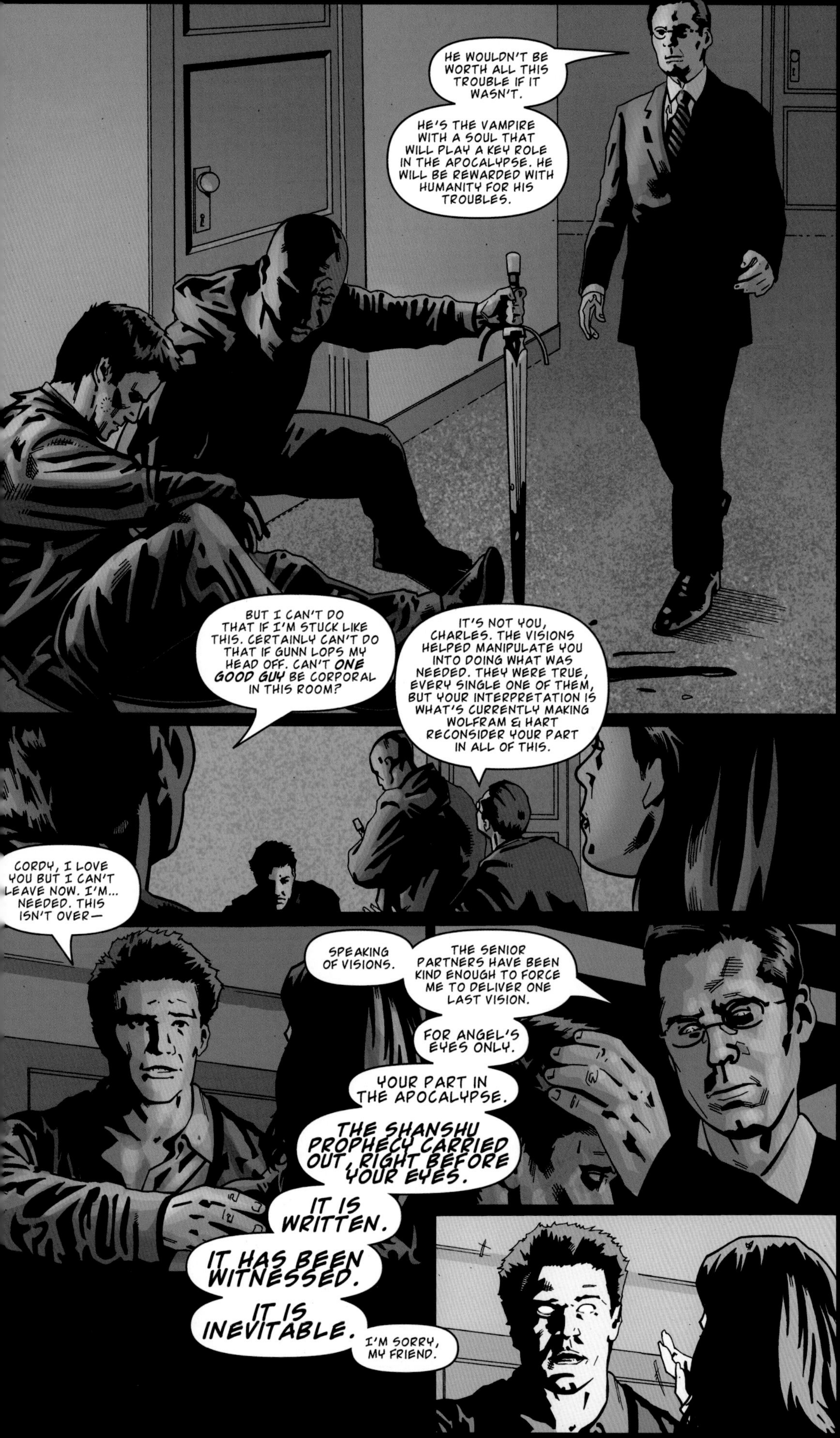
HE WOULDN'T BE WORTH ALL THIS TROUBLE IF IT WASN'T.
HE'S THE VAMPIRE WITH A SOUL THAT WILL PLAY A KEY ROLE IN THE APOCALYPSE. HE WILL BE REWARDED WITH HUMANITY FOR HIS TROUBLES.
BUT I CAN'T DO THAT IF I'M STUCK LIKE THIS. CERTAINLY CAN'T DO THAT IF GUNN LOPS MY HEAD OFF. CAN'T **ONE GOOD GUY** BE CORPORAL IN THIS ROOM?
IT'S NOT YOU, CHARLES. THE VISIONS HELPED MANIPULATE YOU INTO DOING WHAT WAS NEEDED. THEY WERE TRUE, EVERY SINGLE ONE OF THEM, BUT YOUR INTERPRETATION IS WHAT'S CURRENTLY MAKING WOLFRAM & HART RECONSIDER YOUR PART IN ALL OF THIS.
CORDY, I LOVE YOU BUT I CAN'T LEAVE NOW. I'M... NEEDED. THIS ISN'T OVER—
SPEAKING OF VISIONS.
THE SENIOR PARTNERS HAVE BEEN KIND ENOUGH TO FORCE ME TO DELIVER ONE LAST VISION.
FOR ANGEL'S EYES ONLY.
YOUR PART IN THE APOCALYPSE.
THE SHANSHU PROPHECY CARRIED OUT, RIGHT BEFORE YOUR EYES.
IT IS WRITTEN.
IT HAS BEEN WITNESSED.
IT IS INEVITABLE.
I'M SORRY, MY FRIEND.

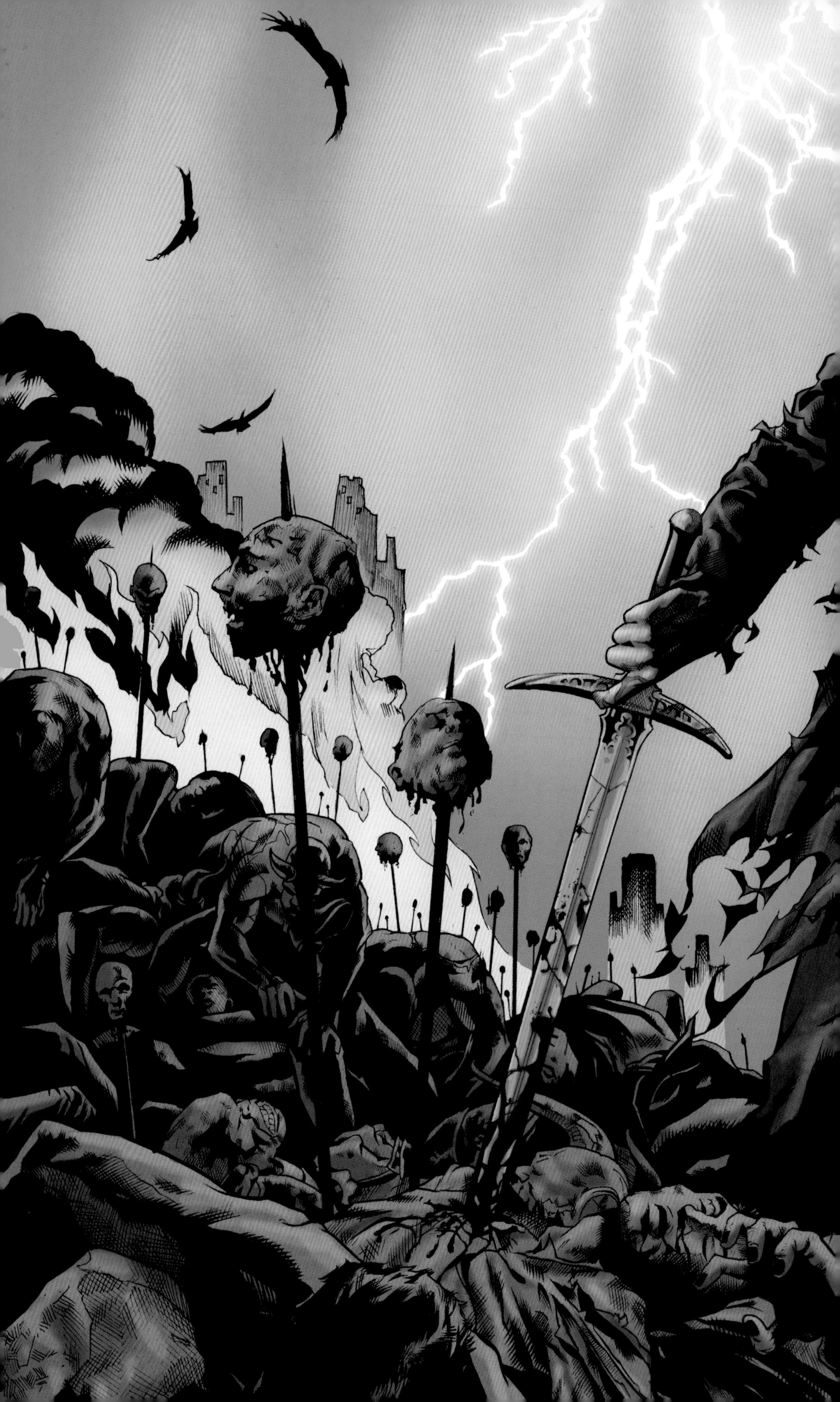

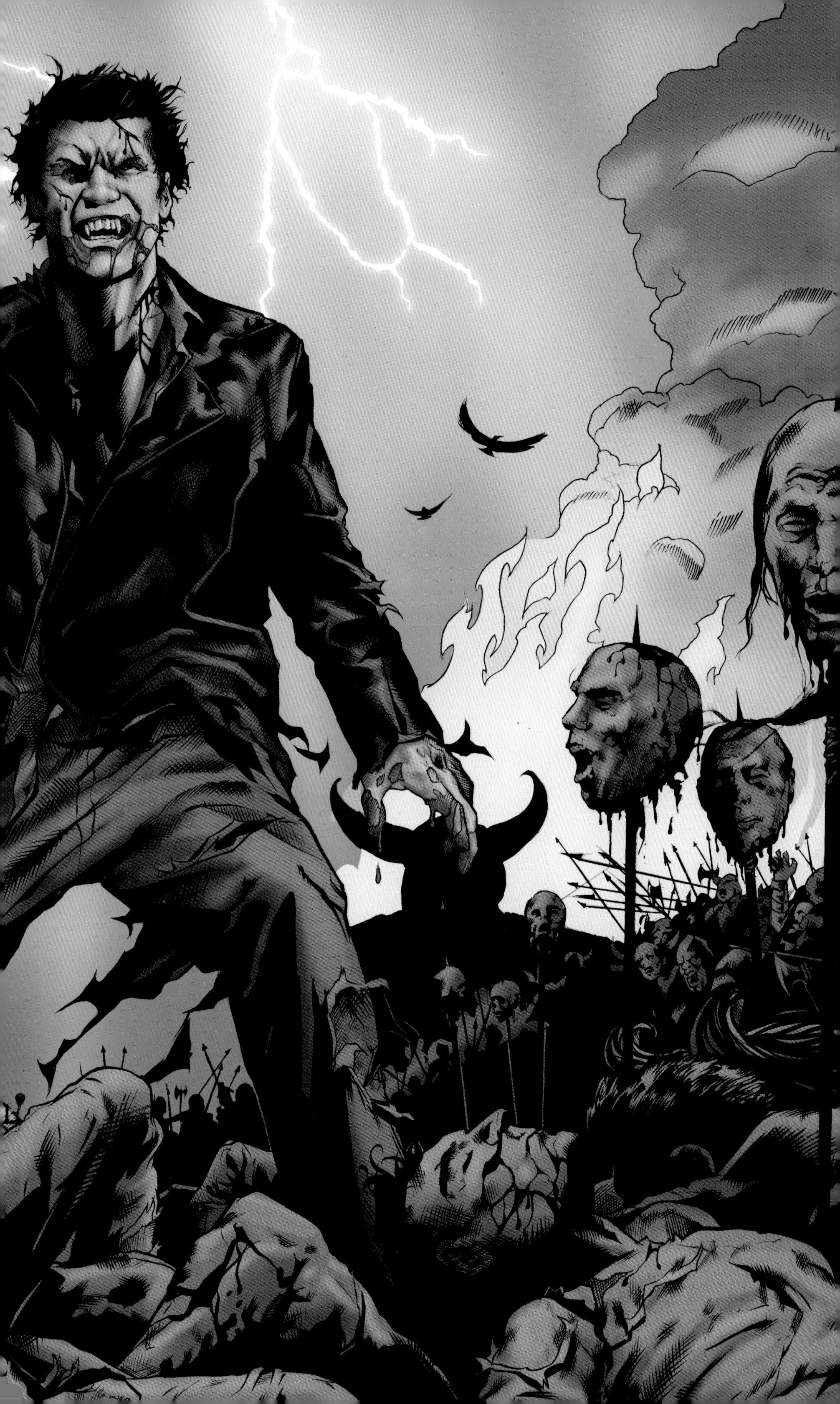

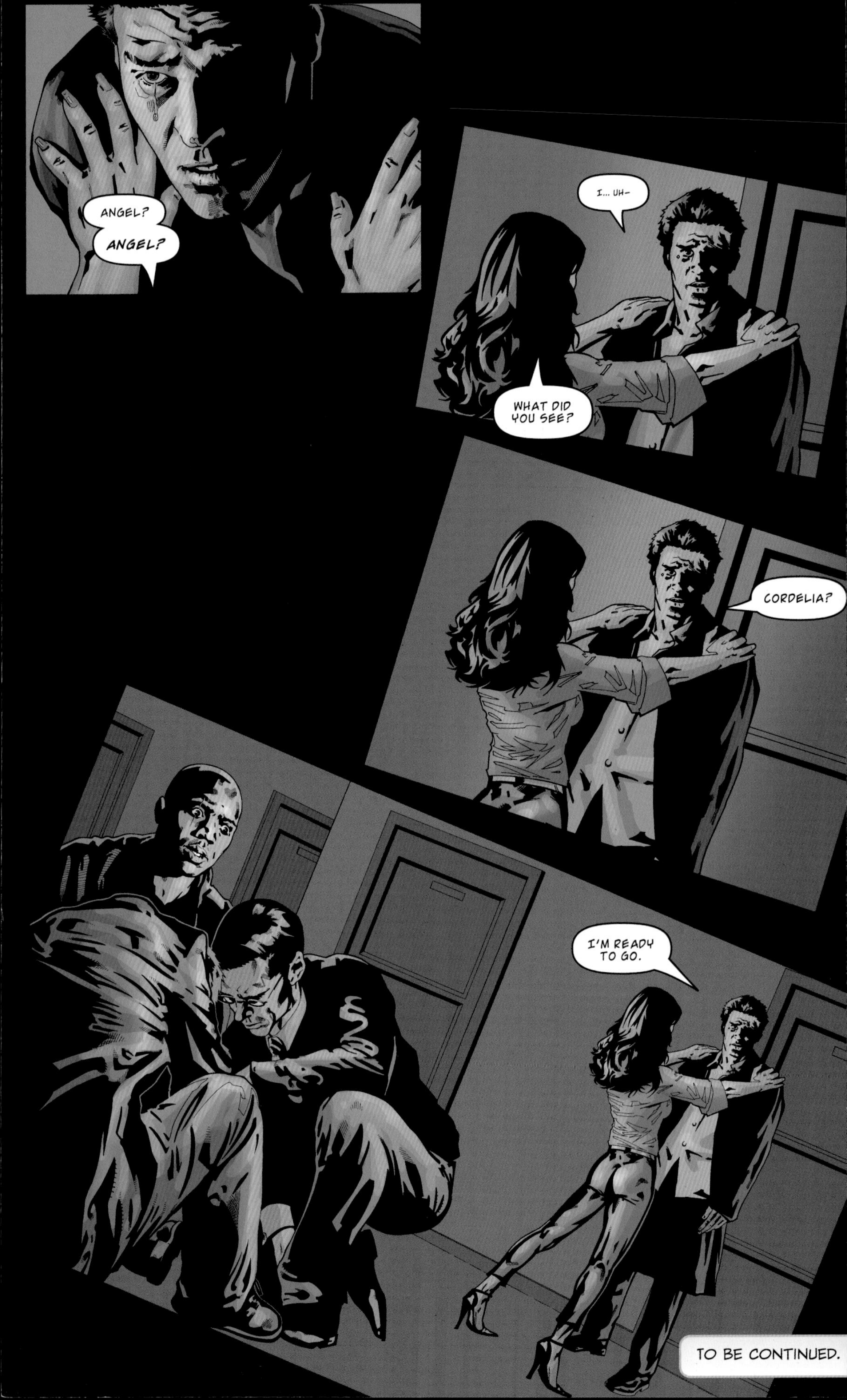
ANGEL?
ANGEL?
I... UH-
WHAT DID YOU SEE?
CORDELIA?
I'M READY TO GO.
TO BE CONTINUED.

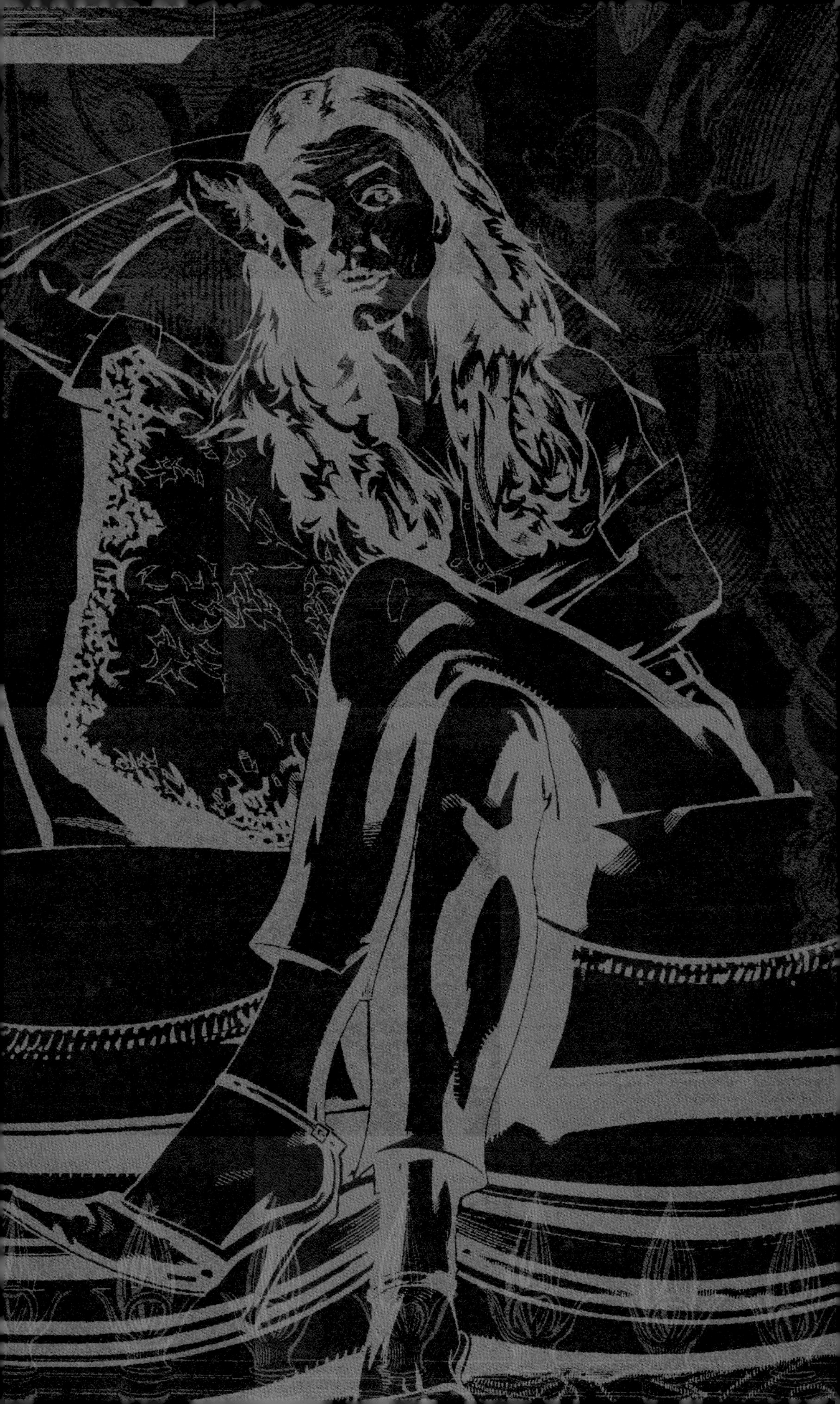

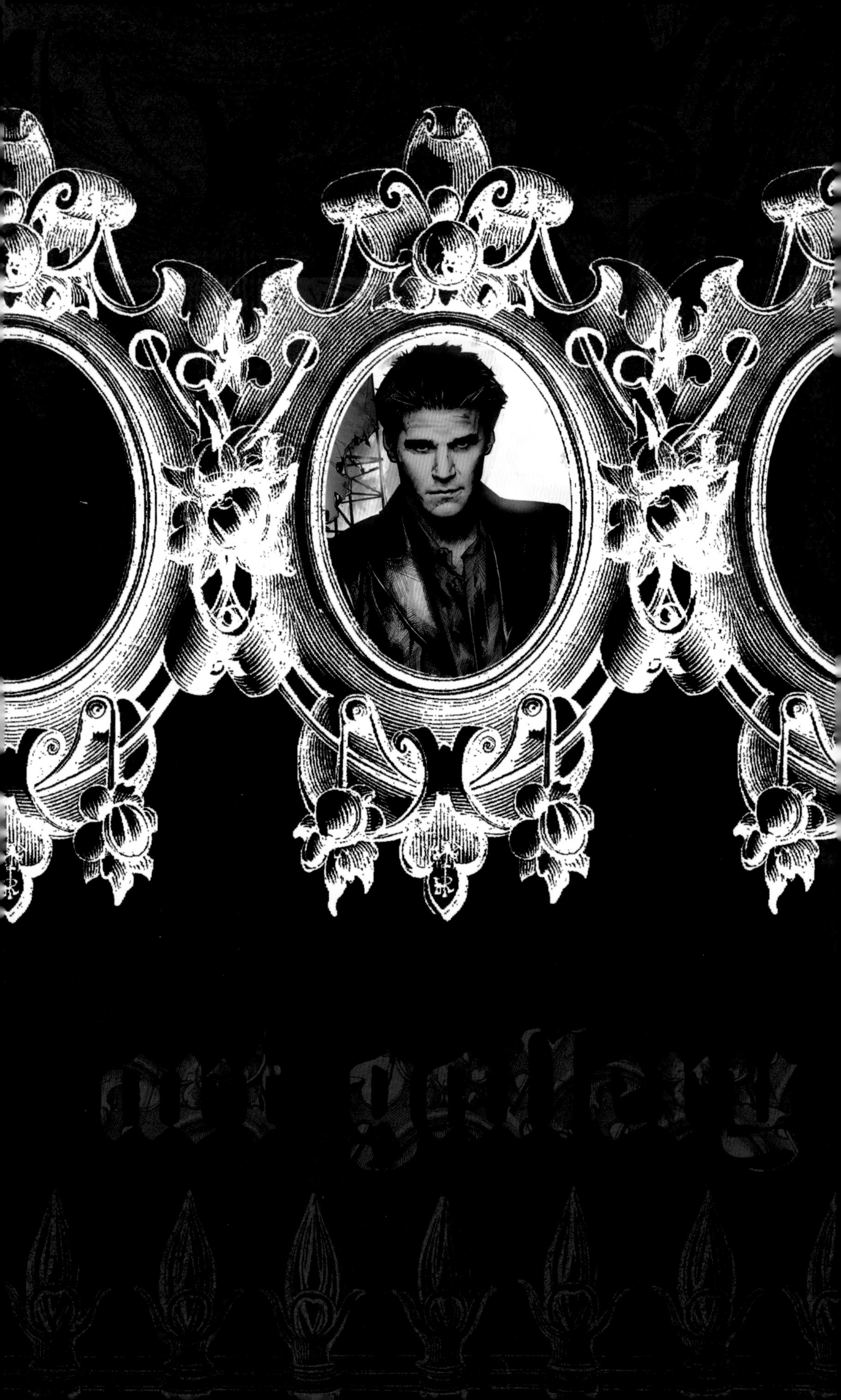

art gallery

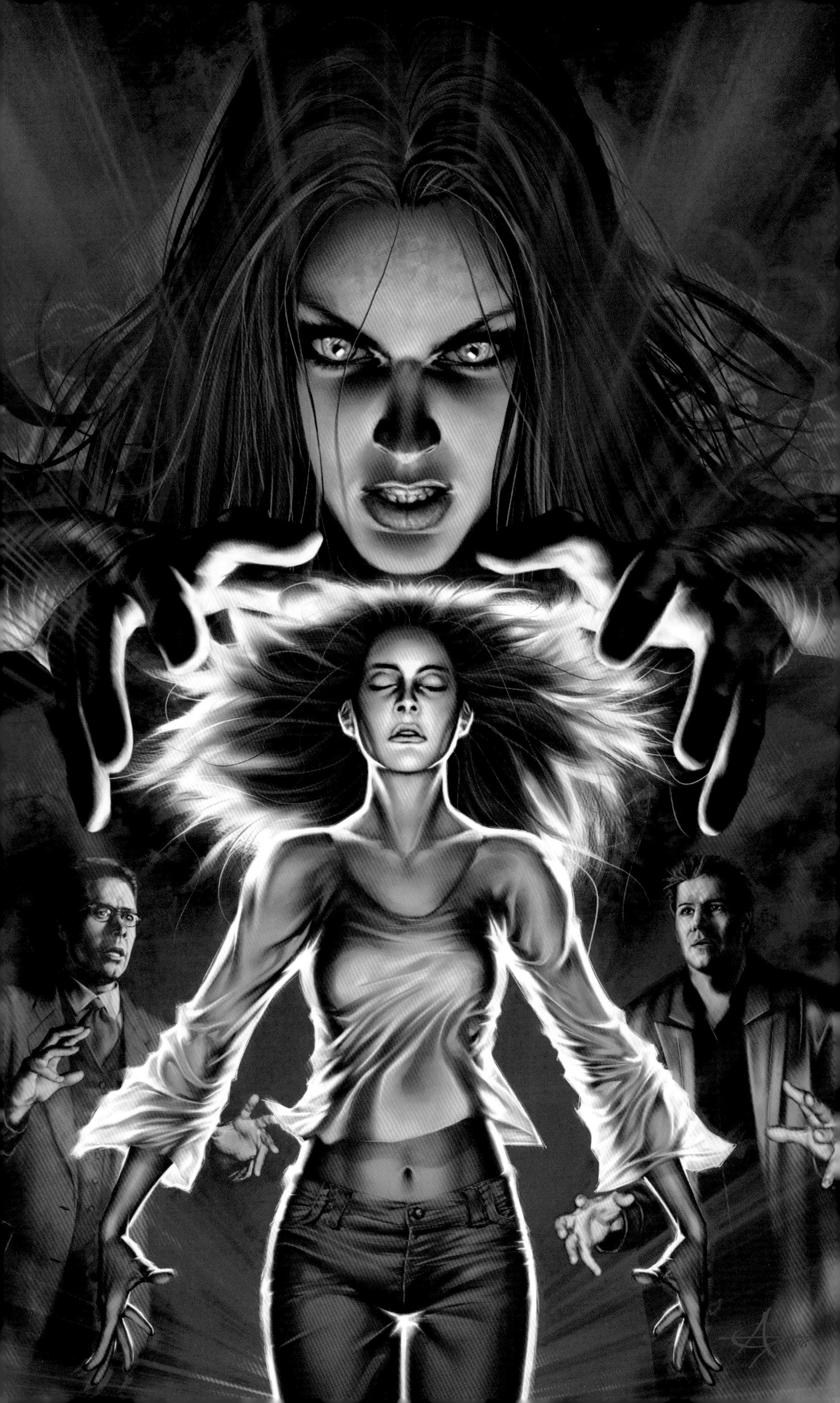

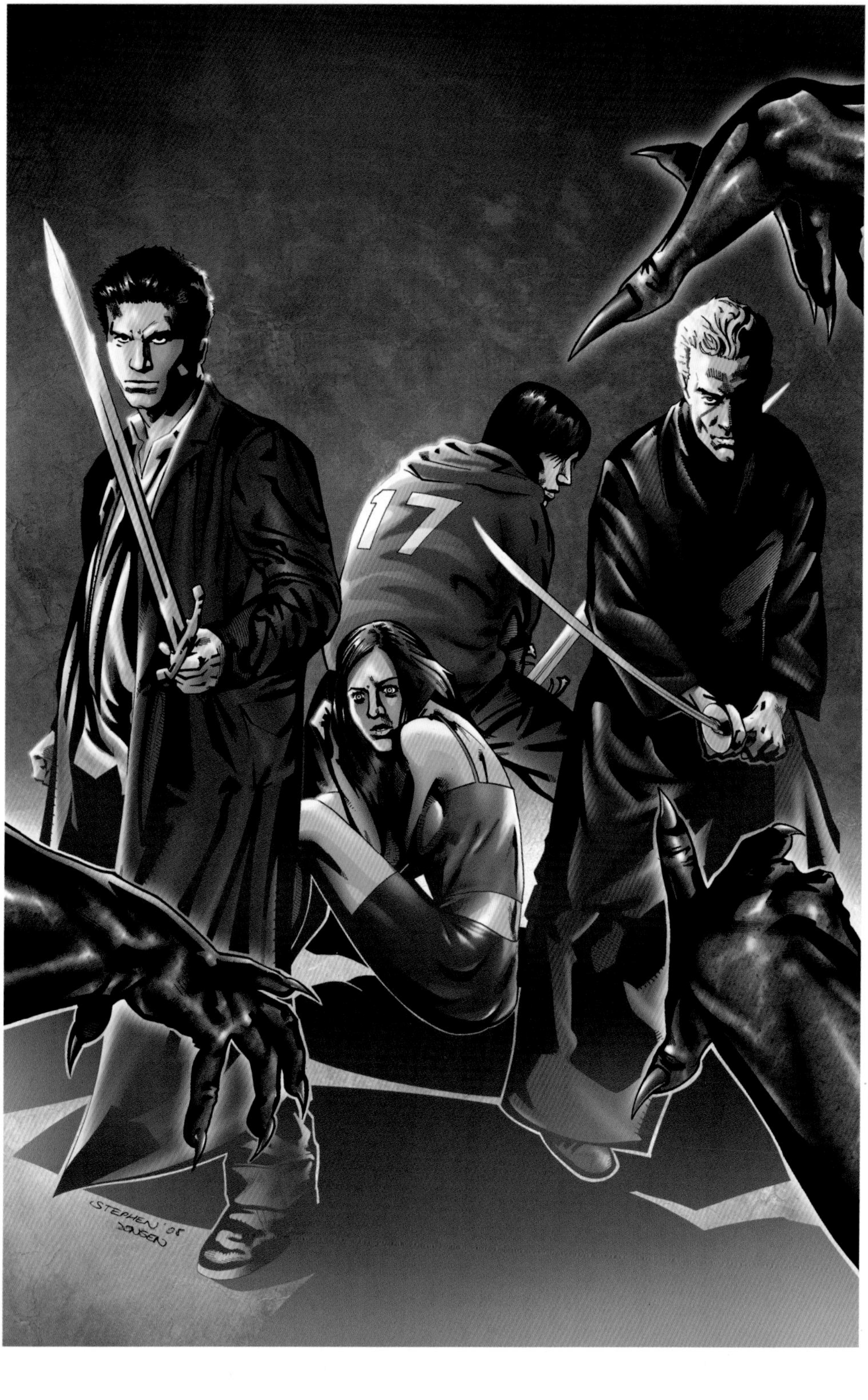
17
STEPHEN '05
JENSEN

Previous Page: Art by Alex Garner

This Page: Art by Stephen Mooney
Colors by Jason Jensen

Opposite Page: Art by Nick Runge

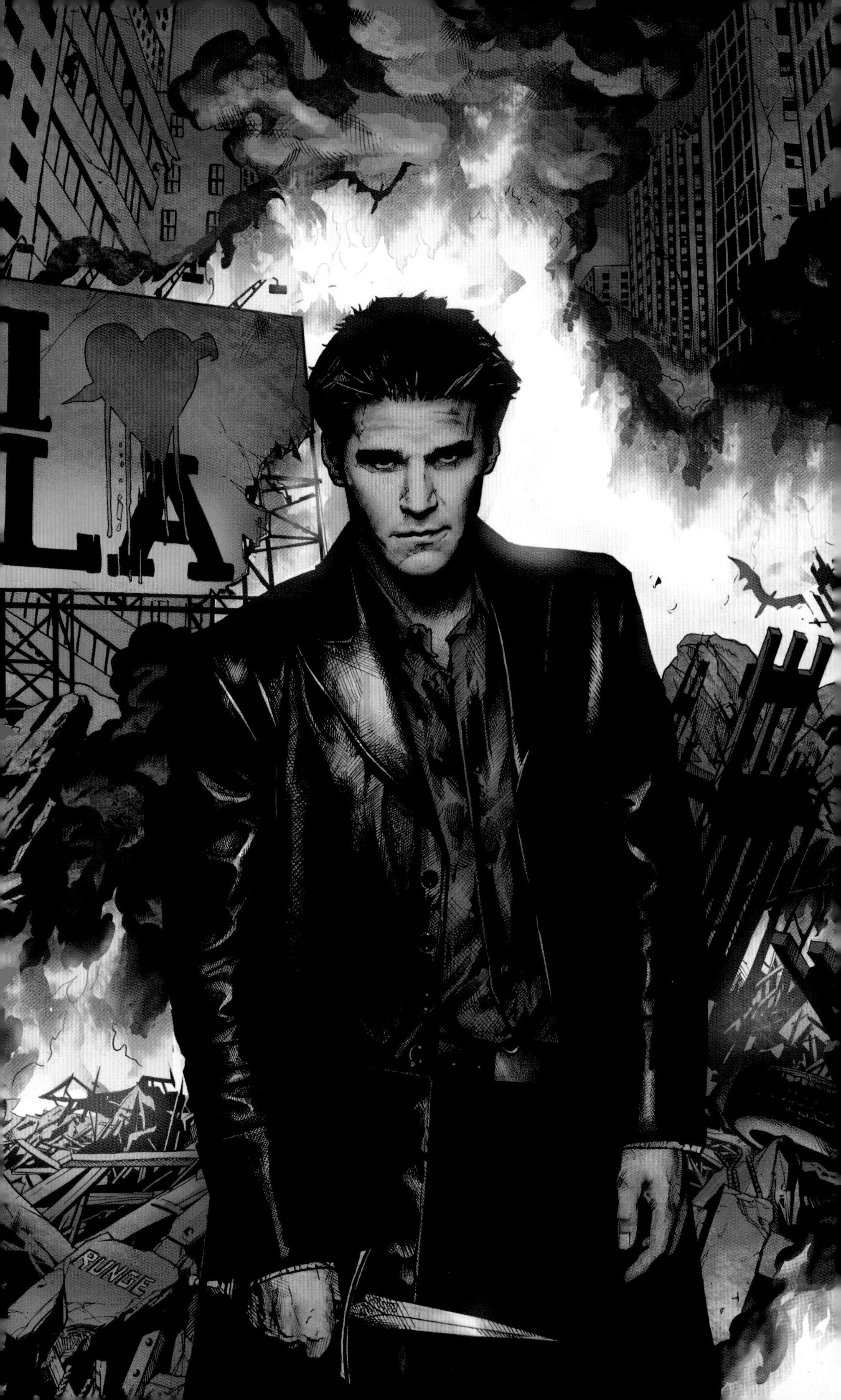
I
L.A
RUNGE

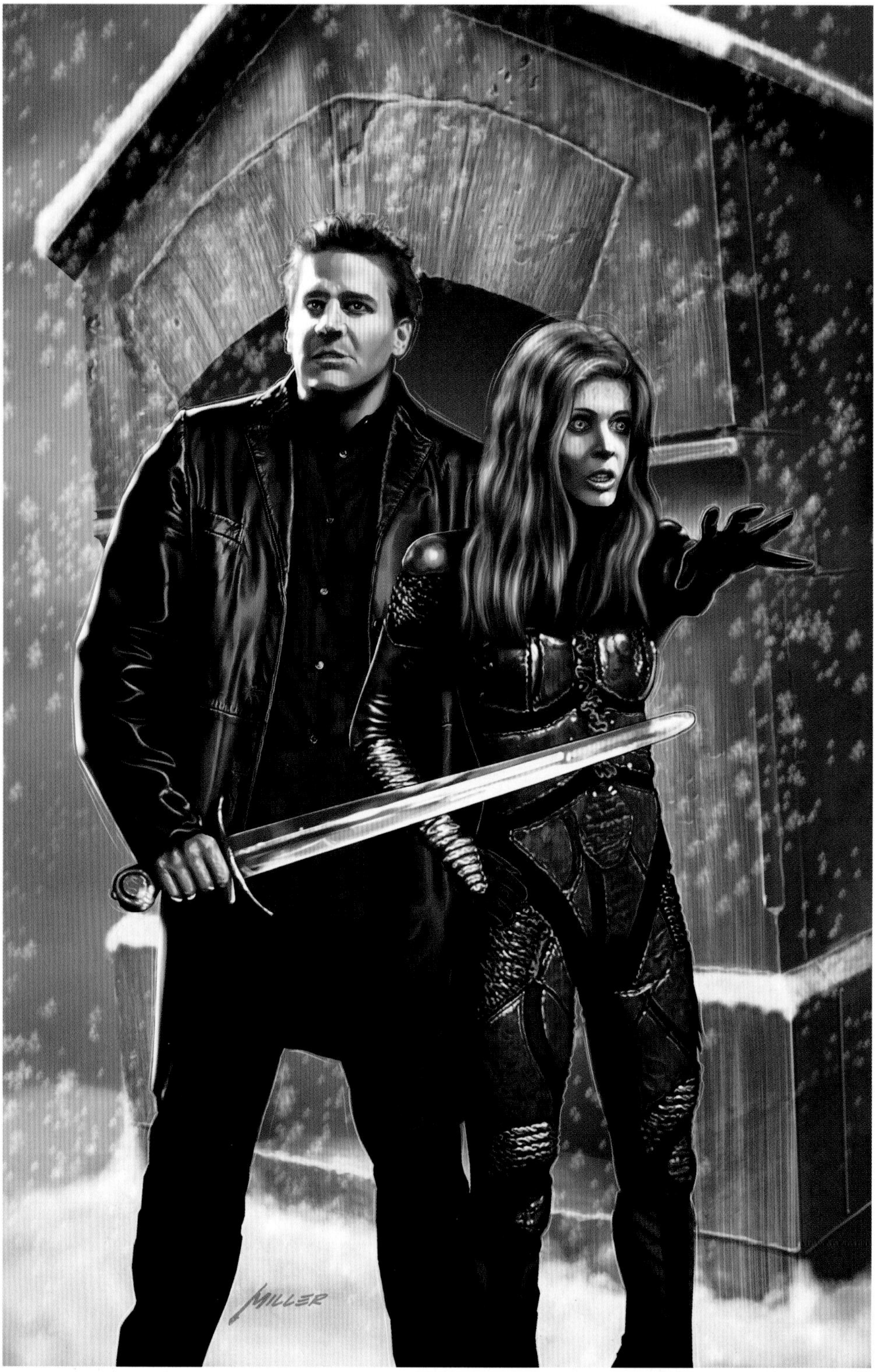
MILLER

This Page: Art by Brian Miller

Opposite Page: Art by Alex Garner

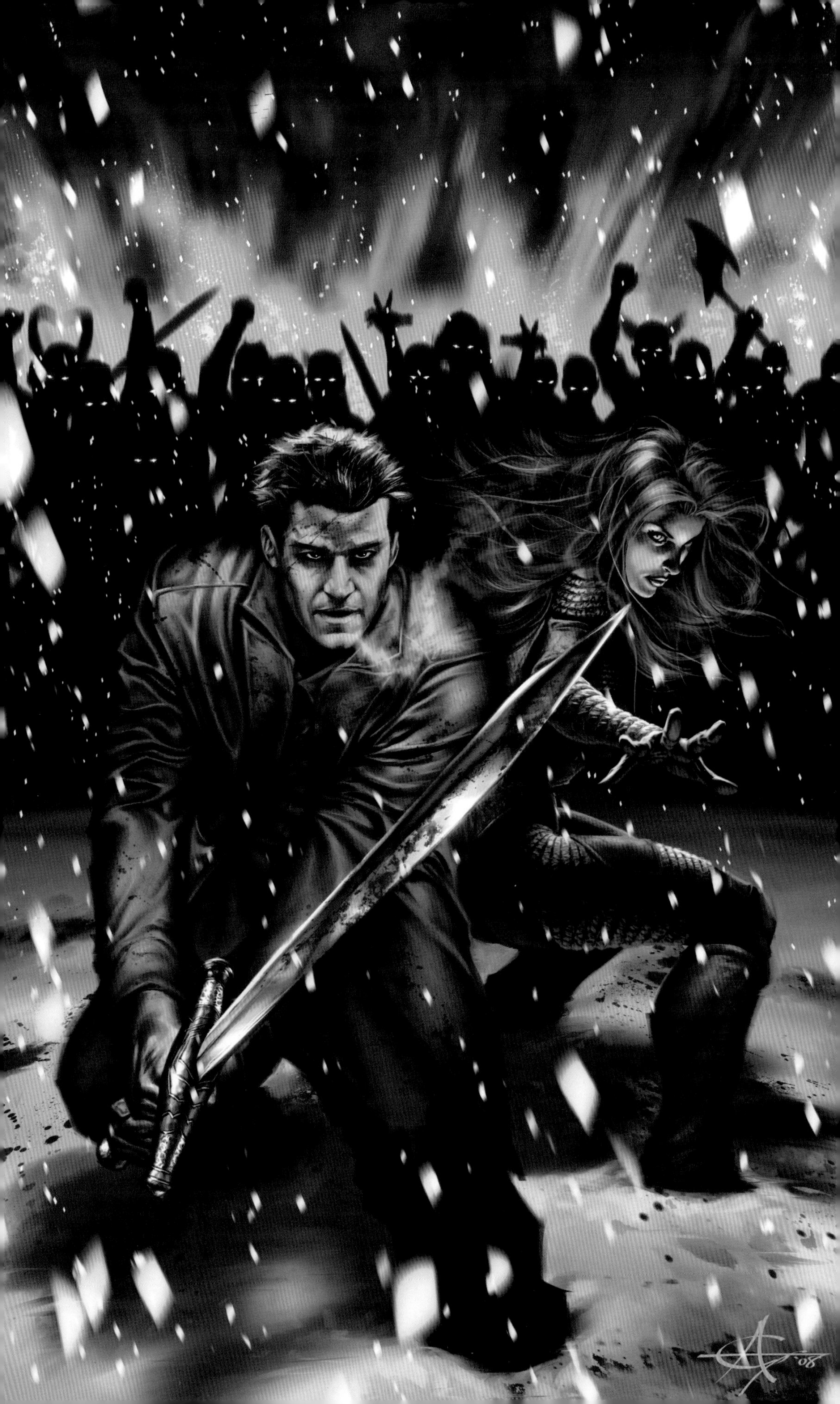

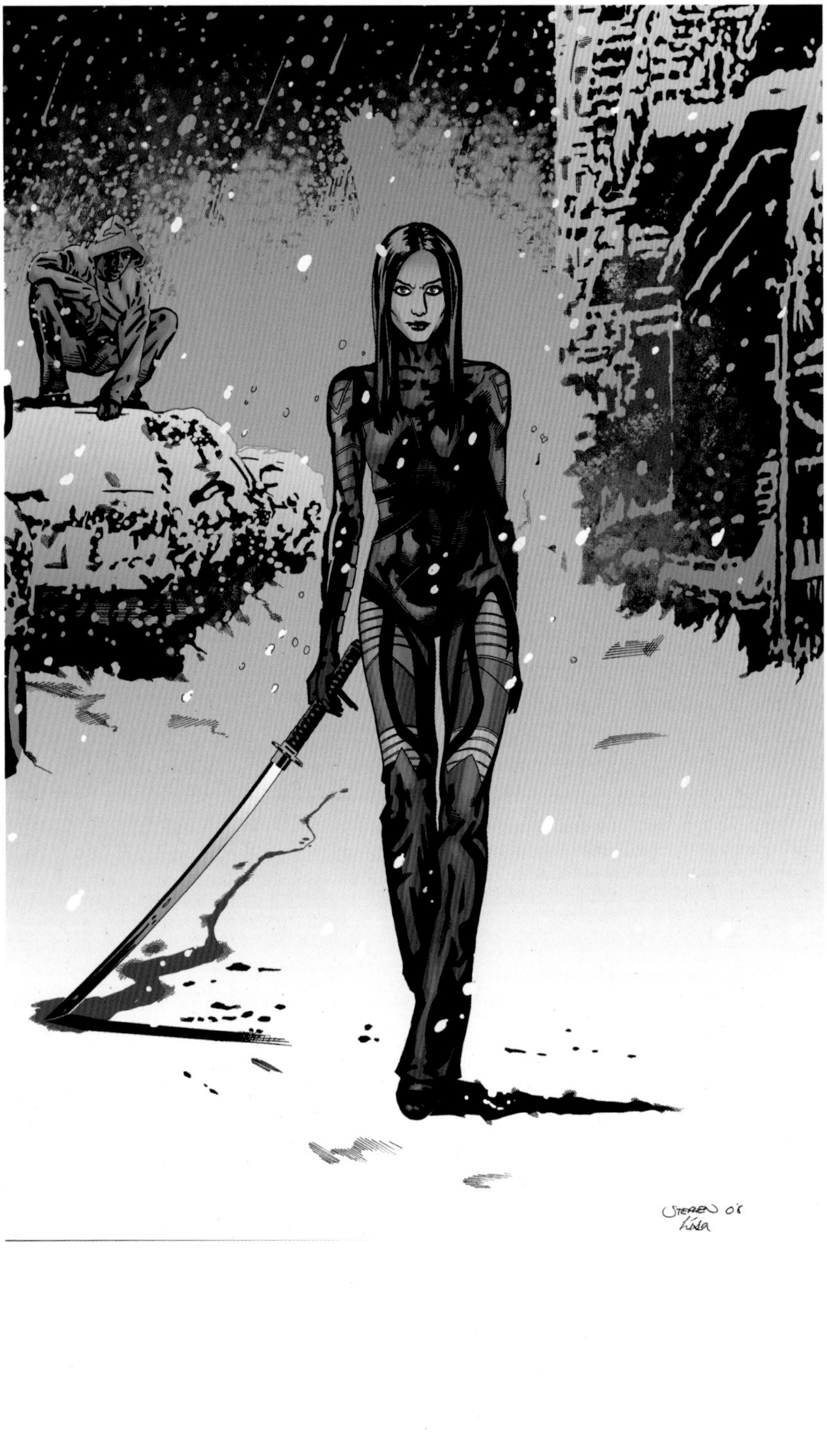

This Page: Art by Stephen Mooney
Colors by Lisa Jackson

Opposite Page: Art by Alex Garner

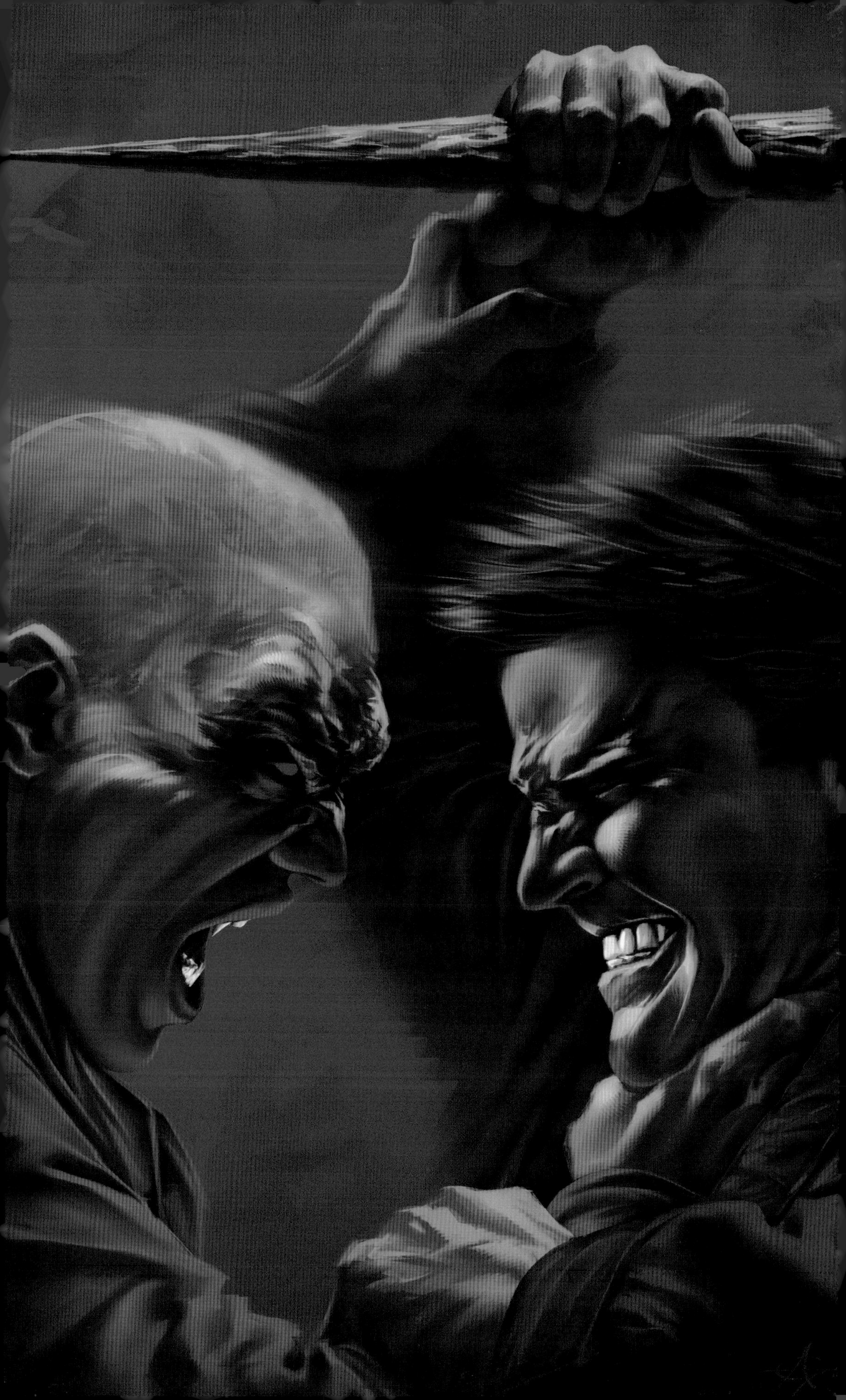

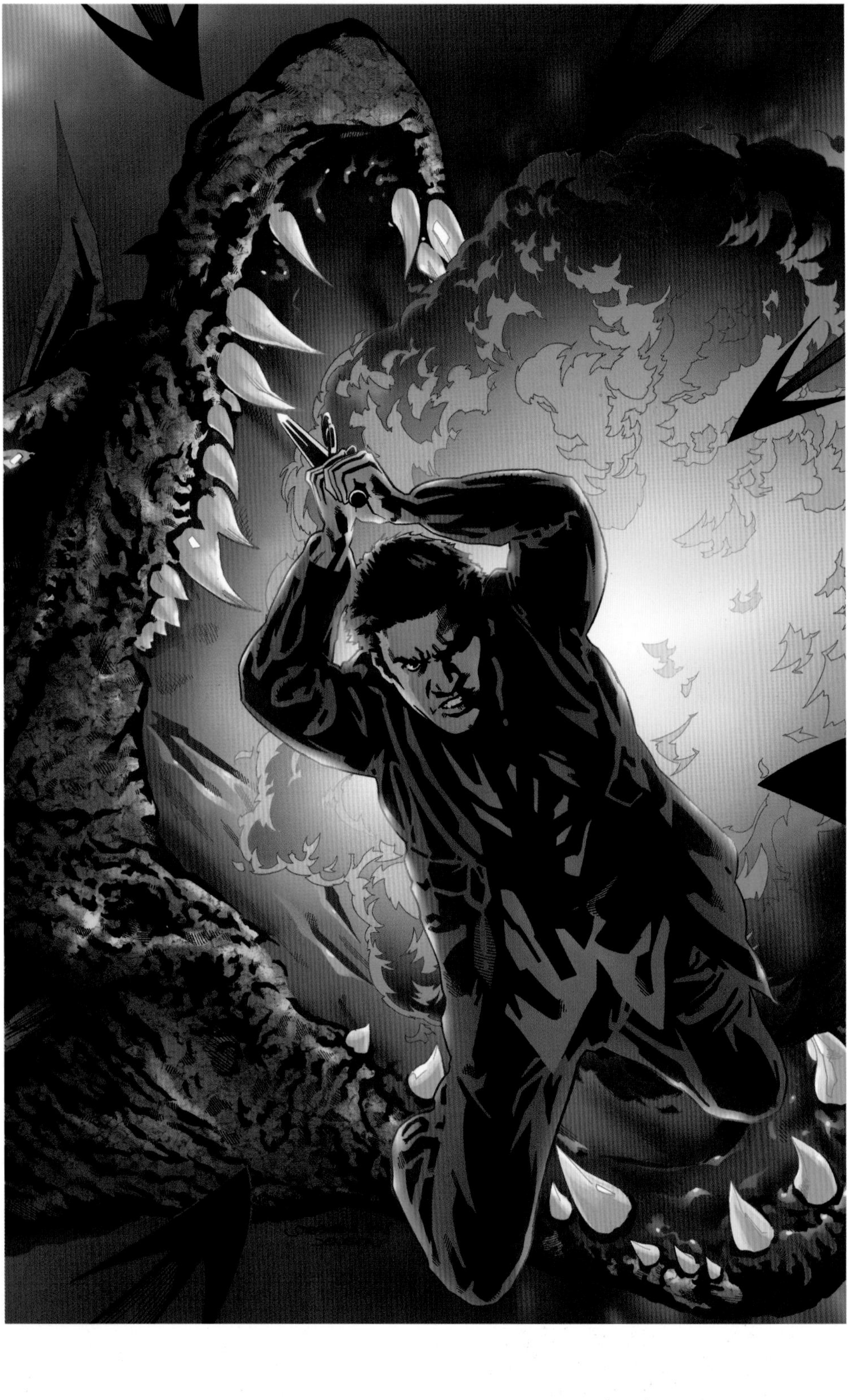

This and Opposite Page: Art by Stephen Mooney
Colors by Jason Jensen

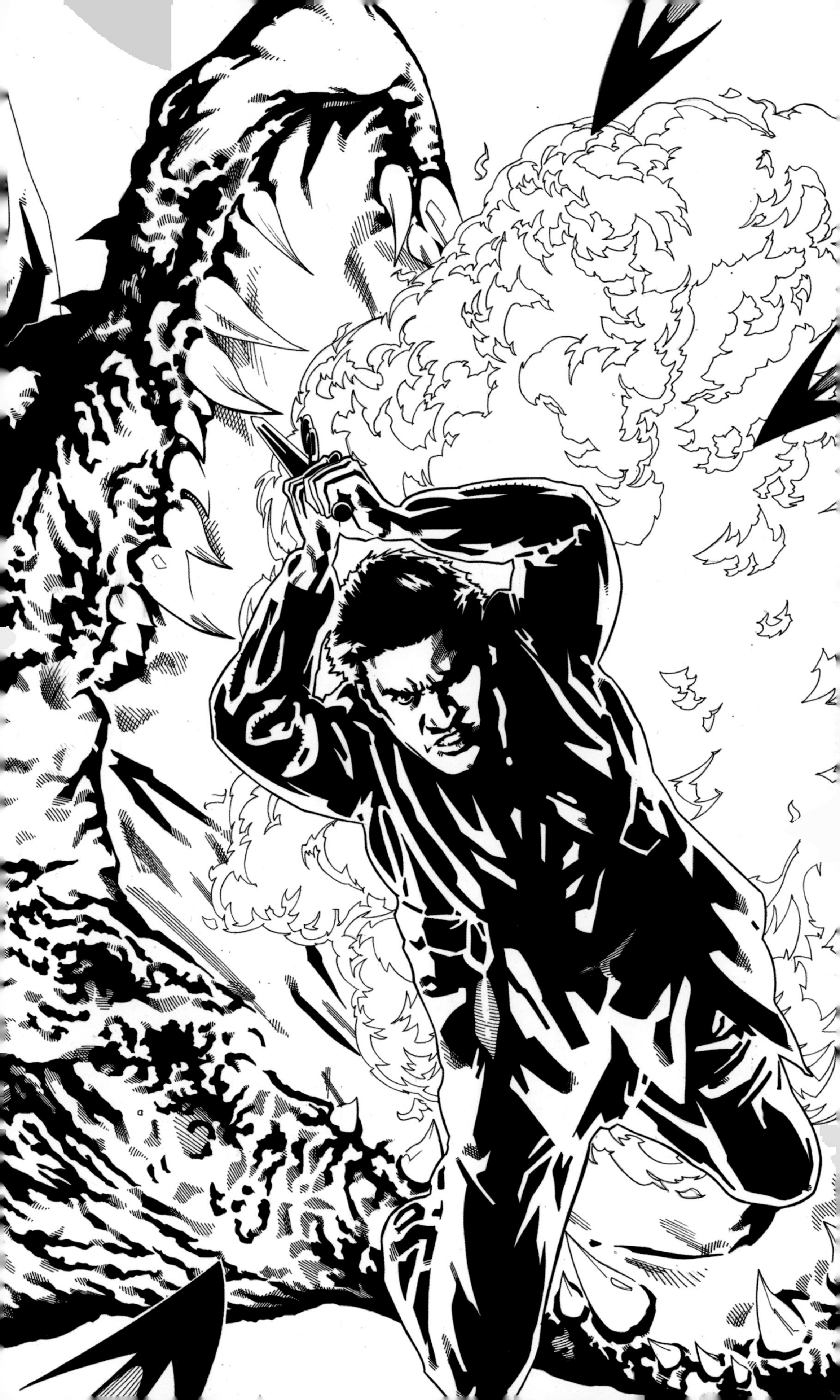

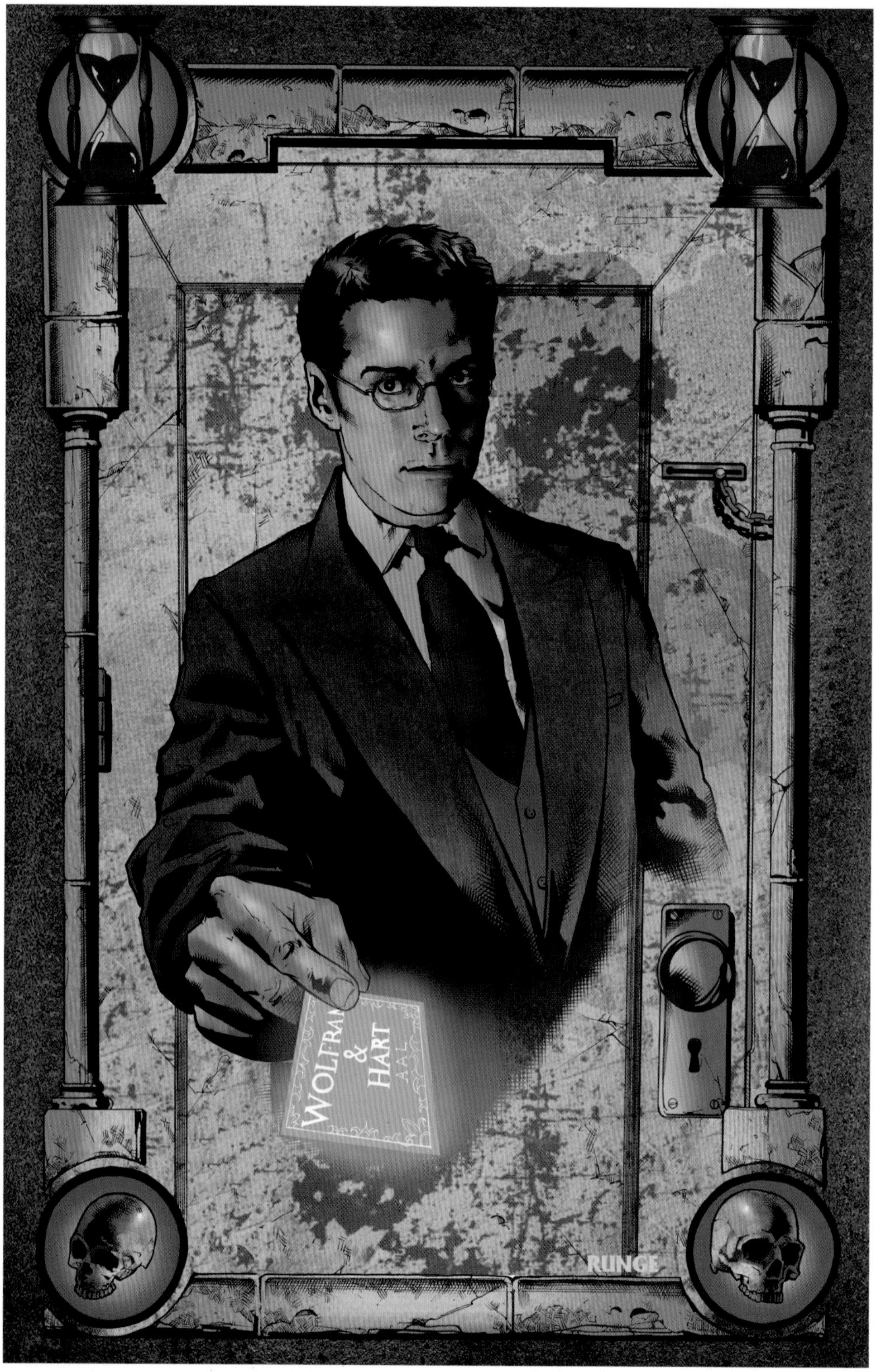
WOLFRAM
&
HART
RUNGE

This Page: Art by Nick Runge

Opposite Page: Art by Alex Garner

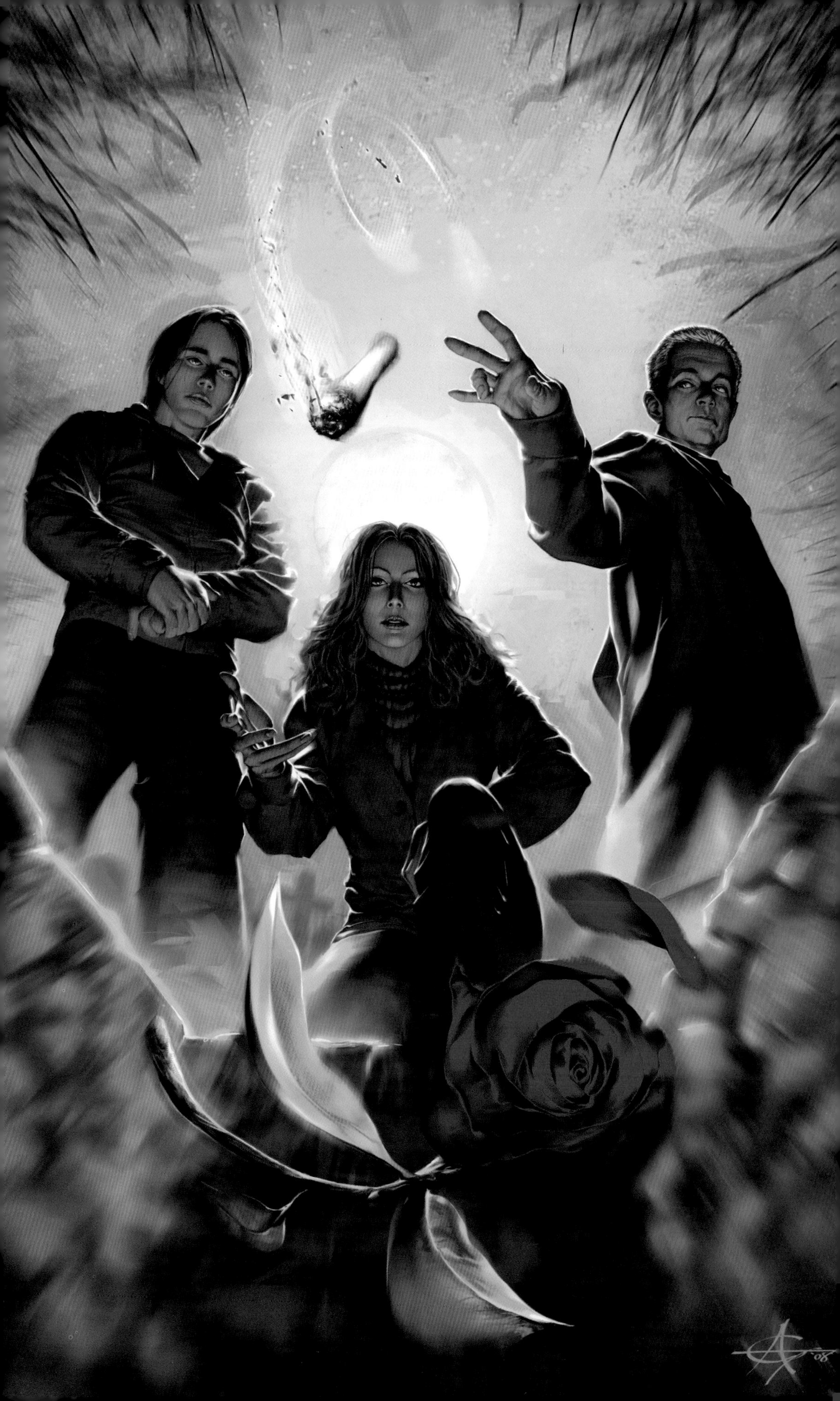

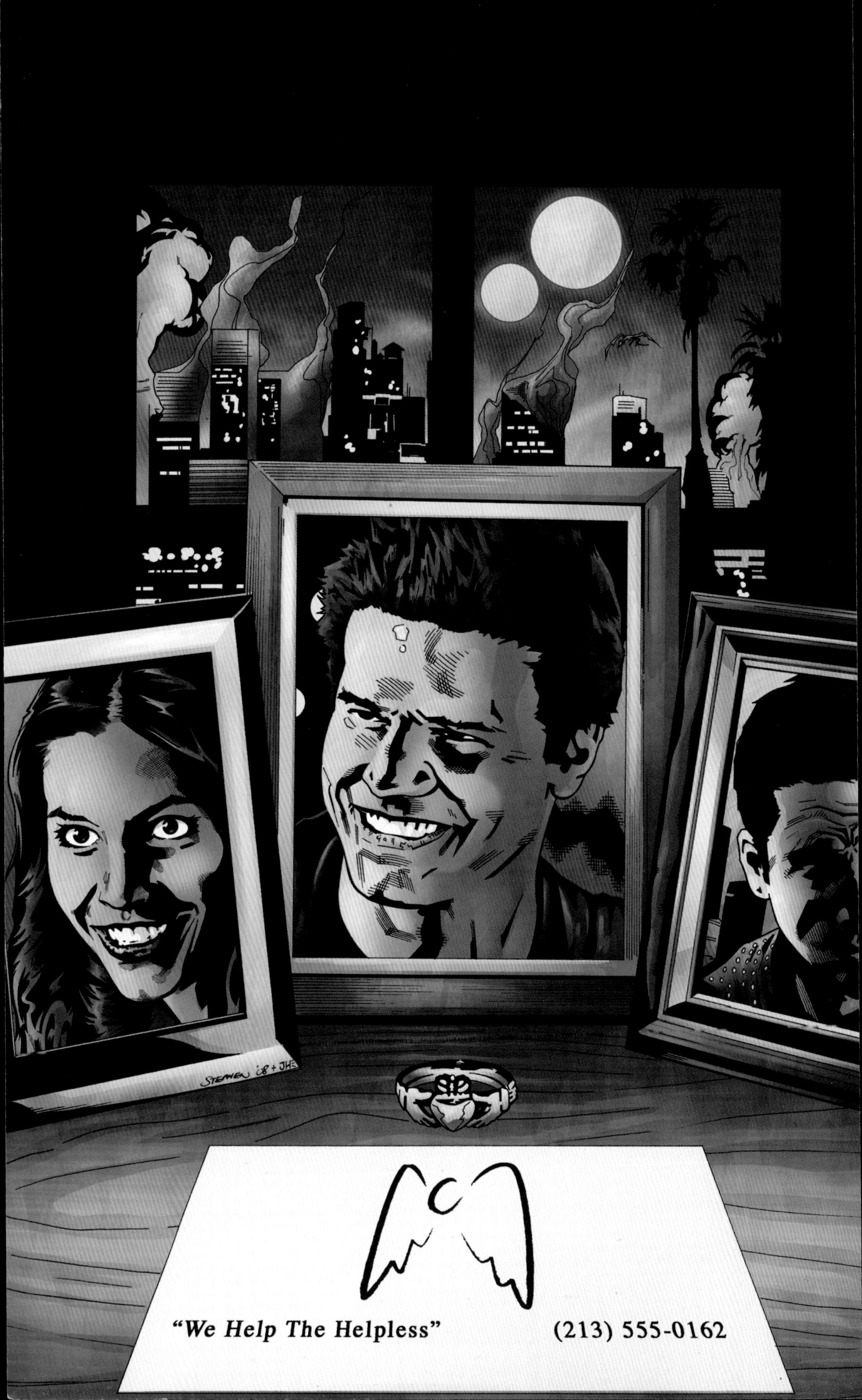
STEPHEN '08 + JHE
"We Help The Helpless"
(213) 555-0162

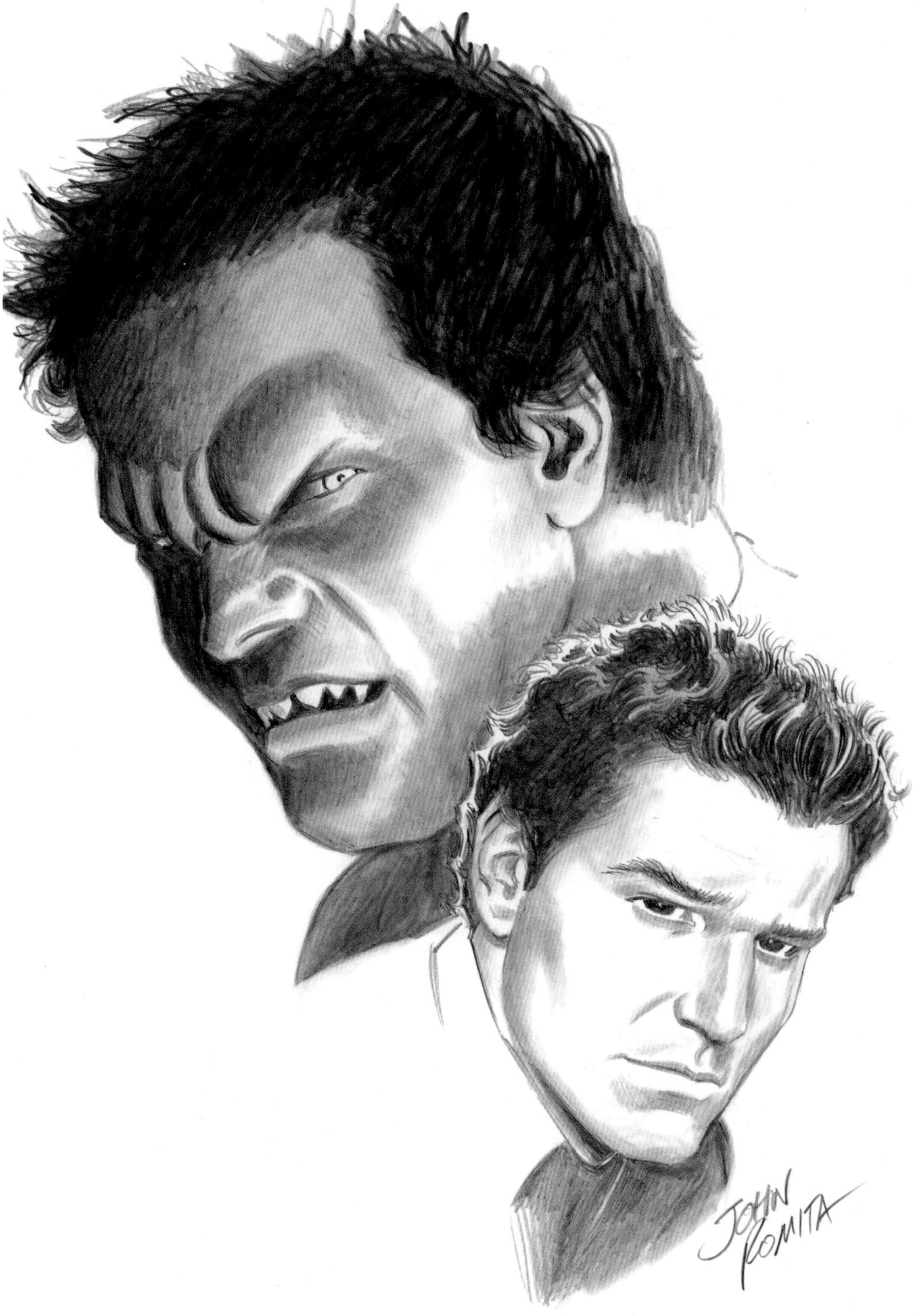
JOHN ROMITA

Opposite Page: **Art by Stephen Mooney**
Colors by John Hunt

This Page: **Art by John Romita**

THROUGH THE FISHBOWL · The On-Set Diary of Betta George

NOTE: The Following was excerpted from the diary of Betta George, telepathic fish and co-star of Angel: After the Fall. This was taken specifically from the days George filmed his scenes for issue 10. The opinions of George are not necessarily those of IDW.

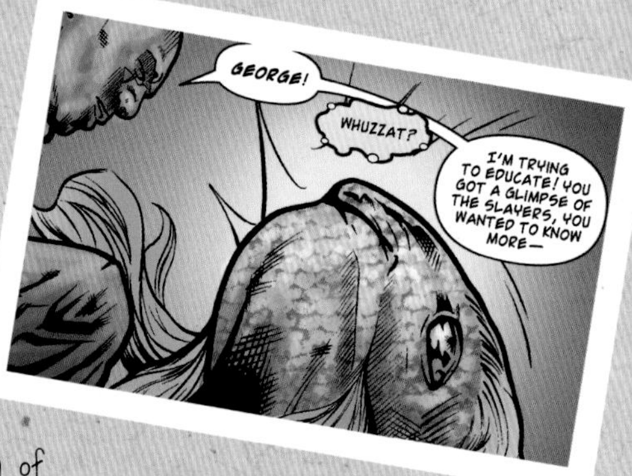
GEORGE!
WHUZZAT?
I'M TRYING TO EDUCATE! YOU GOT A GLIMPSE OF THE SLAYERS, YOU WANTED TO KNOW MORE—

ISSUE 10, PAGE 7

So far, this shoot has been a weird one. My character started as a slave and is now a prisoner. The other actors get to ride on the backs of dragons and fight dinosaurs; I get tied to a bed. But hey, it's a job. And it's high profile, right? I mean, it must be, I'm getting a ton of emails about it already. Most of them start with "You're not canon" and end with "seriously, a fish?".

Gunn, my co-star for the bulk of my scenes, is an interesting guy. He's polite, doesn't step on my lines (it's happened before, looking at you, William the Bloody!) But, well...

...take the other day, when Gunn drained a production assistant dry, right in front of the crew. Sucked her blood, and then pointed at me and said "the fish did it." AND THEY SIDED WITH GUNN. I complained to Whedon, who shrugged and explained Gunn was actually on the show so he's more important. I was shocked, what show was Whedon talking about? I gotta consult Wikipedia later.

Anyway, at least I'm not tied to a bed today. Good, enough of that stupid bed, let's move onto something more cinematic... Like, oh, say, a basement. Fantastic. Prisoner in a basement. Someone's been watching *Silence of the Lambs*. At least Gunn isn't making me put the lotion in the basket.

We filmed my close-up last. Gunn, of course, being the star of Whedon's imaginary series, gets to shoot his footage first.

For my coverage, Gunn's back in his trailer taking a nap. That's not even HIS leg kneeing me in the fish-stomach. But rest assured, that is most definitely MY stomach. I have the bruises to prove it. We tried a stunt double for the first couple of issues but the footage didn't match. That's what you get for dressing a short Mexican dude in a fish costume and trying to pass him off as me. Truth be told, though, I miss Pablo. He had a lot of great stories. Oh, and he never blamed me when production assistants popped up dead on set.

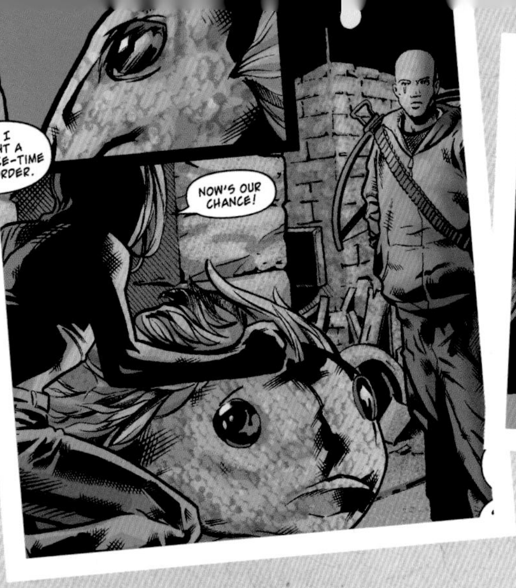
NOW'S OUR CHANCE!

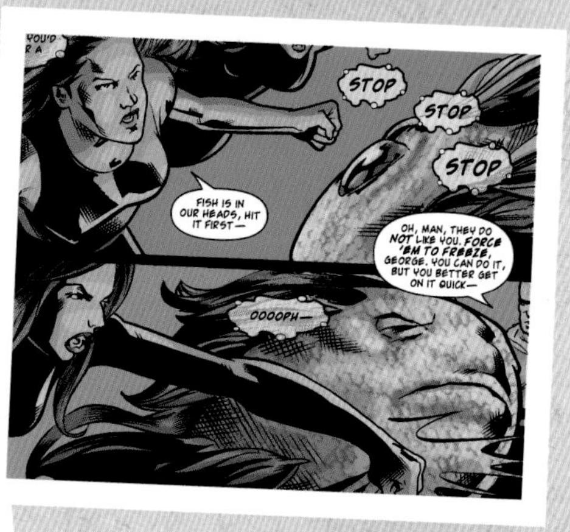
STOP
STOP
STOP
FISH IS IN OUR HEADS, HIT IT FIRST—
OH, MAN, THEY DO NOT LIKE YOU. FORCE 'EM TO FREEZE, GEORGE. YOU CAN DO IT, BUT YOU BETTER GET ON IT QUICK—
OOOOPH—

ISSUE 10, PAGE 8

Got a lot of great close-ups here, nice splash shot. The dialog, however, yikes. "Stop! Stop! Stop!" I fear that this is EXACTLY the kind of lazy writing that will prevent me from even be nominated for a Best Supporting Actor Eisner. I just know Jimmy Olsen's gonna take it. It's his year. Or maybe that Luke Cage dude. Bendis gives that guy, like, pages of monologues. I get "stop!" "stop!"

The slayer ladies were nice. But I will say this: the fact that they were trapped in a five-minute time loop made it really difficult for them to learn lines, which led to cue cards, which prevented them from being 100% in the scene with me. I heard one of them just booked a couple of panels in the next *Scott Pilgrim*. Good for her!

ISSUE 10, PAGE 15

This was a huge character moment for me. Gunn, while completely insane and evil, is actually able to help me channel my power in ways never thought possible. A few of the crew actually CRIED when we shot this. Oh sure, it might have been because Gunn had just killed that Production Assistant, OR, more realistically, it might have been because I pulled off such a powerful scene so very well.

Can I actually push people to do what I want? Oh man, if that were true, there would be plenty of emailers and web boarders that would suddenly stop typing about how I'm not really "canon" and how it's a "disgrace" to the memory of some "TV show" by having me in the book. But no, I can't push people. Heh, that would be cool.

Oh, I should point out that the Slayer Lady actually punched me on this page. She said it was on accident, and then muttered "but maybe it will help your acting and reacting seem more real" and then I said "what did you just say?" and a time-slip occurred and she had no idea what I was talking about. And then Gunn tried to bite Ryall. It was awkward.

Ryall blamed me, by the way.

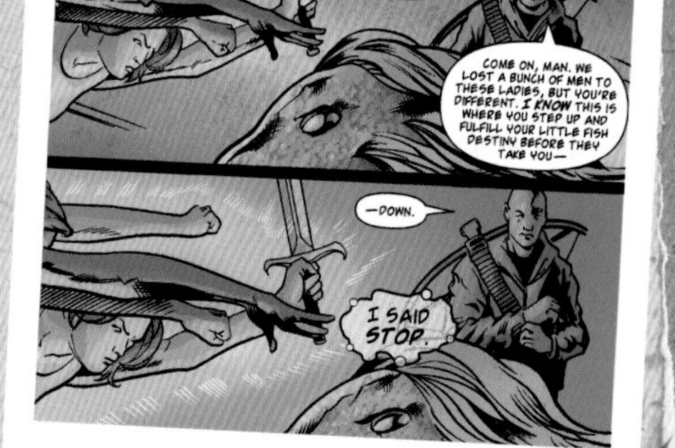
THEY'RE NOTHING! THEY'RE OBSTACLES!
COME ON, MAN. WE LOST A BUNCH OF MEN TO THESE LADIES, BUT YOU'RE DIFFERENT. I KNOW THIS IS WHERE YOU STEP UP AND FULFILL YOUR LITTLE FISH DESTINY BEFORE THEY TAKE YOU—
—DOWN.
I SAID STOP.

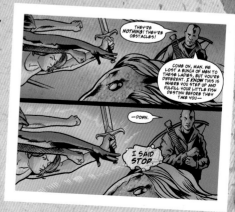

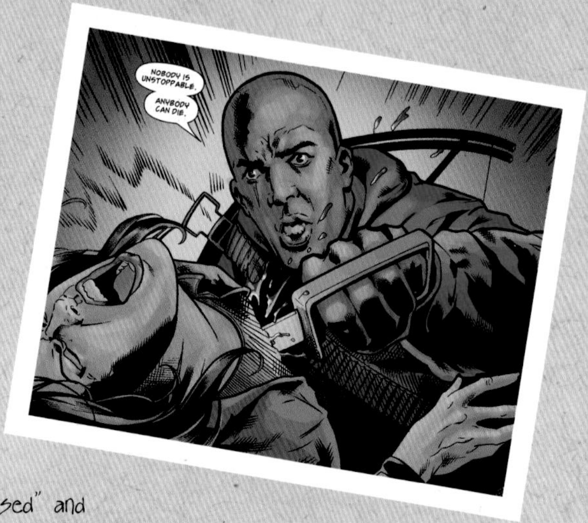
NOBODY IS UNSTOPPABLE.
ANYBODY CAN DIE.

ISSUE 10, PAGES 16-17

Oh man was this weird. The script said "Gunn wedgies slayer." Gunn "improvised" and stabbed her. What the hell was that about? I went right up to Lynch (egotistical jerk, but very very handsome) and asked him what was stopping Gunn from stabbing ME out of nowhere. Lynch looked me up and down and said, "Have you checked out my frat zombie book yet?" I think maybe he was drunk. God, I hope he was, sober people shouldn't act like that.

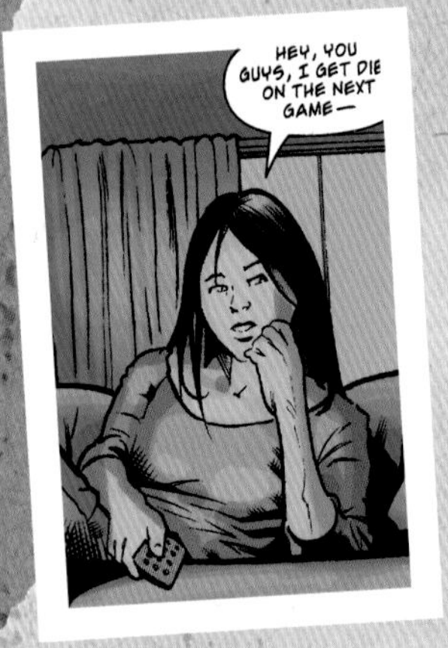
HEY, YOU GUYS, I GET DIE ON THE NEXT GAME—

ISSUE 10, PAGE 18

This should have been a real treat, working with Beck, one of my co-stars from *Spike: Asylum* and *Spike: Shadow Puppets*. I didn't have to be on-set for Beck's scenes, but I thought it would be cool to stop by the set and read my lines to her, you know, help her out.

BIG mistake, let me tell you. Beck was all "why did YOU get to go canon? I was the break-out star of *Asylum* and *Shadow Puppets*, available now on amazon.com." To make matters worse, TMZ was on set and caught the whole thing. So embarrassing.

ISSUE 10, PAGES 20-21

I appreciate the fact that the writers FINALLY saw fit to let me get OUT of that awful hotel set, believe-you-me. But they made it snow, which is hell on the gills. I asked if I could have a production assistant hold an umbrella over me when we weren't filming, but Whedon said something about how it wasn't in the budget.

How was ONE umbrella not in the budget but all that make-up to hide the Dragon's plastic surgery scars IS? Oh sure, a fish can suffer in the snow, but God forbid a comic reader notices liposuction scars on a giant mythological beast.

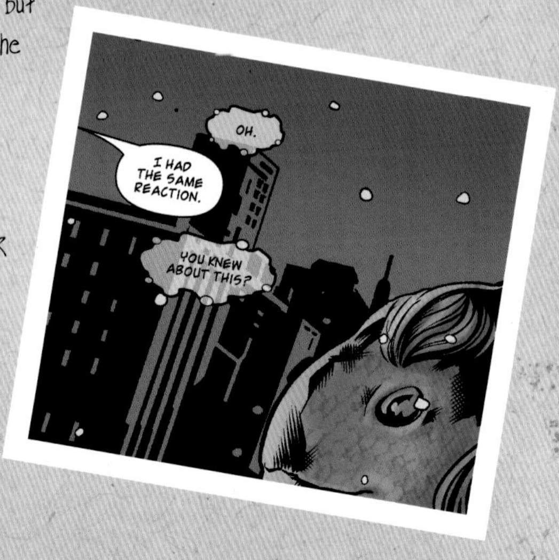
OH.
I HAD THE SAME REACTION.
YOU KNEW ABOUT THIS?

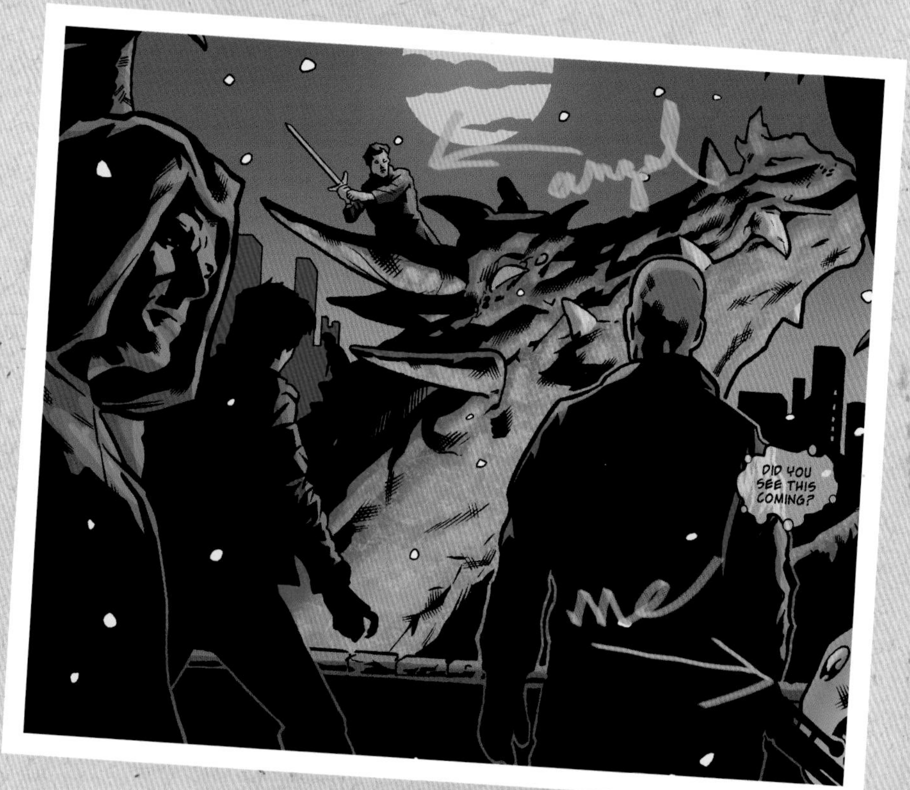
angel
DID YOU SEE THIS COMING?
me

It's treatment like this that is for serious making me feel better about sneaking my resumé out to other comic companies. I think I'd be a great fit over at Green Lantern Corps. I could be Limpet, the Green Lantern from Sector Awesome. Gotta remember to call my agent, ask if he's heard anything.

ISSUE 10, PAGE 22

Finally I get some face-time with the title character. He didn't say much to me. He was busy buddying up to Gunn between takes, asking Gunn if he could get him anything to eat, asking Gunn if he was comfortable, begging for Gunn's forgiveness. There was an awkward air between them. They have history that I can't even begin to fathom. I asked Whedon what was up with that, and he looked at me and was all "have you seriously not seen the show?" and I had to think quickly and say "oh sure, it was great." I don't know if Whedon believed me. But seriously, what show is he talking about? Is he messing with me?

After this issue wrapped, we all went out to a pub and celebrated. Kind of a little "Issue 10 wrap party." It was a blast, the slayer girls are really nice when they're not leaning into punches, and Gunn loosened up a little. That is, until he drained a busboy. It got awkwardly quiet in the place until Angel ran up to ANOTHER busboy and bit him for a second, before laughing and saying "just kidding, I don't do that anymore" which everyone thought was a riot except for Gunn. That really rubbed him the wrong way. Whatever, Gunn, lighten up. Angel's hilarious; he should have his own show.

questions and answers

Brian Lynch asked the good people of the IDW *Angel* forums to pose any questions they had about *Angel: After the Fall* issues 9–12. Now, he will answer them with the strength of roughly two men. Let's go!

QUESTION 1

These issues are packed with the climaxes you've been working toward since issue 1. From the talk between Wesley and Illyria at the end of #9, to everyone finding out about Angel's humanity, to the Angel/Gunn showdown, the bombs planted in earlier issues are going off one after the other. Which of the big moments was most exciting to write, and why?

—Patrick Shand

Now would be a great time to point out that Pat Shand has reviewed every issue of *Angel: ATF* (and *Spike: ATF*, and any Whedon-related book) over at **http://buffyversecomics.blogspot.com**. The reviews usually go up the day the comics come out, and reading his thoughtful and in-depth reviews has become a bit of a ritual. To thank him for making working on the book all the more fun, I named one of Gunn's gang after him. I wish there was more I can do. I tried to change Spike's name to "Pat Shand" but Ryall was all "are you drunk?" to which I could only reply "maybe… and VERY."

Pat is right about the bombs going off one after the other. Set-up over, now we plunge into the meat of the story, the moments we've been waiting to show. Wesley and Illyria's reunion was great fun to write, as was tackling Angel and Gunn's reunion, especially as it went sour. But of all the issues in this volume, I'd have to say the greatest joy came from penning Cordelia's dialog. For one thing, I didn't know I was going to get a chance. She wasn't in the original series outline. In fact, Joss said her story was over, her death was final, and if she was going to come back it would have to be for a great reason.

As we got closer to writing Angel's near-death issues, I knew it was going to be very odd to have Angel simply watching the action from a disembodied state without anyone to talk to. That's when the idea to use Cordy came to me. And once I decided I was definitely going to use her, all these other reasons for her return started clicking. OF COURSE the Powers-That-Be would send her, they want Angel to go calmly and peacefully. And of course she wouldn't care what her mission was, she was going to help Angel any way she could.

Cordelia was always one of my favorite characters on *Buffy* and *Angel* so writing her pages was a real honor. I was in a good mood any day Cordelia and Angel had dialog. It was an honor to give her life again. I hope I did the character justice.

QUESTION 2

1. Is there any character that you feel "translates" less well than others to the comic medium? And which character do you feel "translates" the best to the medium?

2. When it comes to bringing dead characters back, what's the bigger consideration: the positive effects this might have on your current storyline, or the negative effects this might have on a previous storyline/scene (e.g., Fred's death in "A Hole in the World," or Wesley's death in "Not Fade Away")?

3. Was there anything in Angel: After the Fall *or* Spike: After the Fall *that the fans just weren't getting, to your surprise/frustration?*

4. Will any more old characters be showing up after Issue 12?

5. If you could choose just one scene (from the ones we—the readers—have seen so far) to be acted out by the televised series' actors, which would it be?

6. "Shipping": mostly flattering or mostly intimidating, from your new perspective as a VIP?

7. Is there any idea (yours or Joss') that you kind of regret scrapping? (If so, can you tell us what it was?)

—Enisy

Great questions. It's weird to see "Question 2" when it is, in fact, questions 2–8, but let's ignore that and answer!

1. I think all the characters work wonderfully in the comic medium. The only problem is you miss all the subtle nuances the actors bring to the dialog, so sometimes it's difficult to gauge tone just from reading it. That said, Angel is helped greatly in comic form, as he's not the most verbose guy in the room but through narration we can really get into his head.

2. Bringing characters back from the dead is tricky. Wesley, for instance, had a very powerful and moving death on the show. I don't want to ruin it by bringing him back and giving him nothing to do. I didn't know if "Ghost Wesley" would work, but it was Joss' idea, and I don't know if you've noticed, most ideas that come from his head are quite wonderful, so I went for it.

I tackled it like this: Wesley is back but he doesn't want to be. He's earned his happy ending, he wants to ride off into the sunset but Wolfram & Hart won't let him. So now he's going to do what he's best at: helping Angel fight the good fight. This was underlined bold-faced at the end of issue 9 when Wesley decides to give up looking for a way out.

Even "neutered" (he can't fight, he can't even turn pages in a book to do research) he's going to be a vital part of the team. Especially towards the end, just you wait. *After the Fall* would be a lesser book without that character, for sure.

3. Not that I thought she'd be the most beloved character in all of Whedon-dom, but a faction of very verbal, very passionate readers hate Spider. I think she's simply misunderstood. Also, I should point out I've gotten emails from people that DO love her. And to them, I want to say "thank you" and "I'm sorry, I don't have Spider's phone number, as she is fictional."

4. Popeye joins team Angel in issue 35.

5. One scene I'd like to have the actors perform. Wow. Angel and Wesley's

conversation in issue 1. Angel's speech in front of the masses in issue 5. The Wesley/Illyria conversation from issue 9. The aforementioned Cordy scenes. Any of Gunn's scenes, really. There is a scene in issue 16 I'd really like to see Mr. Boreanaz tackle.

6. I stay out of "shipping" conversations. Everyone's got an opinion as to who their favorite character should wind up with, and it's a testament to the actors and creators of *Angel* and *Buffy* that people get that passionate about it. Let's move on!

7. Not really, I'm pleased with how the story came out. At one point, one of the champions fighting Angel in issues 5 and 9 was going to be Pavayne from the "Hell Bound" episode of *Angel* (he was last seen held prisoner in Wolfram & Hart's basement). He was going to be dragging Angel on a "greatest hits" of his failures, and because of Pavayne's amped up hell powers, said failures were going to kick Angel's ass. Eventually he was going to be taken in by Gunn and then used to trap each character in their own "greatest hits" (or, you know, their own personal hell). That might have been fun, but it was cut for numerous reasons (time and story being just two).

QUESTION 3

Angel: After the Fall *is often considered a blessing for the fans of* Angel *that have always wondered what happened to Angel and Co. after the infamous alley fight at the end of "Not Fade Away." As a writer and fellow fan of the series, what has been the greatest highlight of writing* Angel: After the Fall *so far? Any fan reactions that have surprised you, either positive or negative?*

—James Sexton

The greatest highlight? Meeting with Joss to talk to him about the series was a highlight of my life, let alone a highlight of working on the series. But seeing pages for the first time, and enjoying how the artists have elevated my script, that's a thrill that I will never, ever get used to.

The weirdest fan reactions? That is easy. Head over to YouTube and type "geeking out" into search. This will take you to a whole crapload of comic reviews from inside a Canadian comic store. Some lady named Leila and some dude who looks like the son from *Family Guy* review comics, and if a new *Angel* is out, they will talk about how they do not enjoy *Angel*. In a way they are the Bizarro Pat Shand, although I must say I get a kick out of watching their reviews. They are frustrated that we don't see the alley fight, they think it's dumb Angel isn't a vampire, but the review usually ends "so all in all, if you're a fan of *Angel*, you should check it oot." Although I just watched a review of *Angel: After the Fall* #14 wherein she says "if things don't change soon, I'm gonna stop reading this." To which I say, "give it three more issues."

QUESTION 4

Brian, with After the Fall *you've managed to develop each major character further. Is there one character whose story you've enjoyed developing most? And Chris, do you have a favorite character in the story?*

—Ethan Connolly

I think it would be a toss-up between Connor and Gunn. Connor because we got to take him in a fun new direction, and Gunn because of the really dark places we got to go with him. I love Gunn on the TV show, and to drag him through all of this, it was exciting.

QUESTION 5

(The obverse of one of Enisy's questions)
Is there any idea of yours (or Joss') that you regret including in the story so far, and if so, can you tell us what it was?

—DeborahMM

I can't think of any. But I do wish we could have given Nina more to do. Just not enough time. I blew it there.

QUESTION 6

What do you think it is about Angel (the character and the show) that continues to inspire such devotion and love from the fans, and makes him such an enduring character?

—Brendan Collins

Oh that's an easy one. Angel gets beat up, Angel loses, Angel gets everything taken away from him, but he keeps on fighting. And he'll do what he thinks is the right thing even if it means he has to suffer for it. Plus he kicks ass and is funny and charming.

Great, now it sounds like I want to date Angel. A new "ship" for people to write slash fiction about! Don't you dare.

QUESTION 7

How were you able to decide which characters would stay in or jump to (or jump back to, as is the case with Connor) the foreground of the story and which characters were going to have to take a back seat?

—Jack Gallegos

I think it's a question of using whoever fit the story best. Absolutely Lorne is really important to Angel's world (and I'm obviously a fan, as readers of *Spike: Shadow Puppets* can attest) but his part of *After the Fall* could be told in a shorter amount of time. Meanwhile, Connor, who didn't get as much screen-time as Lorne on the TV show, fit into the themes and the story much much easier. In fact, more than I thought he would. It gets to a point where the characters kind of take over and you just hold on and transcribe.

QUESTION 8

(Dominic and Jean-Vic had similar questions, so let's put 'em together and answer both in one fell swoop! Take that, two birds, you didn't see that stone coming, did you?)
How do you manage fan expectation? The fight in the alley was such a stirring moment that for a long time seemed like the last testament to Angel and Co. Now that

you have been given the reigns to the next chapter in Angel's saga, how did you go about the plotting processes knowing how loyal and demanding Angel fans are?

—Dominic Martorana

The Angel Universe is full of fan battles for their favorite character. Namely Angel and Spike, and Illyria and Fred. Were you ever afraid that you might alienate a certain fan base by writing characters a certain way?

—Jean-Vic

I love reading fan reaction to the book, but if I were to think about fan expectation while writing it, I'd be too crippled with fear. You can't please everybody. For instance, when the series was announced, I got a ton of emails saying "oh man, Spike better be a lead" but an equal amount of emails stated "please don't have Spike in it." Still others said "I know a thousand billion readers that won't read the book if Cordelia isn't in it" but an equal amount (yes, a thousand billion other people) said that they wanted her to rest in peace. So I just had to write the best story I could, and not worry about expectations.

QUESTION 9

A lot of us fans were concerned about After the Fall, *mainly because of Joss' feared absence and the canonical issue. Now, I and others are very happy with your work Brian (and of course the artists' and Chris' as well) and are ready to accept* After the Fall *as canon, not mainly because of Joss' input, but because it's a great story. But just because I'm such a geek, I'm asking you to tell us how much Joss is involved, and how much control you have. I would also love to know how much influence Chris and the artists have.*

—Caroline Levén A.K.A. Skytteflickan88

Joss sat me down and told me all his ideas. The gang being trapped in hell, Gunn's situation, Wesley's condition, even the ultimate resolution of the series, he had a lot. I then told him mine, he sent me notes with more ideas, I wrote more, the back-and-forth went on for a while, and then I wrote up an extensive outline for the series based on everything we had talked about.

He was great about answering questions, from important ones ("Wesley's situation, is he walking around opening doors like Lilah or is he walking through doors like Spike in season 5?") to really dumb ones ("What if Angel was a human?").

Here is an exchange from our emails, for your reading pleasure:

ME: So I'm thinking that maybe Gunn would want to cause a reversal of what happened, so everything goes back to how it was. Problem is, whatever he wants to do would either send things back, or make things worse (like, "end of everything that is and will be" worse). In fact, maybe as it gets closer to zero hour on doing whatever Gunn has to do, it's very clear that it WILL wipe everything out, but Gunn is fine with that.

I'm babbling, but sometimes, sometimes babbling leads to good ideas. Or sometimes, it leads to a limerick. Either way, entertainment!

JOSS: There once was a vampire named Gunn

Who nearly destroyed everyone
When he tried to undo
All the shit he'd been through
So his life would be like Season One.

Your babbling was good babbling. But the limerick is ass.

Even his emails are more creative than my scripts. Damn him.

QUESTION 10

1. How much of the story has been changed due to fan reaction or more to the point, over reaction?

2. What topic receives the most positive and negative feedback from the fandom?

3. Why can't Brian be in charge of the next Angel *series?*

4. Can Buffy crossover, if both stories lined up magically to somehow connect? If the answer is yes, does that also apply to Giles, Xander, and Willow?

— Cheryl

1. Not much at all has been changed due to fan reaction. Little things have been changed, Spike's Spikettes were always destined to don the battle gear and become an army, but we got them out of bikinis and into said battle gear a little quicker once fans were all sorts of "bikinis??? Ew, ick."

There was one plot point that was taken out in anticipation of fan reaction. When Angel and company went to the Hyperion Hotel in issue 9, they were originally going to run into a cult of Cordelia worshippers who were awaiting her return. This was going to be my nod to a character I felt was vital to the world of *Angel* but couldn't be in the series.

"She will come again to judge the living and the fashion-impaired… and her kingdom will have no pleather." The plan was to drop hints that this cult existed all throughout the books, with Pro-Cordy graffiti on the walls, etc. But when the Cordy fans started popping up and posting passionate posts on the webboards, I kinda realized that a Cordelia Cult declaring that she will return would obviously make the real-life Cordelia Cult think Cordelia WAS returning, which would lead to MORE passionate posts and decreased enjoyment of the series when she didn't return.

2. I think Spike's ladies are the most poorly received aspect of the series, and either Angel's surprise humanity, Connor's evolution, or Gunn, in general, receive the most accolades.

3. My day job is screenwriting, I write the *Angel* book in my spare time, so for the last year, I haven't had any spare time. I got married last December so I can't wait to show my wife that her husband will not be at the computer 24/7 forever. Plus, there are tons of amazing writers, *Angel* doesn't need me.

4. Joss can use Angel n' Spike in the *Buffy* series, and the reverse is true over here. In fact, there was talk about having the Vampire Buffy be the one who re-vamps Angel IF he gets re-vamped.

QUESTION 11

How did you feel about the show's cancellation, and how did you react to the final episode?

—The Real Inadia

Finally, the Real Inadia steps forward. I am SO sick of all these phony baloney Inadia-wannabes asking questions. I was heartbroken when the show was cancelled, but I thought the final episode was perfect on all levels.

QUESTION 12

First of all, I'd like to congratulate Brian Lynch on the amazing work he's done so far! Seriously, sometimes I think Joss Whedon himself is the one writing the comics, just because of how brilliantly they are written!

So, my question:

We've seen there are some slayers in HelLA, will their presence there be explained in the future? And also, I've heard there will be a sequel to After the Fall *called* Angel: The Aftermath. *Does this mean the end of* ATF *will be inconclusive, in a "Not Fade Away" kind of way? (I really hope not!)*

—Maíra Macedo

Thank you for your kind words!

Their slayers are explained, I think. If not, I'll do it here: there were slayers (or girls with slayer abilities) in LA when it went to hell, Gunn rounded them up and imprisoned them.

Angel: After the Fall will have an ending. It would be a cop-out to not end a year-plus storyline. But it's not Angel's last story by any means.

QUESTION 13

In regards to the return of Gwen, Nina, Kate, and Groo to Angel's world, what led to the decision to bring back each of these characters in ATF, *and was there any non-deceased characters that you did want to bring back but for whatever reason couldn't or was nixed?*

—Buffyversefantic

Ooooh, good questions. I will check them off for you. Nina and Gwen were decided on by Joss and I. We agreed the comic medium suited these ladies well. Kate and Groo were my idea. But when I brought up Groosalugg, Joss lit up, he was very happy about that idea. As well he should, Groo is one of the most underappreciated characters in Angel's world.

As for characters I wanted to bring back but couldn't, I can't think of any. At one point I toyed with a few of Wolfram & Hart's deceased employees being sent to deal with Gunn, but I nixed it.

I don't think I would have made Connor such a big part of the book if Joss hadn't come up with such a great idea for him. Making him the most well-adjusted super heroic character in the book? Genius.

QUESTION 14

Brian and/or Chris,

If you could go out for a pint (of beer, I would hope!) with any character from Angel: After the Fall, *whom would you pick, why, and what would you talk about?*

Many thanks and congratulations to everyone involved for such a wonderful series! Angel: After the Fall *is now one of my favorite seasons of* Angel.

—Sophie

For me, I'd say Spike or Angel. If Angel would open up a bit, he's not the chatty type. That said, I don't think I could keep up with Spike. So maybe, if it's an option, Cordy?

And thank you for the sweet, sweet compliments. You are nice.

QUESTION 15

*1. If you were given permission to write a crossover graphic fiction story with AtS and any other similar-but-unrelated TV show or movie (*The X-Files; Supernatural; The Blair Witch Project; *etc.), which one would you choose?*

2. If you could choose any famous author (Stephen King; Ray Bradbury; etc.) to write a novelization of After the Fall, *who would you pick?*

3. Tell us the history of Betta George's incorporation into the plot. Was he a late addition to it—in other words, was it decided to add him to After the Fall *after the story had already been fleshed out? Or had you and Mr. Whedon planned to include him all along, even before the story was written? (Either way, I'm glad he's here!)*

—Rebecca Taylor

1. I would want Angel and company to cross over with the characters in *Everybody's Dead,* a wonderful horror/comedy series now available in trade paperback. Angel would be all "these characters are wonderful and so well-written" and then Joss Whedon would step into the comic and go "why didn't I create this?"

My point is everyone should hunt down and buy *Everybody's Dead.*

2. I wanna do it!

3. The series that put Franco and me on Joss' radar, *Spike: Asylum,* was also the series that introduced Betta George. I think issue 3 had just come out, and Joss and I were talking via email about *After the Fall,* and he ended the email with "and let's find a place for the fish." Which was scary because he dies in issue 4. So when *Shadow Puppets* came out we resurrected him.

We still didn't know where we were going to put him, and for a while it looked like we didn't have a place at all so he was going to fall by the wayside. I was reading the rough outline for the first chunk of *After the Fall* stories and noticed that Gunn's prisoner, then a bald psychic with no eyes, had powers very similar to George.

The character was whiny, which meant his interactions with Gunn wouldn't have been much fun. George, however, was a smart ass, and would call Gunn on his grandstanding. The problem was, we needed George to be way more powerful than he was in *Asylum* and *Shadow Puppets*, so I had Gunn train him. It turned out to be a great fit, as Gunn, evil and messed up as he was, had some nice moments with George as a result of having to help him realize his true potential.

Poor whiny bald psyhic. He never got his shot.

QUESTION 16

Reading this book I've been blown away by several of the cliffhangers, namely Angel's humanity, the return of Fred, and that amazing apocalyptic vision at the end of issue 12. What parts of the story so far have left you with that jaw-dropping feeling?

—Tom Griffiths

The scripts for issues 12–17 were all very, very exciting to write. After so much build up, writing the pay-offs is such a blast. Wesley's revelations in issue 12, for one. Again, writing Angel and Cordy's dialog was so much fun. And even though they're not in this book, issues 15–16 were the most emotional to write. And while I haven't finished writing 17 I can imagine those last couple of pages will stir some emotions.

This whole experience has been jaw dropping. I get to continue my favorite TV show of all time. With Joss Whedon! Even when the deadlines are mounting and I feel stressed about how much work it is, I take a step back and I remember how lucky I am.

Thanks guys, for being a part of it. I love talking to you guys about the series, be it on the Internet or at comic book conventions or in my front yard at 3 AM (okay, that only happened one time and I'm not sure the dude knew I wrote *Angel*, in fact I'm not sure he knew I wrote anything, he was too into himself and his weird drunk vomiting).

Hope this explained some stuff. I gotta get back to writing, see you all in volume 4!

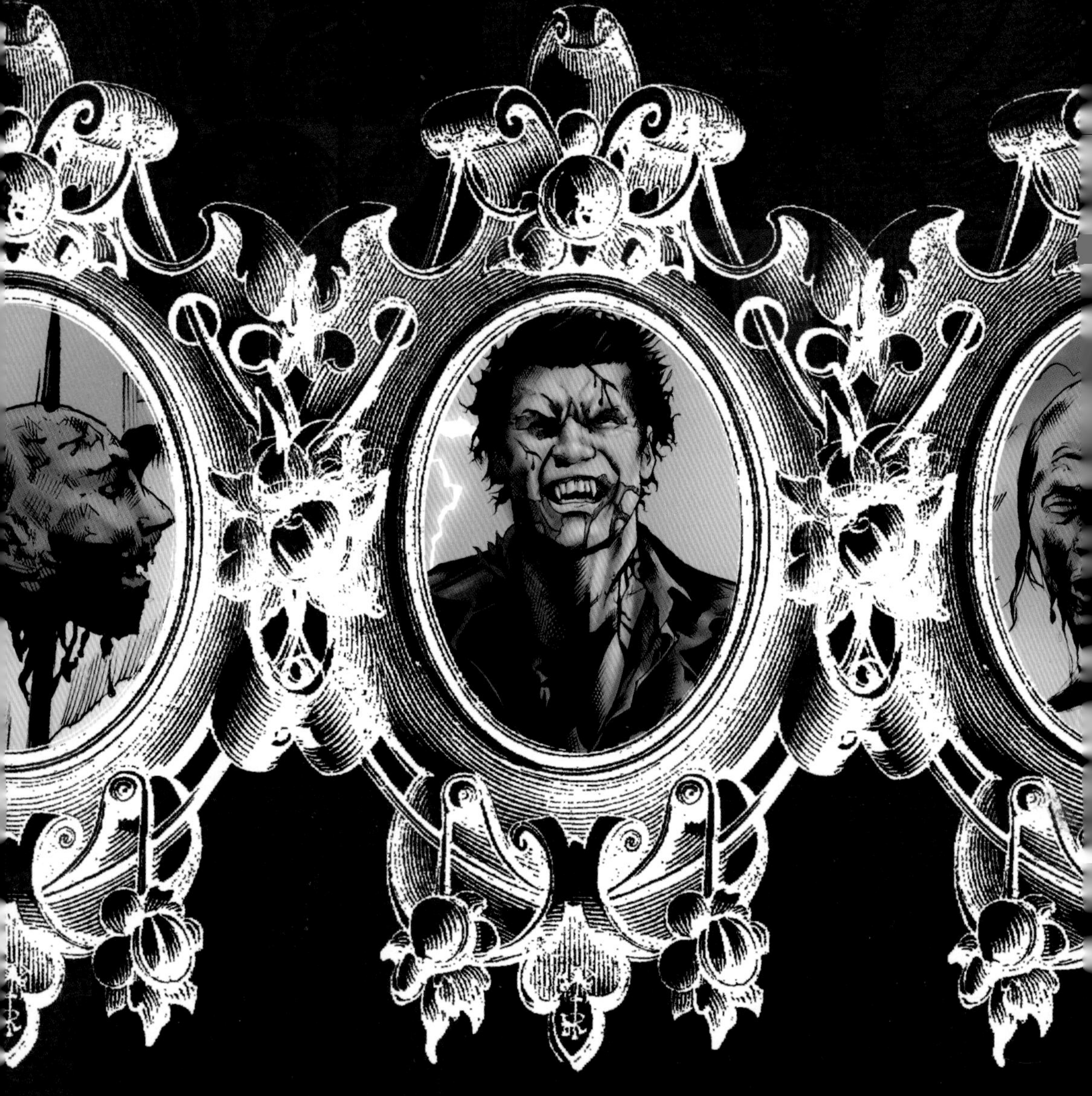

ANGEL™

—AFTER THE FALL—

VOLUME 3